Tragedy and Theory

Michelle Gellrich

Tragedy and Theory

The Problem of Conflict
since Aristotle

PRINCETON UNIVERSITY PRESS • PRINCETON, NEW JERSEY

Copyright © 1988 by Princeton University Press
Published by Princeton University Press, 41 William Street,
Princeton, New Jersey 08540
In the United Kingdom: Princeton University Press, Guildford, Surrey

All Rights Reserved
Library of Congress Cataloging in Publication Data will be
found on the last printed page of this book

ISBN 0-691-06738-4

Publication of this book has been aided by a grant from
The Andrew W. Mellon Foundation

This book has been composed in Linotron Sabon

Clothbound editions of Princeton University Press books
are printed on acid-free paper, and binding materials are
chosen for strength and durability. Paperbacks, although satisfactory
for personal collections, are not usually suitable for library rebinding

Printed in the United States of America by Princeton University Press,
Princeton, New Jersey

For Jesse

On account of wonder men began and continue to philosophize, marvelling in the first place at obvious perplexities
[τῶν ἀπόρων], then proceeding little by little and puzzling
about greater things, such as occurrences in the moon and
the sun and the stars and the origin of everything. Now he
who feels perplexed and amazed thinks he is ignorant; . . .
thus if men philosophized in order to escape ignorance, it is
clear that they pursued science [τὸ ἐπίστασθαι] for the sake
of knowing [τὸ εἰδέναι] and not for any practical use.

Aristotle, *Metaphysics*

CONTENTS

THIS PROJECT took shape around questions elicited by my readings in the theory of tragedy. In an effort to understand salient differences characterizing the great documents on drama from Aristotle to Nietzsche, I became aware of a break in the theoretical tradition, which had received little attention. Although nineteenth- and twentieth-century accounts defined tragedy routinely in agonistic terms, older views, notably Aristotle's in the *Poetics*, were remarkably unforthcoming on the topic of conflict. An important turning point appeared to occur with Hegel, whose *Vorlesungen über die Ästhetik* offered an approach to drama that departed from earlier classical and Renaissance orientations because of its unmistakable emphasis on contradiction and struggle. Although I realized that Hegel often was acknowledged as a key influence on modern accounts of tragedy, I discovered that the nature of his influence had not been very thoroughly studied, especially in America and England, nor, in particular, was his model of conflict understood as transitional in the history of critical theory. The argument of my book began in reflections on the significance of the break marked by the *Vorlesungen über die Ästhetik*, on the reasons for the muted understanding of it in the twentieth century, and more generally on the relationship between Aristotelian and Hegelian theories of tragedy.

My approach developed around the philosophical frameworks that structure Aristotle's and Hegel's pronouncements about tragedy and particularly their attitudes toward conflict. Given the organic character of the systems produced by these two thinkers, such a direction of study was perhaps inevitable. In any case, the acroamatic nature of both the *Poetics* and the *Vorlesungen über die Ästhetik* motivated an exploration of the foundations supporting the dramatic theories elaborated in each work. This method subsequently informed my investigation of Renaissance criticism and German Romantic theories of the tragic sublime, which compose an important part of my argument about critical responses to conflict. Thus, this book, which got under way as a result of essentially historical questions, was molded early on by an effort to explain how seminal ideas in accounts of tragedy are expressions of systematically determined interests, typically latent in dramatic theory, but intelligible once a fuller view of a theorist's corpus is adopted. For these reasons, my approach toward the absence of attention to conflict in Aristotelian-based theories and its emergence in Hegelian thought has not been ordered chronologically. Rather, I have made the conceptual and synchronic focus of my study into the organizational rationale for the chapters, since this orientation, and not an essentially historical approach to ideas, led to insights into tragic theory. Readers looking for the history of an idea will consequently not find one in the following pages. Indeed, part of my claim is that conflict cannot have the status of an "idea" within a system whose guiding principles are not conducive to reflection upon it.

There is an equally pressing reason for my disengagement from a chronological order of exposition. One of my major claims about theorists in the dramatic tradition is that they have typically adopted a historical view of their own contribution. They have seen the beginnings of their ideas in earlier thinkers and ultimately in the great predecessor Aristotle. This tendency has supported a genetic fallacy—an erroneous assumption about the developmental, evolutionary movement of the idea of conflict in the history of criticism. Because my own aims with respect to this assumption are revisionist, I have attempted not to repeat as a principle of organization in the book the concept of historical genesis, which I am trying to expose as mistaken.

In elaborating my argument, I have depended on a general understanding of literary theory worth making explicit at the outset. Beginning with Aristotle's institutionalization of poetics as a discipline, or *techne*, one of the main aims of theory has been to ground literary exegesis (or, in the case of the *Poetics*, literary *praxis*) in a framework of conceptual generalizations and systematic rules. Because the principles of theory are typically taken to be derivative of the texts to which they revert when they are used as guidelines for evaluation, they presumably account for the main features of a work and illuminate "what it is" (τί ἐστι), to use Aristotle's formulation. The circularity of this structure in the philosophy of Aristotle and in later theory has not, until recently, been felt as problematic. To the contrary, it has been thought to produce clarity. While I take such clarity seriously in my analyses of the insights into tragedy occasioned by a particular theory, I also attempt to trace its enabling conditions in the exclusionary premises of the system. In other words, I see the productive energy generated by theory in close relation to its repressive tendencies as a "discipline." By assuming a panoptic view of the field, the theorist seeks to master the material at his disposal and thus lay claim to authority. The visual terminology controlling such a notion of *theoria* is of course as old as Western philosophy itself and as central to the work of Plato and Aristotle as it is to the work of Hegel. Relying on this traditional understanding of theory as a special mode of seeing, my own discourse tends toward metaphors of power, control, and surveillance in describing the strategies engaged by systematic approaches to tragedy. Readers will find, to some degree, an affinity between this perspective and the work of Michel Foucault. His arguments about the relationship between discipline, power, and knowledge suggest the extent to which specular and spatial notions are implicated in the concept of theoretical mastery of a "field" or "subject matter." I would qualify this indebtedness, however, by saying that the following pages were never conceived as an effort to implement a Foucaultian archaeology in a new area of inquiry. The debt is more general and extends, as well, to such diverse thinkers as Paul de Man, Jürgen Habermas, and Frank Kermode, all of whom have provided ways of addressing the exclusionary biases that necessarily attend theory's claim to authority and coherence.

In this context, I should also note that for purposes of my argument I do not differentiate between *theory* and *criticism*, largely because the texts that I study fall as much under one category as under the other. While interpretations are rarely extensive or close in theoretical works, the tenets of a system are ususally explicated in terms of examples drawn from plays, which in turn become integrally identified with the theorist's central defining ideas. Such is the case, for example, of Sophocles' *Oedipus Tyrannus* in the *Poetics* and his *Antigone* in the *Vorlesungen über die Äesthetik*. But if this fact influences my tendency to interchange *theory* and *criticism*, it also motivates my effort to develop readings that foreground what is excluded in systematic accounts. In the process, I suggest that the ostensibly panoptic view generating a theorist's claim to have encompassed and defined his subject matter militates against close reading, since that activity turns out to be preeminently subversive of the generalized validity of theoretical principles.

If my orientation toward theory and tragedy is shaped by a variety of modern thinkers, so too is my approach to an understanding of conflict in tragic plays. Again, my readings move within the ambience of contemporary critical discussion without seeking to implement the ideas of a specific critic or "school." I have drawn eclectically on deconstructive critiques of binary structure and dualism in Western philosophy, which have been especially useful in helping me articulate an initial impression about the differing and even adversarial tendencies of theory and tragedy. While systematic thought about plays strives for coherence, consistency, and totality, the plays themselves enact conflicts that disrupt such expectations and defer what might broadly be called closure or centeredness. My argument is not, however, a reiteration of the simple view that tragic conflict fragments order—a point hardly worth repeating. Rather, I claim that it is not assimilable to theoretical models of centered structure, including Hegel's dialectical version. To submit conflict to the pattern of a philosophically grounded system, that is, to the controls of reason, however reason may be conceived, is to tame its subversive vigor and master its violence within containing frameworks whose legitimacy the plays themselves have already called into question. The latter point is crucial, for it guides my critiques of Aristotle, Hegel, Renaissance critics, and Schiller, whose widely disparate positions on tragedy nonetheless ultimately share a commitment to a principle, or *arche*, of structure that halts the disruptive energy of conflict in tragedy.

But while my borrowing from deconstruction, notably from the work of Jacques Derrida, is apparent in these matters, I also diverge from it in an important respect. I assume a difference between theoretical and literary discourse that is eroded in deconstructive efforts to foreground the rhetoricity and tropology of philosophical texts. The book does not offer arguments in explicit defense of this difference. Nor does it investigate the possible disruption of rational thought patterns in philosophy through the rhetorical play of language. If I had taken this course, the result would have been, in all likelihood, an appreciation of the conflicts within philosophical discourse that undermine theoretical principles, just as the conflicts of dramatic tragedy defer the stability of a center that secures order. I have foregone a "rhetorical" approach to theory in this study not only because I conceive its methods and ends to be essentially different from those of the tragic plays I examine, but also because I do not subscribe to a position that radically reduces philosophical discourse to the play of tropes. In ascribing a foundational role to "rhetoricity," such a position produces a myopic preoccupation with turns of phrase that are taken *tout court* as decisively disenabling of the whole. In short, my interpretations of philosophical texts in the following pages are far less oriented toward figures and tropes of language than are many deconstructive readings.

I have thus come to approach attitudes toward conflict in critical documents on drama in terms of a tension between the systematic aims of theory and the subversive interests of tragic plays. To appreciate this tension, I try to elucidate both the reach and inadequacies of the most influential accounts of tragedy in our tradition. That these accounts are derivative of broader philosophical programs, which both ground and direct them, is no accident. In the case of tragedy, the urge to theorize seems directly linked to the quest for intelligibility, which Aristotle claims is especially provoked by whatever resists understanding and challenges our efforts at assimilation. Aristotle, of course, also thought that this challenge was effectively met by his responses in the *Poetics*. In many ways it was, even profoundly so. But if that document is one of the earliest and greatest witnesses to the sense-making operations of the critical intelligence, it is no less witness to the limitations engendered by the project of theoretical mastery.

ACKNOWLEDGMENTS

AMONG THE MANY PEOPLE who made this project possible, I wish to express my gratitude first to Thomas Rosenmeyer. Not only did he suggest the topic of the dissertation that eventuated in the present book, but he was a generous and an acute reader of the manuscript at various stages of its development. I also wish to thank my other friends and colleagues who have taken time to register their criticism and advice, including Norman Rabkin, Phillip Damon, Michael Bernstein, Donald Mastronarde, Charles Witke, Ludwig Koenen, Anthony Edwards, GailAnn Rickert, Ruth Scodel, Steve White, and Nicholas White. My research assistant at the University of Michigan, Jennifer Carozza, spent many hours preparing the bibliography and helped ready the text for submission to the Press. Katherine Paine, at Louisiana State University, aided me with computer-related problems and kindly ensured that the final printing ran smoothly.

For a leave from teaching in 1985, which allowed me to finish the manuscript, I am indebted to the joint support of the American Council of Learned Societies and the Department of Classical Studies at the University of Michigan.

Patricia and Ted, my parents, have profoundly influenced the ideas of this project and the process of its completion. Their loving encouragement has been unflagging over the years.

Jesse, my husband, has been so closely involved with the genesis and evolution of the book that I feel the finished product is as much his as mine. The dedication is a small expression of gratitude for the deep and abiding ways in which he has nurtured me and supported my work.

NOTE ON TRANSLATIONS

ALL TRANSLATIONS from Greek, Latin, French, and German are my own, unless otherwise indicated. I have translated foreign terms the first time they occur in the text. I also have listed them in the Index, with the translation in parentheses.

Tragedy and Theory

Introduction

Sometimes it appears that the history of interpretation may be thought of as a history of exclusions, which enable us to seize upon this issue rather than on some other as central, and choose from the remaining mass only what seems most compliant.
                              —Frank Kermode, *The Genesis of Secrecy*

WHEN ARISTOTLE observed in the *Metaphysics* that people began to philosophize out of wonder, he expressed a basic human need to find explanations for phenomena in the world, especially those that appear to resist understanding.[1] What inspires *aporia* or provokes doubt also sets in motion the urge for establishing order. This striving for comprehension diminishes the helpless ignorance we feel in the grip of enigmas and ultimately produces the *epistemai*, or systems of knowledge, that ensure us a rational existence. In the dynamic interplay of wonder and intelligibility, Aristotle suggests, the philosophical frame of mind, more or less developed in all human beings, moves.

But as the *Metaphysics* bears out, there is also a threshold, albeit a tenuous and fluid one, between philosophically driven interest in objects whose provocativeness yields rational understanding and philosophical exclusion of what cannot be accounted for more or less systematically. Theorizing seems to hover on shifting boundaries between objects that can be included and those that do not fit its containing structures. In deference to these variable lines of demarcation, Aristotle ranks *epistemai* according to the degree to which they admit of systematic rigor: theoretical knowledge, particularly metaphysics, ranks uppermost in the hierarchy because it concerns

[1] Aristotle, *Metaphysics*, ed. with comm. by W. D. Ross, 2 vols. (1924; reprint, Oxford: Clarendon Press, 1958), 982b11–23.

the necessary and universal, whereas productive and practical forms of knowledge, often called *technai*, rank lower because they concern things that exist for the most part and that are consequently only probable.[2] The precise criteria distinguishing the objects of knowledge in this epistemological schema are less important for our purposes than the common denominator supposedly enabling our philosophical treatment of them. The material studied by an *episteme* or a *techne* must possess sufficient regularity to be learned and taught. Only the necessary and universal or the probable and likely satisfies such a condition.[3] This is why, in Aristotle's view, we cannot have knowledge of the random and indeterminate, for they are simply unamenable to systematic reflection, which seeks for order in proportion to the relative orderliness of its material.[4] Although the basic gesture of knowledge is incorporative and aimed at comprehending the world rationally, it delimits its range in areas where the material of investigation resists classification. Not everything is susceptible of philosophical understanding. At the margins of methodical thought are recalcitrant wonders, accidents, and indeterminacies that cannot be approached through reason.

While Aristotle's conception of the *epistemai* and *technai* has had a profound impact on our ways of formulating the nature of philosophizing, my purpose in adumbrating some of his ideas is to draw attention to his influence on literary theory and drama. By considering the production of poetry, and of tragedy in particular, as material conformable to the demands

---

[2] For these classifications, see *Metaphysics*, 1.1–2, and *Nicomachean Ethics*, ed. J. Bywater (1894; reprint, Oxford: Clarendon Press, 1959), 6.3–8. Also see Ross's commentary on the *Metaphysics*, loc. cit., and W.F.R. Hardie, *Aristotle's Ethical Theory*, 2d ed. (Oxford: Clarendon Press, 1980), pp. 221–23, 338–57.

[3] See *Nicomachean Ethics*, 1139b25–28; *Metaphysics*, 1027a20–22; *Posterior Analytics*, ed. with comm. by W. D. Ross (1949; reprint, Oxford: Clarendon Press, 1965), 1.1, 71a1.

[4] See, for example, *Metaphysics*, 1027a20–22, and *Posterior Analytics*, 87b19–22. We will discuss this distinction between the "always," the "usual," and the "indeterminate" in chap. 2.

of a *techne*, Aristotle initiated a theoretical tradition that has persistently sought to approach drama as a system of patterns, which responds to expectations of order.[5] The systematic view of tragedy, beginning with the *Poetics*, has typically subscribed to the fundamental assumption that plays submit to reason. Within such an approach, indeterminacies and wonders that provoke irresolvable *aporia* are relegated to the margins of study or regarded as unfortunate anomalies.

This consequence is apparent in the long-lived and resilient principles first elaborated by Aristotle in his dramatic theory. A tragedy, he argues, must be a unified totality, its parts so closely related that the removal of any one of them would topple the whole; it must be perspicuous, designed to conform to the limits of what the mind can grasp; the actions of its characters must be intelligible in terms of a moral purpose that is unitary or at least stable; it should avoid the irrational and, if it cannot, try to exclude it from the action of the play.[6] These principles are both prescriptive for the dramatist and, according to Aristotle, descriptive, drawn from an investigation of how existing dramas, especially the best tragedies from fifth-century Greece, operate. In other words, the order residing in such principles is to be sought and cultivated by the aspiring playwright, the practitioner of the art, but it is also objectively present in literary works to which the art of poetry, as a theoretical study, is directed. In the *Poetics*, we first encounter the effort of philosophy to incorporate poetry, and tragedy in particular, into its orbit of the rationally intelligible, by submitting its production to the controls of a *techne*.

Beginning with their canonization in the Renaissance, Aristotle's principles have assumed a kind of institutional power over the centuries. Their status, however, has come into question in our time with increasing pressure. To put briefly a case that has been argued more fully elsewhere, because the Aris-

---

[5] *Techne* is always grounded in a rational principle; see *Nicomachean Ethics* 1140a8–10.

[6] See *Poetics*, ed. with comm. by D. W. Lucas (1968; reprint, Oxford: Clarendon Press, 1980), especially chap. 6.

totelian view treats poems as objects possessed of their own intrinsic order, it assumes that unity, coherence, and totality are ontologically present in the work of art and constitutive of its objective form, whereas these elements are instead produced through the interpretive process.[7] The modern critique of objective form addresses Aristotle's failure to differentiate between the object of study and the activity of understanding, or to put it in another way, between the order inherent in the material of *theoria* and the order generated by *theoria*. Focusing on the central importance of the theoretician's expectations in approaching his subject matter, these recent departures reject, more or less explicitly, the Aristotelian view of autotelic form as the presence of order, in favor of a more dynamic concept that takes into account the role of the constituting subject. In this shift of approach, form and its attendant characteristics are said to be produced by the interpreter in a process that strives for order, totality, and closure. The *theoros*, in short, is no disinterested spectator. His anticipations, predispositions, and methodological framework not only shape the object of study but determine value. An important consequence of this reorientation is that a play, for example, is conceived not as a self-contained and autonomous reification of meaning, but as a repository of virtual forms and

---

[7] For a critique of the ontology of objective form in literary texts, see Paul de Man, "Form and Intent in the American New Criticism," in *Blindness and Insight: Essays in the Rhetoric of Contemporary Criticism* (New York: Oxford University Press, 1971), pp. 20–35. He relies on the work of Hans Georg Gadamer, *Truth and Method*, tr. Garrett Barden and John Cumming (New York: Seabury Press, 1975), and Martin Heidegger, *Being and Time*, tr. John Macquarrie and Edward Robinson (New York: Harper, 1962), chap. 5. The critique is implicit in much poststructuralist criticism; see, for example, Frederic Jameson, *Marxism and Form: Twentieth-Century Dialectical Theories of Literature* (Princeton: Princeton University Press, 1971), pp. 306–416, and Jonathan Culler, *On Deconstruction: Theory and Criticism After Structuralism* (Ithaca: Cornell University Press, 1982), pp. 180–280. A more general philosophical treatment of the institutional interests of interpretation is by Jürgen Habermas, *Knowledge and Human Interests*, tr. Jeremy Shapiro (Boston: Beacon Press, 1971), chaps. 7–11.

meanings that are constituted by the interpreter addressing the text, who molds it by the questions posed and the responses expected.

While the shift in critical theory initiated by such hermeneutic critiques has stimulated numerous reevaluations of our approaches to such literary works as the lyric poem and the novel, it has not, somewhat surprisingly, prompted adequate reconsiderations of tragedy.[8] If we approach the tradition of dramatic theory from the vantage offered by recent hermeneutical developments, provocative avenues of inquiry are opened. Once attention is directed to the dialogical context within which poetic order emerges, it becomes possible to explore the extent to which tragic plays, rather than bearing out salient principles of traditional dramatic theory, resist them and withstand the modes of understanding that they make possible. In other words, the interests of theory may be shown to collide with or diverge from the interests of tragedy.[9] This book is concerned with studying such points of friction or divergence. My purpose is to explore how seminal documents in the history of dramatic theory have typically excluded from their formulations of tragedy material that is not amenable to the theoretician's conceptual framework. In turn, such exclusions shed light on the ideas or values that tragedy in some

[8] See, for example, Roland Barthes, *S/Z* (Paris: Seuil, 1970), on the Balzacian novel; Jonathan Culler, *Flaubert: The Uses of Uncertainty*, rev. ed. (Ithaca: Cornell University Press, 1985); Jacques Derrida, *Dissemination*, tr. Barbara Johnson (Chicago: University of Chicago Press), pp. 175–285, on the poetry of Mallarmé; Frank Kermode, *The Genesis of Secrecy: On the Interpretation of Narrative* (Cambridge, Mass.: Harvard University Press, 1979), on narrative. Recent works on tragedy that have made indirect uses of these developments include Timothy Reiss, *Tragedy and Truth* (New Haven: Yale University Press, 1980), and Charles Segal, *Dionysiac Poetics and Euripides' Bacchae* (Princeton: Princeton University Press, 1982).

[9] On the oppositional role between theory and literature, see especially Michel Foucault, *Power/Knowledge: Select Interviews and Other Writings, 1972–1977*, ed. Colin Gordon (New York: Pantheon Books, 1980), pp. 78–133; Frank Kermode, *The Genesis of Secrecy*, pp. 1–21; Culler, *On Deconstruction*, pp. 89–110, 156–79; Steven Knapp and Walter Benn Michaels, "Against Theory," *Critical Inquiry*, vol. 8, no. 4 (1982): 723–42.

way threatens and that theory tries to protect, through a selective appropriation of texts. In this perspective, I suggest that philosophical or systematic expectations of order are guided by a set of interests that is repressive and that demonstrates its repression through its distinct modes of partiality.

Though I am concerned with elucidating various forms of theoretical closure in influential accounts of tragedy, I propose no polemical thesis. Rather, in focusing on the implications of certain lacunae in theory, my aims are heuristic, geared toward a process of discovering what motivates particular limitations inherent in the chief models of tragedy that have informed dramatic criticism since the time of the *Poetics*. Within this framework, I try to draw attention to features of tragic drama that elicit what Aristotle called wonder, particularly the type of wonder arising from doubt or irresolvable *aporia*. The approach of literary theoreticians to such enigmas in tragedy, to indeterminacies that resist assumptions of unity, order, and coherence, is broadly speaking the subject of this book.

THAT THERE ARE some unmistakable gaps in Aristotle's account of tragedy has been remarked often. Critics have noted the lack of discussion about gods, necessity, or fate; the tendency to avoid treatment of specific ethical contents in the plays, aside from the most obvious points related to an agent's social status; and the absence of a concept of the "tragic hero."[10] But another lacuna is discernible in the *Poetics*, one that has not been observed, for the most part, though it deserves careful scrutiny. I refer to the experience of conflict in the Greek plays, which modern critics typically regard as essential to tragedy but about which Aristotle is reticent.[11] This

---

[10] See, among others, John Jones, *On Aristotle and Greek Tragedy* (New York: Oxford University Press, 1962), pp. 11–62; Gerald Else, *Aristotle's Poetics: The Argument* (Cambridge, Mass.: Harvard University Press, 1963), pp. 305–07; William K. Wimsatt and Cleanth Brooks, *Literary Criticism: A Short History* (New York: Alfred A. Knopf, 1965), pp. 51–53.

[11] Two scholars who have noted the peculiarly modern nature of the critical emphasis on conflict are George Kimmelman, "The Concept of Tragedy in

reticence is all the more striking since it can be traced well beyond the *Poetics* and through the major theoretical documents on tragedy in the Renaissance and in the neoclassical period. Despite their characteristic eclecticism and often greater reliance on Latin than on Greek sources, these documents bear a heavy imprint of Aristotelian ideas and maintain his silence on the subject of conflict. Indeed, so influential is the classical account that not until the turn of the nineteenth century, when Hegel develops a dramatic theory that eventually rivals Aristotle's, does the agonistic side of tragedy surface as a central topic of theoretical investigation. In the *Vorlesungen über die Ästhetik*, the German philosopher offers the first major critical exposition of tragedy that focuses on contradiction and struggle. Hegel's contribution has not been adequately appreciated in this light. Although it is commonly recognized that his theory focuses on conflict, it is generally not perceived that this orientation initiated a remarkable shift of approach in literary theory about tragedy after the eighteenth century. This shift, however, does not have the character of a sudden, radical break with the past. As suggested in readings of some of Hegel's older contemporaries, such as Friedrich Schiller and A. W. Schlegel, the change is well under way already in Romantic revisions of neoclassical ideas about drama.[12] But the impressive comprehensiveness of Hegel's dramatic theory and its seminal influence on later thinkers make his lectures particularly pivotal documents in the evolution of modern criticism.

The contribution of Hegel is of particular importance in this project, since his attention to conflict raises the question why it did not become prominent in theoretical formulations until his time. Though he does not address the problem, Hegel nonetheless invites us to explore the reasons for the exclusion

---

Modern Criticism," *Journal of Aesthetics and Art Criticism* 4 (1945–1946): 141–60, and Stuart Hampshire, "On Tragedy," in *Moderns on Tragedy: An Anthology of Modern and Relevant Opinions on the Substance and Meaning of Tragedy*, ed. Lionel Abel (Greenwich, Conn.: Fawcett, 1967), pp. 267–71.

[12] These developments are studied in chap. 4.

of conflict from Aristotelian accounts of tragedy. My approach in confronting this question is via the essential premises about dramatic consistency, intelligibility, and unity articulated in the *Poetics* and later absorbed into the mainstream
of literary study. These premises can be effectively secured
only if obstinately unsystematic and destabilizing movements
of language and action in tragedy are bypassed or somehow
brought to heel. Dramatizations of tragic conflict, as we will
see, are problematic for critical approaches based on assumptions of normative order because they are subversive. Typically they question a culture's truths and systems of knowledge, overturn standards of rational consistency, and upset a
basis in the tragic action from which resolution, synthesis, or
catharsis might come. In short, conflicts in tragedy indirectly
challenge the terms on which such critical accounts stand;
they seem to assault a basic assumption of theory, namely,
that its material can be adequately known in terms of definitions, categories, and methodical classifications of meaning.[13]
Aristotle, I will argue, sidesteps the challenge. While his aim is
to delineate what is involved in the art of composing the best
plays, this productive *techne*, as I have already said, has an
interpretive side. It invites us to consider tragedy (*theorein*)
within a set of expectations that implicitly relegates to the periphery the recalcitrant, subversive aspects of drama, including its agonistic elements. Hegel introduces ways of neutralizing the disruptive strategies tied to tragic collision and thus
breaks Aristotle's silence on the topic. But traditional assumptions about unity and coherence are nonetheless so binding on
his views that he ends up taming conflict and reducing it to his
own philosophical terms of order.

While the sense-making, organizing operations of dramatic
theory serve systematic interests, they also perform a definite

---

[13] This assault on theory is provocatively discussed by Foucault, in terms of
"an insurrection of subjugated knowledges," in a lecture anthologized by
Gordon in *Power/Knowledge*, pp. 78–92. For a recent work that studies this
dynamic in relation to tragedy, see Stephen Booth, *King Lear, Macbeth, Indefinition, and Tragedy* (New Haven: Yale University Press, 1983).

cultural function: they so digest tragedy into a form both intelligible and safe that its threatening, enigmatic aspects are transformed. In the oldest preserved responses to tragedy that we have available, this cultural function becomes apparent. Plato reminds us that from the early stages of Western tradition tragedy, more than any other type of literature, has been feared as a menace to philosophical thinking, moral order, and social stability.[14] This famous detractor of art and drama reveals a profound sensitivity to the subversive side of tragedy and particularly tragic conflict. His suspicion and critique single out agonistic experiences presented by the tragedians that undermine values which Greek philosophy works hard to stabilize. We can appreciate the cultural significance of Aristotle's project against the backdrop of this Platonic attack. Without ever addressing his predecessor directly, Aristotle proceeds in the *Poetics* to establish a line of approach to the Greek plays that, by virtue of its scientific method and structural focus, both excludes the kinds of issues that preoccupied Plato and secures a place for tragedy in culture and the arts. If conflict does not figure as an item in Aristotle's treatment of drama, it is because his insistence on the *logos* of tragedy precludes attention to precisely those elements that unsettle logical, ethical, and social order.[15]

In noting Plato's preoccupation with conflict in tragedy and Aristotle's subsequent reorganization of approach to the Greek plays, I am pointing to a tension in the critical tradition that is apparent at least through seventeenth-century discussions of drama and even later. Attacks like Plato's continue to be launched in the Renaissance and in the neoclassical period, usually from religious partisans who would eliminate from the social sphere practices such as drama that threaten to corrupt

[14] See his critique of poetry in the *Republic*, ed. John Burnet (1903; reprint, Oxford: Clarendon Press, 1965), book 2, 376c–book 3, 398b; book 10, 595a–608b.

[15] On Aristotle's *Poetics* as a response to Plato, see Else, *Aristotle's Poetics*, pp. 1–38, 304–06, 636–41; Thomas Gould's review of Else's edition and commentary in *Gnomon* 34 (1962): 641–49; *Poetics*, ed. Lucas, pp. xiv-xxii.

society and demean the dignity of human kind.[16] Many of the most famous treatises on tragedy in these centuries are apologetic and, by meeting such onslaughts in one form or another, perform a cultural function similar to the *Poetics*: they are implicitly designed, at least in part, to neutralize moral outrage and fear of social dissolution by accommodating tragedy to structures that are institutionally acceptable. While the service performed by such theoretical works is undoubtedly valuable in establishing a cultural space for tragedy, what is lost in the process is a context for appreciating the adversarial, culture-questioning spirit of many classical and Renaissance plays, which dramatize conflict in ways that undermine the stability sought by systematic accounts.

Thus, I am not suggesting that for centuries no one talks about struggle in tragedy or that theorists of drama before Hegel, because they were obtuse, failed to catch on to the importance of conflict in plays. Comments on tragic conflict appear as far back as Plato, though they are typically in the form of polemical attacks and rejections. But the tradition of dramatic theory beginning with Aristotle distinguishes itself from such commentaries by assuming that its material is substantial enough to warrant methodological rigor and by developing itself around a set of interests that establishes the systematic nature of the plays. It is within such a context that we can begin to appreciate the reasons for the exclusion of tragic conflict from theoretical inquiry.

A deeper appreciation must await the discussion in subsequent chapters. But for now let me clarify briefly an assumption of Plato's critique of tragedy, which has wielded a powerful influence on theories whose basic premise is the rationality of dramatic art. In Plato's philosophy, strife is valorized as evil, as a lapse from what is best in the world, namely, the harmonious hierarchy of man, his society, and his

---

[16] See Jonas Barish, *The Antitheatrical Prejudice* (Berkeley: University of California Press, 1981), chaps. 1–6, and Russell Fraser, *The War Against Poetry* (Princeton: Princeton University Press, 1970).

universe under the controlling force of *logos*.[17] Investing the highest values in unity and oneness, Plato adopts a consistently negative tenor toward conflict, whether it be psychological, social, or metaphysical. His attitudes were highly formative of Aristotle's views. But decisive though the Platonic identification of *stasis* and irrationality was in setting subsequent attitudes, it was not the first or the only philosophical rendering in early Western thought of the nature of conflict. Aristotle had at his disposal pre-Socratic concepts, in which strife figures as a fundamental principle of structure in the cosmos, responsible for things coming to be or passing away in timely fashion, and thus, in a basic sense, a manifestation not of chaos or anarchy but of *logos*.[18] These pre-Socratic notions do not provide an adequate framework for understanding the tragic dramatization of conflict in fifth-century plays. But the adoption of such notions might have allowed the author of the *Poetics* to "rationalize" *stasis* and, despite Plato's critique, bring it within the pale of his theory. This move is made by neither Aristotle nor his Renaissance and neoclassical followers. But it is made by Hegel.

Hegel's theory of tragedy is based on a conception of *Kollision*, as he calls it, that owes something to pre-Socratic ideas.[19] Borrowing from such thinkers as Anaximander, Her-

[17] On the centrality of ideas about unity and harmony in Plato's philosophy, see Nicholas P. White, *A Companion to Plato's Republic* (Indianapolis: Hackett, 1979), pp. 9–60, and Julia Annas, *An Introduction to Plato's Republic* (Oxford: Clarendon Press, 1981), pp. 72–108, 178–81.

[18] See, among others, Gregory Vlastos, "Equality and Justice in Early Greek Cosmologies," in *Studies in Presocratic Philosophy*, vol. 1, *The Beginnings of Philosophy*, ed. David J. Furley and R. E. Allen (New York: Humanities Press, 1970), pp. 56–91, and Charles Kahn, *Anaximander and the Origins of Greek Cosmology* (New York: Columbia University Press, 1960), pp. 119–65.

[19] Hegel's studies of the pre-Socratics are contained in the first part of the *Vorlesungen über die Geschichte der Philosophie*, vol. 17, pp. 204–434 of *Hegels Sämtliche Werke*, ed. Hermann Glockner, 20 vols. (Stuttgart: Friedrich Fromann, 1927–1930). All references to Hegel are to volumes in this edition, unless otherwise indicated. The impact of pre-Socratic ideas on his theory of tragedy will be studied in chap. 1.

aclitus, and Empedocles the notion of *eris,* "strife," as a force of universal order, Hegel develops a model of conflict that eliminates the problems of chaos, dissolution, and irrationality with which it was tied in the Platonic tradition. Thus, he can attend to an experience in the Greek plays bypassed in earlier critical accounts and at the same time not risk the more basic institutional interests of theory in order, formal unity, and closure. Excluded, once again, by this new approach is whatever remains recalcitrant to the appropriating gestures of the systematic critical mode. Hegel's theory produces interpretations of strife in tragedy that may be reassuring in their conformity to a dialectical schema of conflict and resolution, but these interpretations are less the expression of the tragic dramatists than of the critic's need to find intelligibility in the experience of disorder.

While I examine this pre-Socratic legacy later in the context of Hegel's dialectical theory of drama, the point I wish to observe here is that the *Vorlesungen über die Ästhetik* elaborates a way of thinking about the violent clashes typical of tragedy that leaves behind a long tradition of Platonically conditioned ideas for a view much closer to Plato's predecessors. A strong link unites Hegelian with pre-Socratic thought against Platonic notions of *eris* as a force of dissolution and evil. That a view of regenerative strife is not to be found in Aristotle's *Poetics,* though it certainly was available to him, indicates that the phenomenon had become problematically charged as a result of his teacher's critique. For a theory set on establishing the logical basis of the tragic *praxis,* the Platonic demotion of conflict to the opposite of reason and order appears to have posed a formidable obstacle. And although we can imagine ways in which Aristotle may have gone around the difficulties, these strategies for various reasons never surfaced in the *Poetics.*

WHY ARISTOTLE'S RETICENCE about the experience of conflict in tragedy has not, by and large, been acknowledged over the centuries may be explained in several ways. First of all, through the neoclassical period, the conceptual closure operative in dramatic theory barred the possibility of reading against the grain of Aristotelian biases. As I already suggested, this closure is determined by interests embedded in philosophical predispositions that attain a kind of institutional status over time. For having established their authority in classical antiquity, they continue to exert a powerful, though usually subterranean, influence on later critical thought. Not only is the production of theory controlled by such interests, but so too is the ability of a critical tradition to read its own biases and understand its own lacunae. Thus, through the seventeenth century, the failure to appreciate the exclusion of conflict in the *Poetics* is neither an oversight nor a deliberate omission. Rather, it is systematically motivated, the result of a system whose center of focus delimits the theoretical purview. While such closure is most easily studied in terms of a specific critical text, we will see that it extends to an establishment of Renaissance and neoclassical critics whose respect for Aristotle and classical thinkers perpetuates a kind of anesthesia to the exclusionary gestures of its great authorities.

Hegel's apparent insensitivity to the nonagonistic bias in classical and neoclassical dramatic theory is more difficult to explain. For even when he directly takes up and interprets Aristotelian concepts in terms of *Kollision*—a frequent procedure in the aesthetic lectures—he says nothing of the fact that he is making over conventional ideas to fit an essentially new formulation of tragic action and character.[20] There is a blind spot in his understanding of the tradition out of which he is working and of Aristotle in particular. Although he is aware of the persistent associations that conflict has had with disorder and irrationality and shows that he is attempting to redefine these associations, he fails to specify the full significance of his project as one whose new emphasis on conflict does not

---

[20] *Vorlesungen über die Ästhetik*, vol. 12, p. 289, on pity and fear; *Vorlesungen über die Ästhetik*, vol. 14, pp. 252–53, on the proper subject of tragedy; and *Vorlesungen über die Ästhetik*, vol. 14, p. 494, on the beginning, middle, and end of dramatic action.

forfeit a longstanding claim for the rationality of tragic drama. This blind spot, rather than being a simple limitation in Hegel's perspective, seems to play a distinctly enabling role in his thinking. For it forestalls direct confrontation with ways in which the systematic categories of a philosophical approach to literary texts, such as Aristotle's, exclude what is not in conformity with their premises. The high degree of coherence in Hegel's theory is purchased largely at the price of an obscurity that protects him from seeing what his own theory leaves out in asserting its dialectical understanding of drama. It will be necessary to take up later in greater detail the systematically motivated nature of Hegel's critical exclusions—their relation, that is, to the interests of his method. For such partiality contravenes the claim he makes to a privileged and impartial understanding of tragedy on the basis of his superior reflective position as philosophical spectator.

In the nineteenth and twentieth centuries, the apparent failure to account adequately for the absence of attention to conflict in the Aristotelian tradition is motivated by other factors. The pervasive modern assumption about the centrality of conflict in tragedy has been attended by misreadings of Aristotle. Repeatedly, the Greek philosopher is so interpreted that his terms are seen from an agonistic perspective. Aristotle, in other words, has been assimilated to a relatively recent way of understanding tragedy. As a result, post-Hegelian critics in general have not been able to appreciate the problems that conflict in tragedy posed for classical and Renaissance theories dedicated to revealing the *logos*, the rational order, in dramatic character and action. Examples from some popular works on tragedy that have appeared over the last thirty years or so bear out this point.

For instance, Helen Gardner finds fault with a modern tendency to see in the past our own preoccupation with the disjunctive, incoherent features of tragic drama. But she also asserts, "From the beginning, in all discussions of tragedy, one note is always struck: that tragedy includes, or reconciles, or preserves in tension, contraries."[21] The dominant chord in contemporary theory has sounded consistently in the history of criticism. In support of this opinion, Aristotle is introduced as the first exponent of the notion of conflict. Gardner brings him into her argument by indicating that the pity and fear complex corresponds to contrary aspects of plot or dramatic character. She does not spend time on this point, however, and passes quickly to writers who render these contrary aspects explicitly as a clash of passions and wills. The brevity of Gardner's treatment suggests that there is not much in the *Poetics* she can gather in support of her assertion, but, on the other hand, she does not admit any difficulty in fitting Aristotle's theory into a historical review of tragic conflict.

Others have also tried to trace the principle of conflict back to the *Poetics*. Robert Heilman bases his view of dividedness on "Aristotle's definition of the tragic hero," though he denies that he is in any sense "claiming Aristotelian protection."[22] Operating within an existentialist framework, he thinks that hamartia implies a "pulling apart . . . within the personality, a disturbance, though not a pathological one, of integration. The character is not 'one,' but divided." *Prohairesis*, Aristotle's technical term for deliberative choice, is often imported into this scheme, for it is thought to imply a crisis of values. The tragic agent, faced with two or more alternative courses of action, agonizes in his deliberations and recognizes that he loses whichever way he goes. Herein lies the tragic double bind, which Aristotle's notion of hamartia is supposed to involve. This interpretation of hamartia is reasserted by T. R. Henn. Using the Platonic language of John Donne's "Good Friday, 1613, Riding Westward," Henn says that the tragic psyche is " 'subject to foreign motions,' that is to external circumstances; it may lose its sense of purpose, its 'naturall

---

[21] Helen Gardner, *Religion and Literature* (London: Faber and Faber, 1971), p. 24.

[22] Robert Heilman, *Tragedy and Melodrama: Versions of Experience* (Seattle: University of Washington Press, 1968), p. 7.

forme' through its own internal conflicts, of which Donne's 'Pleasure or business' are secondary manifestations."[23]

Psychological and existentialist views of conflict are not the only ones that critics have tried to ground in the *Poetics*. Francis Fergusson's ritual theory of tragedy, which borrows heavily from Aristotle, centers on the importance of the agon in dramatic action.[24] Henry Myers says that the "beauty of tragedy" resides in the *metabasis*, which harmonizes the conflicting opposites of good and evil to form a "law of values."[25] Neither Fergusson nor Myers is concerned particularly to trace conflict back to Aristotelian ideas. But the assumption that the *Poetics* deals with conflict appears implicitly in the simple inclusion of one or more of its key terms in their discussions of tragic division.

To a certain extent, Aristotle's comments allow the connection that critics often want to see between the *Poetics* and the modern perspective on tragic struggle. *Hamartia* or *prohairesis* could imply an inner division between a good person's character and the flaw that pulls him or her in the opposite direction; and *metabasis* or *peripeteia* could signify a turning point in a clash between rivals. But Aristotle argues none of these positions and in several ways reveals that he does not imply them either. To assume that the Greek philosopher must have formulated what is now taken for granted is to confound a basic orientation of his poetics. Overlooked in all the cases cited here is Aristotle's distinct bias against a conflictual understanding of character and action.

In pointing out the tendency of twentieth-century critics to see a kind of continuity between classical attitudes and their

[23] T. R. Henn, *The Harvest of Tragedy* (1956; reprint, London: Methuen, 1961), p. 94.

[24] Francis Fergusson, *The Idea of a Theatre: A Study of Ten Plays, the Art of Drama in Changing Perspective* (Princeton: Princeton University Press, 1949).

[25] Henry Myers, "The Tragic Attitude toward Value," in *Tragedy: Modern Essays in Criticism*, ed. Laurence Michel and Richard B. Sewall (1963; reprint, Westport, Conn. : Greenwood Press, 1978), pp. 161–74.

own emphasis on strife, I am not simply calling attention to the reasons for a skewed understanding of Aristotle. Although I want to bring into view a mistaken appreciation of the *Poetics*, the reach of my argument is that the focus on tragic conflict needed specific and propitious conditions in critical theory to take shape and that these conditions did not emerge until the late eighteenth and early nineteenth centuries.

In order to appreciate the influence of these later developments, I will turn in the first chapter to Hegel's *Vorlesungen über die Ästhetik* and isolate the strategies he employs in formulating his seminal account of tragic conflict. An understanding of the difficulties posed by strife for earlier dramatic theorists can emerge most effectively, I think, in a context where its associations with disorder and irrationality are quite forthrightly addresssed and neutralized, as they are by Hegel. My discussion centers on his reliance in the aesthetic lectures on ideas about struggle and contradiction elaborated in the "philosophical history" of the *Phänomenologie des Geistes* and the *Vorlesungen über die Philosophie der Geschichte*. In reading Hegel on drama it becomes apparent that his influential conception of tragic conflict, as a struggle between equally valid but mutually exclusive ethical claims, is determined by a philosophical system with a vested interest in the mediation of conflict through the process of dialectical *Aufhebung*.[26] Indeed, the major tenets of the theory of tragedy in the *Vorlesungen über die Ästhetik* are fully comprehensible only against the backdrop of Hegel's larger conception of history as the violent self-embodiment of Spirit (*Geist*) in space and time. His model of conflict offers an opportunity to study the ways in which theoretical discourse works to control the disjunctive or indeterminate elements of the plays that it treats. The limitations of Hegel's "synthetic" approach to tragedy— the resistance of the literature to the conceptual framework of

---

[26] *Aufhebung* is a complex philosophical term, whose various senses Hegel exploits in his discussions of dialectic. The word, which is treated in chapter 1, means a raising or an elevation; a suspension; and an annulment or a dissolution.

interpretation—surface in his readings of tragic drama, particularly Sophocles' *Antigone* and Shakespeare's *Hamlet*, which are treated extensively in chapter 1.

This study of Hegel's efforts to regulate tragic conflict under the force of his dialectical structure establishes the ground for appreciating why it is excluded in literary theory predating him. Focusing on Aristotle, chapter 2 sets the anti-agonistic strain of the *Poetics* not only in the context of the *Nicomachean Ethics* and the logical treatises (particularly passages from the *Prior* and *Posterior Analytics*), but also in terms of Plato's critique of tragedy in the *Republic*. I argue that one of the central claims of the *Poetics* about the *spoudaiotes*, "goodness" or "seriousness", of the tragic agent is launched in implicit opposition to Plato's charge that the figures of drama are morally degenerate and that tragedy is, if not an infantile form of play (*paidia*), a dangerous indulgence of human weakness and instability. Moreover, Aristotle's pivotal notion of *spoudaiotes* carries a whole set of ethical assumptions with it that act as deterrents to a discussion of tragic conflict. Although the assumptions are not quite explicit in the *Poetics* itself, they become apparent in the framework of the *Nicomachean Ethics*, where one can discern the nonconflictual bias built into the term. This bias has a social side and a psychological side, both of which are explored in the chapter, through a reading of several fifth-century plays, including the *Oresteia*, *Ajax*, *Trachiniae*, *Heracles Mainomenos*, and *Bacchae*.

With the insights into an Aristotelian approach derived from a close analysis of the *Poetics*, I proceed in chapter 3 to a study of Renaissance and neoclassical dramatic theory. Given the sheer number of critical works on tragedy in the sixteenth and seventeenth centuries following the rediscovery of the *Poetics*, I have selected representative texts on drama in this period that have proven to be seminal. These include Antonio Minturno's *L'Arte Poetica* and *De Poeta*, Julius Caesar Scaliger's *Poetices Libri Septem*, Sir Philip Sidney's *Defense of Poetry*, Pierre Corneille's *Trois Discours*, and John Dryden's

An Essay of Dramatic Poesy. My effort is to show how these works reflect an appropriation of Aristotle's *Poetics* as a didactic treatise whose orientation could be assimilated to the rhetorical interests of Horace's popular *Ars Poetica.* Because this moralization of Aristotle was adumbrated in the twelfth-century Arabic commentary on the *Poetics* by Averroës, I will study briefly how Renaissance didacticism is anticipated in this earlier text and in its Latin translation by Hermannus Alemannus. Averroës' influence in the Middle Ages appears to have been negligible; nevertheless, he was quoted fairly often and approvingly by cinquecento critics, who found in his work confirmation of the predominant view that tragedy promotes ethical ideals and stabilizes the values of a culture. Although some of this moralizing criticism can justly claim a source in the Greek philosopher, most of it represents the continuation of a Roman tradition of rhetorical theory whose overtly moral preoccupations are superimposed upon the more subtle ethical strains of the *Poetics.* In any case, the convergence of Aristotle and Horace in the sixteenth and seventeenth centuries produces a hardening of the nonagonistic approach to tragedy and perpetuates assumptions about the values of moral, social, and individual harmony that forestall attention to the tragic dramatization of conflict. Christopher Marlowe's *Doctor Faustus,* William Shakespeare's *King Lear,* John Webster's *Duchess of Malfi,* and Pierre Corneille's *Le Cid* and *Horace* are studied in this connection.

Chapter 4 attempts to isolate one of the major intellectual developments in the eighteenth century following Dryden, which disrupts the neoclassical tradition of ideas about drama and introduces sustained reflection on the role of tragic conflict. In German Romantic theories of the sublime, particularly Friedrich Schiller's, we encounter ways of thinking about tragedy that emphasize struggle and opposition. As in the case of Hegel, however, this new attention to conflict is problematic, for it seeks to regulate the experience under the control of moral reason or some other analogous faculty aligned with humanity's end or destination (*Bestimmung*). A theoretical principle of order once again preempts and contains dramatizations of strife in tragedy and assures the determinacy of value as well as the individualistic integrity of tragic character. The theoretical limitations of this model are probed against several plays from classical Greece, a culture to which the German Romantics repeatedly turned in developing their literary exemplars.

In all these chapters my procedure is to test the viability of critical attitudes and positions against a variety of plays, frequently those addressed directly by a theorist. In exposing the constraints that theoretical principles generate for interpretation, I speak often of a playwright's resistance to critical assumptions about order in tragedy. To avoid the impression of anachronism, let me say that although the formulations of such order are temporally subsequent to the tragedy, the act of interpretation engages critic and literary work in a way that makes it possible to address textual resistance to theoretical strategies. I stress *textual resistance* because I am not embarked on an effort to discern authorial intention or argue for the tragic dramatist as revolutionary. Rather, I am concerned with the interpretive potential of texts and with the theorist's deferral of what is potentially disruptive to his claims. In foregrounding such deferrals, I realize that my own readings, which themselves are produced within the closure of a critical model, are marked by their own forms of exclusion.

CHAPTER ONE

Hegel: Conflict and Order

Without contraries is no progression. Attraction and Repulsion, Reason and Energy, Love and Hate, are necessary to human existence.
—William Blake, *The Marriage of Heaven and Hell*

WHEN HEGEL was delivering the *Vorlesungen über die Ästhetik* in Berlin during the 1820s, other prominent German literati were engaged in discussions of tragedy that emphasized conflict. I mentioned both Friedrich Schiller and A. W. Schlegel in this connection, but one could also cite Goethe as a forerunner of Hegelian ideas. Eckermann's *Gespräche mit Goethe* contains remarks about the Greek tragedians, notably Sophocles, that are in line with Hegel's later formulations of ethical struggle, and Wilhelm Meister's critique of *Hamlet*, which focuses on the battle within the heroic soul, exemplifies a burgeoning interest in psychological dilemmas.[1] This preoccupation is continued in English Romantic criticism, particularly of Shakespeare, and eventually develops into the kind of widespread character criticism in the twentieth century that stresses the tragic implications of inner dividedness.[2] Although

[1] Johann Wolfgang Goethe, *Gedenkausgabe der Werke, Briefe und Gespräche*, ed. Ernst Beutler, 28 vols. (Zurich: Artemis Verlag, 1948), *Johann Peter Eckermann's Gespräche mit Goethe in den letzten Jahren seines Lebens*, vol. 24, pp. 601–11, *Wilhelm Meister's Lehrjahre*, vol. 7, pp. 260–64.

[2] See Samuel Taylor Coleridge, *Shakespearean Criticism*, ed. Thomas Middleton Raysor, 2 vols. (Cambridge, Mass.: Harvard University Press, 1930), vol. 2, pp. 181–98 on *Hamlet*; William Hazlitt, *Characters of Shakespear's Plays* (London: J. M. Dent and Sons, 1906); A. C. Bradley, *Shakespearean Tragedy: Essays on Hamlet, Othello, King Lear, and Macbeth* (London: Macmillan, 1905); A.J.A. Waldock, *Hamlet: A Study in Critical Method*

these earlier speculations are evidence that Hegel's views were not entirely new, his theory is nonetheless distinguished from others by its remarkable consolidation of ideas and orientations popular in his time and influential for later thinkers.[3]

Hegel's conceptual model of dramatic conflict, as I have indicated, seems to be indebted to pre-Socratic philosophy, though the influence is not directly acknowledged by him and must be inferred from his other writings. As Walter Kaufmann has pointed out, Hegel was the first not only to establish the history of philosophy as an area of central importance for students, but to direct attention to the major contributions of the Greeks. About the *Vorlesungen über die Geschichte der Philosophie*, he remarks, "almost two thirds of the history of Western Philosophy is taken up by Greek philosophy. The pre-Socratics get three times as much space as all of medieval and Renaissance philosophy taken together."[4] Given this interest, it is perhaps not surprising to find several key pre-Socratic ideas at the heart of Hegel's views of conflict and dialectic.[5] These ideas may be briefly summarized by scrutinizing some aspects of the fragments of Anaximander, Heraclitus, and Empedocles.

Anaximander, according to the only and highly disputed fragment of his work that we possess, conceives of a cosmological scheme in which the elemental powers, all equals, are in a constant state of war, one periodically ascendant over its opposite—for example, the wet over the dry—and thus compelled to pay penalty and retribution (δίκην καὶ τίσιν) to the wronged party, who subsequently gains advantage.[6] Thus the

(Cambridge: Cambridge University Press, 1931); H. B. Charlton, *Shakespearian Tragedy* (Cambridge: Cambridge University Press, 1948).

[3] One of the best scholarly attempts in English to evaluate Hegel's contribution to dramatic criticism is still A. C. Bradley's lecture in *Oxford Lectures on Poetry* (1909; reprint, London: Macmillan, 1959).

[4] Walter Kaufmann, *Hegel: Reinterpretation, Texts, and Commentary* (Garden City, N.Y.: Doubleday, 1965), pp. 278–81.

[5] On Hegel's use of the pre-Socratics in formulating his own dialectic, see Hans Georg Gadamer, *Hegel's Dialectic: Five Hermeneutical Studies*, tr. P. Christopher Smith (New Haven: Yale University Press, 1976), pp. 5–34.

[6] Anaximander, Frag. 112 (DK 12), in *The Presocratic Philosophers: A*

Anaximandrian law of the universe is a *lex talionis*, predicated on cosmic strife and the distribution, "according to the ordinance of time," of compensation and punishment to the offended and offending parties.[7] The metaphor shaping this formulation is drawn, of course, from the realm of human social and political activity and thus, perhaps, bespeaks a sense of life informed by necessary strife and a system of rewards and punitive measures. In this view, conflict would be part of a self-balancing system, whose equilibrium is constituted in the reciprocal process of making up for transgressions and excesses.

Heraclitus claims that "war is the father of all, the king of all," and that "it is necessary to know that war is common and strife is justice, and all things come to be by strife and necessity."[8] These pronouncements, as recent scholarship has shown, go beyond those of Anaximander, since they construe *"dike* not merely as compensation for crime or excess but as a total pattern that includes both punishment and crime itself, as necessary ingredients of the world order."[9] Conflict, or rather war (*polemos*), is generalized for the structure of op-

---

Critical History with a Selection of Texts, ed. G. S. Kirk and J. E. Raven (1957; reprint, Cambridge: Cambridge University Press, 1975); from Simplicius, *Physics* 24, 17. "ἐξ ὧν δὲ ἡ γένεσίς ἐστι τοῖς οὖσι, καὶ τὴν φθορὰν εἰς ταῦτα γίνεσθαι 'κατὰ τὸ χρεών διδόναι γὰρ αὐτὰ δίκην καὶ τίσιν ἀλλήλοις τῆς ἀδικίας κατὰ τὴν τοῦ χρόνου τάξιν.' "

[7] See Charles Kahn, "Anaximander's Fragment: The Universe Governed by Law," in *The PreSocratics: A Collection of Critical Essays*, ed. Alexander R. D. Mourelatos (Garden City, N.Y.: Anchor Books, 1974), p. 105.

[8] Heraclitus, Frags. 214 and 215 (DK 80 and 53), in *The Presocratic Philosophers*, ed. Kirk and Raven.

> εἰδέναι χρὴ τὸν πόλεμον ἐόντα ξυνόν, καὶ δίκην ἔριν,
> καὶ γινόμενα πάντα κατ' ἔριν καὶ χρεών.

(214)

> πόλεμος πάντων μὲν πατήρ ἐστι, πάντων δὲ βασιλεύς, καὶ
> τοὺς μὲν θεοὺς ἔδειξε τοὺς δὲ ἀνθρώπους, τοὺς μὲν δούλους
> ἐποίησε τοὺς δὲ ἐλευθέρους.

(215)

[9] *The Art and Thought of Heraclitus*, ed. with comm. by Charles Kahn (Cambridge: Cambridge University Press), p. 207.

position that informs all things and produces *logos*; the universe is orderly not in spite of but because of strife and the violent opposition of the elements. In particular, Heraclitus echoes in these fragments the prayer of Achilles in his speech of regret over the quarrel of Agamemnon and controverts Homer's association of Ares, the war god, with destruction and loss:[10] from a cosmic perspective, conflict and justice are not antithetical but one, and their identity constitutes the *kosmos* of the natural world as well as of human life.

In addition to rejecting the Homeric assertion in the *Iliad* about the destructiveness of strife, Heraclitus is also, apparently, departing from Hesiod's formulation in the *Works and Days*, where two types of *eris* are distinguished, one that spurs evil war and battle (πόλεμόν τε κακὸν καὶ δῆριν) and another that is far better for people, moving them to toil (ἐπὶ ἔργον) and making them compete with one another for excellence.[11] Such a dual evaluation, which can be more easily squared with the view of Anaximander, is superseded by Heraclitus, who "is best appreciated if we think of him as accepting the distinction for the sake of argument, and then equating evil Eris with the principle of Justice."[12] Heraclitus, in short, has a more radical conception of conflict than either Hesiod or other extant pre-Socratic philosophers and proffers a much stronger identity of strife and order. This difference, however, is less important for our purposes than the organizing function that they all attribute in their various ways to *eris*.

Empedocles' views may also be mentioned in this context, though they have more in common with Hesiod and Anaximander than Heraclitus. He presents a cosmic cycle in which struggle (*neikos*) is not ranked with disorder, chaos, and evil, but allotted status as a genuine principle of creation. From one point of view, it is destructive of the perfect unity of the Sphere

---

[10] Homer, *Homeri Opera*, ed. David B. Munro and Thomas W. Allen, 4 vols. (1920; reprint, Oxford: Clarendon Press, 1962), vol. 2, 18.107.

[11] Hesiod, *Works and Days*, ed. with comm. by M. L. West (Oxford: Clarendon Press, 1978), ll. 11–16.

[12] Kahn, *The Art and Thought of Heraclitus*, p. 206.

under the ruling power of *Philotes*, while from another, it is productive of the separation of elements into parts necessary for the composition of more complex entities.[13] In other words, the possibility of cosmogony and zoogony depends on Strife's fragmentation of the One into parts that, in turn, under the gradual reassertion of Love, become constitutive of complex living things. This interpretation is still controversial in some respects, for it is drawn from recent scholarly attempts to reformulate along new lines the orthodox position about Empedocles' cosmic cycle.[14] But the interesting details of exegesis on this debated issue are not so important for our purposes as a fact that few would now dispute: that Empedoclean philosophy presents us with a double view of strife as an annihilating and a vitally generative force.

These pre-Socratic accounts are exemplary in specifying a two-sidedness in *neikos*, which is rehabilitated by Hegel and made into a fundamental premise of his dialectic. Conceiving of *Kollision* as simultaneously destructive and revitalizing, he creates the building blocks of his philosophical history *(philosophische Geschichte)* and renders conflict a suitable structural principle for his rationalizing account of tragedy.[15] Admittedly, there are important differences between these pre-Socratic notions of conflict and Hegel's view of regenerative strife. For example, the triadic dialectic developed by Hegel includes a moment of synthetic *Aufhebung*, as we will see, which becomes in turn an element in another conflict between

[13] See Frags. 423 and 424 (DK 17), in *The Presocratic Philosophers*, ed. Kirk and Raven.

[14] Jean Bollack, *Empédocle*, vol. 1, *Introduction à l'ancienne physique* (Paris: Les Éditions de Minuit, 1965); Friedrich Solmsen, "Love and Strife in Empedocles' Cosmology," *Phronesis* 10 (1965): 109–48; Uvo Holscher, "Weltzeiten und Lebenszyklus," *Hermes* 93 (1965): 7–33. These works and the debate they have entailed are reviewed by A. A. Long, "Empedocles' Cosmic Cycle in the Sixties," in *The PreSocratics*, ed. Mourelatos, pp. 397–425.

[15] For a modern theory of tragedy also based on a dual valuation of violence, see René Girard, *Violence and the Sacred*, tr. Patrick Gregory (Baltimore: Johns Hopkins University Press, 1977).

opposites. This triadic structure guarantees the forward thrust of the dialectic, as a principle of progress in history. None of the pre-Socratic thinkers discussed here formulates such a moment of synthesis. Typically, their conception of opposites in conflict involves the same elemental powers, bound in a periodic order of reciprocity and symmetry, which constitutes a continuous equilibrium. While acknowledging this difference, we can nonetheless appreciate Hegel's adaptation of a characteristic pre-Socratic idea, which redirects critical thinking by breaking with Platonic and Aristotelian attitudes.

Because Hegel's theory of history is basic to his theory of tragedy, we will begin our study by focusing on the *Vorlesungen über die Philosophie der Geschichte* and on portions of the *Phänomenologie des Geistes*.[16] These texts develop the thesis that conflict, far from posing an ultimate threat to order and stability, is a crucial transitional experience in a world-historical process, which generates ever higher levels of social and spiritual perfection. In this dialectical scheme, human action (*Handlung*) has a key role insofar as it is the vehicle for the expression of interests that clash violently and that are finally mediated to usher in a more advanced stage of consciousness. Essential to Hegel's conception of history, action also has a central part in his ideas about drama and motivates

[16] The introduction to the *Vorlesungen über die Philosophie der Geschichte* is edited by Johannes Hoffmeister under the title *Die Vernunft in der Geschichte* (Hamburg: F. Meiner, 1955). I have used Eva Moldenhauer and Karl Markus Michel's edition of the *Vorlesungen über die Philosophie der Geschichte*, vol. 12 of *G.W.F. Hegel: Werke in zwanzig Bänden* (Frankfurt: Suhrkamp, 1970), which relies on the Hoffmeister text. A new English translation of *Die Vernunft in der Geschichte* is by H. B. Nisbet, *Reason in History* (Cambridge: Cambridge University Press, 1975). For a recent discussion of Hegel's text, see George Dennis O'Brien, *Hegel on Reason and History: A Contemporary Interpretation* (Chicago: University of Chicago Press, 1975). References to *Vorlesungen über die Philosophie der Geschichte* will be abbreviated in subsequent notes as *VPG*. For all other works of Hegel, I use Hermann Glockner's edition, *Hegels Sämtliche Werke*, 20 vols. (Stuttgart: Friedrich Fromann, 1927–1930). *Phänomenologie des Geistes*, vol. 2, will be abbreviated in subsequent notes as *PhG*.

his preoccupation with rivalry and reconciliation, with the *tragische Kollision* as a manifestation of rational order.[17] Within this context, we can appreciate the genesis of several notions about tragedy, which have subsequently been assimilated into the mainstream of critical thinking.

BEFORE EXAMINING Hegel's historical works, it is useful at the outset to differentiate between two conceptions of history that make their way into his aesthetics and dramatic theory. One has been discussed frequently by commentators interested in his system of modes but is of minor importance for the issues we will be examining. I refer to Hegel's organization of artistic forms into a chronological sequence beginning with "symbolic" modes of expression among the Egyptians, of which monolithic sculpture is representative, and passing progressively through more spiritually complex creations of the "classical" and "romantic" phases.[18] As a chronological pattern into which artistic modes are fit for purposes of classification, history, in this traditional usage, appears simply as an external temporal field that is articulated and organized by the philosopher.

But in Hegel's aesthetics, history is also, and more typically, an internal principle of structure in art and constitutive of its form. This historical aspect, especially significant for understanding the essential characteristics of tragedy, is elaborated in the general remarks opening the *Vorlesungen über die Ästhetik*, contained under the title "Das Kunstschöne oder das Ideal."[19] In these pages, artistic beauty is conceived as an evolving process in which the divine principle enters into the temporal, human world and undergoes various forms of de-

---

[17] For a recent evaluation of the importance of "action" in Hegel's thought, see Charles Taylor, "Hegel and the Philosophy of Action," in *Hegel's Philosophy of Action*, ed. Lawrence S. Stepelevich and David Lamb (Atlantic Highlands, N.J.: Humanities Press, 1983), pp. 1–18.

[18] See *Vorlesungen über die Ästhetik*, vol. 12, pp. 114–32; hereafter abbreviated as *VA*.

[19] *VA*, vol. 12, pp. 212–406.

termination (*Bestimmtheit*) in particular works of art. We discover what is involved in this determination after Hegel poses the questions that guide his analysis: "In what way can the Ideal, despite its going out into externality and finitude, and thus into the non-Ideal, still preserve itself; on the other hand, in what way is finite existence in a position to take on the ideality of artistic beauty?"[20]

In answering these questions, Hegel suggests how thoroughly the nature of *Kunstschöne*, "artistic beauty," is implicated in the problems of history. *Die Bestimmtheit des Ideals* necessarily involves "active movement and development" (*thätige Bewegung und Entfaltung*), an expansion into particularity and the "opposition of the broken and confused life of the world."[21] Thus the divine Spirit loses itself in the fragmented conditions of space and time, taking on the one-sidedness and division (*Einseitigkeit und Entzweiung*) that Hegel says are inseparable from development, but by doing so is allowed to pervade that world and finally reassert itself in ideal form. Different artistic forms are then ranked according to the stage or stages in this process that they embody and especially according to the manner in which they present the reassertion of the Ideal. Furthermore, the criterion for ranking is implied in the very notion of *Bestimmtheit*: the more the work of art enters into the contradiction and division attending determinacy, the better it conforms to its intrinsic principle.

Thus we find Hegel proposing in the *Vorlesungen über die Ästhetik* a hierarchical schema of arts that intersects with the chronological system of symbolic, classical, and romantic modes, but according to which the historical component is essentially internal to the work of art and understood as the embodied, temporalized Ideal.[22] Hegel's fusion of these two classificatory systems, which is complicated by the different ways in which he manipulates the idea of history, has given rise to

[20] *VA*, vol. 12, p. 240.
[21] *VA*, vol. 12, p. 244.
[22] *VA*, vol. 12, pp. 107–32.

some perplexity. But as Anne and Henry Paolucci remark, the double classification can be extremely efficient. For instance, it allows that "poetry, though characteristically romantic, has passed, historically, through symbolic and classical phases before attaining in modern times that precise relationship between content and form that defines the romantic type of expression. Thus, Greek tragedy is romantic in comparison with Greek sculpture, yet classical in comparison with Shakespearean tragedy."[23] Though in this passage the Paoluccis reserve the term *history* for the sequential unfolding of modes over time, the relationship between form and content to which they refer is a way of talking, in common literary parlance, about the embodiment or sensible manifestation of the Ideal, which is also conceived by Hegel as a historical process, but one contained within the work of art as its principle of structure.

Let us look more closely at this hierarchical schema in which the historical component may be said to inform art. The types on the lower end of the scale, architecture and sculpture, are characterized by an appearance of "inactive, infinite repose" (*thatlos ewige Ruhe*).[24] Because the "terror of division still lies dormant" in these works of art, they bear a sense of calm and proud solidity. There is no attempt to embody action in them, only a permanent restfulness and a tranquil gaze. "These are situations which certainly transfer to the independent form of God a determination, yet a determination that does not pass over into wider relations and oppositions, but remains closed in itself and has for itself its own security."[25] If Spirit at this stage "takes a rest" in its physical form, it comes to active movement in other kinds of art and in increasingly violent ways, until in poetry it reaches a peak of agitation and conflict.

In Hegel's account, then, the three major poetic genres, epic,

[23] *Hegel on Tragedy*, ed. Anne and Henry Paolucci (1962; reprint, New York: Harper and Row, 1975), p. xviii.
[24] *VA*, vol. 12, pp. 243, 269.
[25] *VA*, vol. 12, p. 275.

lyric, and drama, contain an element of disruption in which "the determination presents itself as essential difference and in opposition against another gives ground to a collision."[26] The Ideal suffers violation in these final stages of embodiment, which present an advance into extreme fragmentation. Given such discord, it is the primary difficulty of art to prevent the destruction of beauty into radical and irresolvable *Differenz*, "difference, differentiation." Coherence must not be threatened by a dissemination of Spirit that does not allow mediation. It becomes imperative, therefore, that the breach of unity be carried only so far that harmony may again be captured. From this perspective, drama, especially tragedy, distinguishes itself in Hegel's view, for he believes it is best suited to reintegrate the broken nature of the Ideal, to cancel division and bring the action back to a condition of repose. Such a dramatic process, which involves simultaneously an annulment or a dissolution of conflict, a suspension of the values in collision, and a raising of these values to a higher level of spiritual consciousness is what Hegel designates by the complex term *Aufhebung*. "Insofar as the collision generally requires a resolution, which follows the conflict of opposites, the situation that is replete with conflict is above all the subject matter of dramatic art, to which is granted the privilege of presenting beauty in its most complete and profound development."[27] The requirement of resolution, the importance of not carrying opposition too far, is expressed by Hegel in terms of a principle of necessity (*Nothwendigkeit*), which issues from the Ideal inherent in art and which is capable of mediating every contradiction.[28] As we will see, this principle is problematic. Although it is asserted to be intrinsic to the work of art and consequently part of the artist's design, it is rather the product of interpretation and identifiable with the activity that Hegel conceives as philosophical contemplation. Necessity is an idea

[26] *VA*, vol. 12, p. 278.
[27] *VA*, vol. 12, pp. 278–79.
[28] *VA*, vol. 14, p. 485.

manipulated by an interpreting consciousness to neutralize forces that disrupt closure and destabilize the conditions for mediation.[29]

Comedy, I should note, appears most consistent with the experience of reconciliation on which Hegel lays such weight, and in the aesthetic lectures it indeed ranks highest among all the arts because of its joyful affirmation of unity and integration. Yet tragedy is the form in which Hegel finds dramatized the great collisions of the Ideal and the most penetrating tests of what constitutes spiritual truth. Thus, the theoretical supremacy of comedy in the system of fine arts is virtually eclipsed by the overriding interest shown in the conflicts and mediations of tragedy; far more attention is paid to the plays of Aeschylus, Sophocles, and Shakespeare than to those of Aristophanes, Plautus, and Molière. The centrality of tragedy in Hegel's thought is confirmed in his tendency to formulate the movement of Spirit (*die Bewegung der Substanz*) out of oneness and into opposition as a *tragische* not a *komische Bewegung*.[30]

The orientation in Hegel's concept of the artistic Ideal toward increasing fragmentation is a result of influence exerted on the aesthetic lectures by his theory of history. In the *Vorlesungen über die Philosophie der Geschichte* and in the earlier *Phänomenologie des Geistes* we find the idea of Spirit as a rational substance—"that through which and in which all reality has its being and subsistence"[31]—realizing itself in the

[29] For a discussion of some controversial problems surrounding Hegel's conception of necessity, see Raymond Plant, *Hegel: An Introduction* (Bloomington: Indiana University Press, 1973), pp. 127–33, 184–89. That Hegel thinks necessity is structured into the work of art is clearer than the more troubled issue of how and if he thinks it is structured into natural and social development.

[30] Otto Pöggeler, "Hegel und die griechische Tragödie," *Hegel-Studien* (Supplement 1 of "Heidelberger Hegel-Tage," 1962), pp. 292–96.

[31] VPG, p. 21. "Durch speculative Erkenntnis in ihr wird es erwiesen, dass die Vernunft . . . die Substanz wie die unendliche Macht, sich selbst der unendliche Stoff alles natürlichen und geistigen Lebens wie die unendlich Form,

process of world history by abandoning its transcendent ideality and immersing itself in the lives of nations and individuals. *Geist* exists only by entering into space and time, according to Hegel; its business is "to come to itself, to produce itself, to make itself into that which it is in itself"—through the history of mankind. "According to this abstract definition, it may be said that world history is the representation of Spirit as it achieves knowledge of its own nature."[32] Thus, *Geist* cannot exist without the world, and yet the world it enters is dispersed, fragmented, inhabited by beings who have only the dimmest consciousness of themselves as vehicles of a rational purpose.[33] It is the project of Spirit to overcome these limitations by embodying itself in finite beings and by bringing these beings in turn to an awareness of themselves as embodied Spirit. Having suffered division and conflict in the course of history, *Geist* achieves a final dialectical mediation, united with humanity in a world that understands itself not only as the product of but as the necessary ground of being for *Geist*. This ultimate self-reflection, in which individuals apprehend themselves as identical with the universal, in which appearance becomes one with essence, is what Hegel calls reason or absolute knowledge.[34]

Revealed in this brief recapitulation are several important

---

die Betätigung dieses ihres Inhalts ist. Die Substanz ist sie, nämlich das, wodurch und worin alle Wirklichkeit ihr Sein und Bestehen hat."

[32] *VPG*, p. 31.

[33] See Charles Taylor, *Hegel* (Cambridge: Cambridge University Press, 1975), p. 104. Taylor's entire discussion of "self-positing Spirit" and historical conflict is useful, pp. 76–147; also see pp. 365–461. Other discussions of *Geist* and historical conflict that have been helpful to me include Walter Kaufmann, *Hegel: Reinterpretation, Texts, and Commentary*, chaps. 1 and 6; Herbert Marcuse, *Reason and Revolution: Hegel and the Rise of Social Theory*, 2d ed. (New York: Humanities Press, 1954), pp. 3–223; J. Glenn Gray, *Hegel and Greek Thought* (1941; reprint, New York: Harper and Row, 1968), pp. 1–16, 53–67.

[34] See Plant, *Hegel*, pp. 124–46, and Taylor, *Hegel*, pp. 465–533. For a penetrating critique of the position of absolute knowledge in Hegelian philosophy, see Jürgen Habermas, *Knowledge and Human Interests*, tr. Jeremy Shapiro (Boston: Beacon Press, 1971), pp. 7–24.

parallels between the aesthetic *Bestimmtheit des Ideals* and the historical *Bestimmung des Geistes*. At the most general level, it is clear that the movement of Spirit in the sociohistorical world provides a model for Hegel's conception of art and of drama, in particular. The necessary collisions attending the incarnation of *Geist* in world history are also central to the advanced artistic forms of determinate Spirit. In this light, tragedy appears as an exemplary artistic expression of a process at work in the larger historical field. In addition to this fundamental parallel, there are others that bear closer scrutiny: (1) the emphasis on action in the self-embodiment of *Geist* and the Ideal; (2) the notion that Spirit operates teleologically, rendering meaningful and coherent what individual persons, from their limited dialectical position, cannot understand; and (3) the idea that this teleology and ultimate rationality are accessible only to one who has attained a privileged vantage point, that of absolute knowledge.

In Hegel's formulation of artistic types, the progressive movement of the Ideal into more differentiated stages of embodiment means a movement into individuated human action. This is why drama, and tragedy especially, which is rooted in action, takes on a position of special importance in the Hegelian scheme. Human passions and activities are the vehicles through which Spirit expresses itself. Thus we find Hegel asserting in his view of tragedy two related premises of his *philosophische Geschichte*: first, "action is the clearest unfolding of the individual, both in respect to his mental disposition and his aims; what a man is in the innermost depth of his being is first brought to realization through his action";[35] and second,

---

[35] *VA*, vol. 12, p. 297. These words echo Hegel's statement about action in *VPG*, p. 57: "We should note in connection with these determinations of the Spirit [in objects, deeds, or works] that a distinction is often made between man's inner nature and his deeds. This does not apply in history; the man himself is the sum total of his deeds. One might imagine a case in which a person's intentions were excellent even though his actual deeds were worthless. And individual instances can certainly occur in which people conceal their real attitudes, but this is not the whole picture. The truth is that there is

the nature of Spirit emerges most fully in human volition and deeds. "The universal must be actual in the individual as something proper to him and his very own [*das Eigene und Eigenste*], but not as a property of the subject as thinker, rather as his character and disposition."[36] In these two points resides a famous Hegelian paradox: what individuals do, though personally motivated and willed, is at the same time guided by *Geist* and consequently subordinated to a rational end. An integral part of his dramatic theory, this paradox is supposed to furnish a solution to some traditional philosophical problems attaching to action—its contingency and resistance to explanations based on rational necessity. It would be helpful to examine briefly the context in which Hegel's view develops.

Individual action, as a product of the will or personal decision making, has from the time of Aristotle posed a difficulty to those who would see in history a rational design. Because the realm of human affairs is shaped by private motives and fortuitous happenings, it appears wanting in a principle of order, a *logos*.[37] What is brought into being by action is contingent, for it admits of being other than what it is, and the contingent, as Hannah Arendt recently argues, has from the beginning of Western philosophy been construed as unamenable to or in some way at odds with reason.[38] Far from deny-

---

no difference between the inner and the outer. In history, especially, there is no need to waste time puzzling over temporary differences between them. The character of a nation is that of its deeds, for the deeds represent the end it pursues."

[36] *VA*, vol. 12, p. 248.

[37] Aristotle's view of history, and its bearing on his theory of tragedy, is a major topic of the following chapter. His attitude about *historie* is expressed in *Poetics*, chap. 9, and indirectly in other treatises, for example, *Metaphysics*, 5.7–9, 6.2–3, and 7.6–10, where the realm of human activity is conceived in terms of its contingent nature. That there can be no *episteme* of history is borne out by the fact that Aristotle does not bring his teleological method to bear on the vicissitudes of human life through time.

[38] Hannah Arendt, *The Life of the Mind* (New York: Harcourt Brace Jovanovich, 1978), vol. 2, *Willing*, pp. 27–32.

ing this perception, Hegel gives it a vivid formulation in a famous passage of the *Vorlesungen über die Philosophie der
Geschichte*.[39] History is a "spectacle of passions" (*Schauspiel
der Leidenschaften*), in which personal interests and the sat-
isfaction of individual impulses are the most potent force.
What makes them powerful, Hegel says, is that "they observe
none of the limitations that law and morality want to impose
upon them, because the power of the natural temperament has
a more direct influence over man than the artificial and pains-
taking inculcation of order and moderation, law and morality."[40] Thus, in beholding history, we see a display of confusion and wreckage in which the desires of individuals compete
without serving any apparent end. The pervasive contingency
of this spectacle defies the possibility that there is a principle
of rational necessity at work in the course of human affairs.

In this passage, the problem of history is posed not only in
terms of contingency—the particular deeds or passions of individuals that could just as well be otherwise—but in terms of
conflict. Particular human aims assert themselves against
others that impede them, and action, consequently, becomes
mired in violent strife, which seems directed to no universal
goal. But while Hegel accepts the validity of an impression
sanctioned by Aristotle, he also submits the *Schauspiel der
Leidenschaften* to a question that allows him to redefine the
initial perception of historical chaos. In fact, the notion of a
history with meaningful form is already implicitly contained
in the metaphor of *Schauspiel*, which suggests a dramatic performance with an ordering hand at work and an interested
spectator. "Even as we look at history as the slaughter bench
on which the happiness of nations, the wisdom of states, and
the virtue of individuals have been sacrificed, a question also
necessarily arises in our thoughts: to whom, to what final end
have these monstrous sacrifices been made?"[41] In this question

[39] *VPG*, pp. 34–35.
[40] *VPG*, p. 34.
[41] *VPG*, p. 35.

is echoed the need of the beholder to eliminate contingency, to find rational meaning in the apparent aimlessness, conflict, and destruction of the past. It is precisely such a need that motivates Hegel's project of a "philosophical history," which attempts to prove that "reason governs the world and that world history, therefore, has progressed rationally."[42]

A major interpretive strategy of this project is to admit that individual competing passions are the mainsprings of everything that has happened in the world, while also asserting that they are at the same time "the means and instruments of a higher and broader enterprise of which they know nothing, but which they unconsciously fulfill."[43] That human beings may, through their actions, produce an effect and serve an end that they do not intend is the work of the "cunning of reason" (die List der Vernunft). The ruse of this principle is to use individuals, while they act on their own will, toward a general end and then to abandon them to destruction, once they have been made to serve the universal. Hegel makes a similar point in the Phänomenologie when he says that the movement of Spirit "has the expression of its necessity in individuals, in whom the universal appears as a pathos and the activity of the movement as individual action, which gives the appearance of contingency to the necessity of the process."[44] The paradoxes of a teleologically controlled contingency, of the necessity in willed acts, of a rational end served by conflict all follow from a basic premise of Hegel's philosophical history and phenomenology of Spirit, that universality (die Allgemeinheit) embodies itself in the particular, in the deeds and passions of individuals.

The case of Socrates exemplifies how these tenets of Hegel's philosophische Geschichte work. His life and death are seen, in the lectures on both philosophy and world history, in terms

[42] VPG, p. 20. "Der einzige Gedanke, den die Philosophie mitbringt, is aber der einfache Gedanke der Vernunft, dass die Vernunft die Welt beherrsche, dass es also auch in der Weltgeschichte vernünftig zugegangen sei."
[43] VPG, p. 40.
[44] PhG, vol. 2, p. 364.

of a struggle between *Sittlichkeit*, the traditional morality of the Athenian polis, and *Moralität*, the right of self-determination, of subjective independence in deciding what to do and what to avoid.[45] Revealed in the *Kollision* between these two different bases of human conduct is the surreptitious progress of Reason in the life of the Greeks, the shift from one order of culture to another. Though Socrates, the individual, is vanquished—and in a way that may appear unfair or irrational—his moral action has an enduring effect on the Athenian people. "The false form of individuality is done away with and in a violent way, by punishment. But the principle will rise up later into its true form," that is, into a form of the world Spirit.[46] The principle about which Hegel speaks is the personal freedom of choosing, which is represented by the Socratic *daimonion*. Thus *die List der Vernunft* turns a clash of values in the ethical life of Athens into a transitional point generating beneficial change. Where there is darkness and destruction, the seeming obliteration of something valuable, *Geist* introduces a purpose, preserving what is good in the process of negating its individual human bearer.

Structuring this view of Socrates and the whole *philosophische Geschichte* of which it is a part is a dialectical understanding of historical action. Only a privileged spectator, a philosopher of history such as Hegel himself, is capable of perceiving that the universal comes into being through the particular and its negation.[47] The agents, on the other hand, as the concept of the cunning of reason suggests, are deficient in the knowledge possessed by a philosophical beholder, ignorant of

---

[45] *Vorlesungen über die Geschichte der Philosophie*, vol. 18, pp. 100–122; *VPG*, pp. 328–30.

[46] *Vorlesungen über die Geschichte der Philosophie*, vol. 18, p. 117.

[47] For a perceptive analysis of the spectator's role in Hegelian philosophy, see Arendt, *The Life of the Mind*, vol. 1, *Thinking*, pp. 92–98. Also, for a discussion of some inconsistencies and cruxes in Hegel's conception of the philosophical spectator, see Shlomo Avineri, "Consciousness and History: List der Vernunft in Hegel and Marx," in *New Studies in Hegel's Philosophy*, ed. Warren E. Steinkraus (New York: Holt, Rinehart, and Winston, 1971), especially pp. 111–12.

the ghostly power operating behind their backs and turning what they do to ends they never imagined. Acting in a cloud, the doers cannot comprehend the higher rational purpose of the confusion in which they are caught up. From their vantage point, the struggle of competing claims is likely to appear senseless. But when scrutinized with a superior mind of reason, collisions and individual losses become meaningful steps leading to a more advanced form of Spirit. History, turning on the deeds of half-conscious agents, such as Socrates, whom Hegel calls "world-historical individuals," takes on an orderly form. Turbulence in the historical field reveals a hidden design centered on decisive collisions instigated by those who have pursued their understanding of spiritual truth to the point of violent confrontation. Conflict, therefore, is ultimately not a force of dissolution or an expression of contingency. On the contrary, conceived philosophically, it is the experience through which the coherence of history emerges, the negativity giving thrust to the dialectic shaping human affairs.

It is precisely in these terms that Hegel seeks to define tragedy and the tragic poet. Like the philosopher of history, the dramatist with a mind of reason brings order to the turmoil of human activity by turning apparently contingent strife into the driving force behind the manifestation of universal law. Where "for ordinary sight only obscurity, accident, and confusion seem to have control, for him is revealed the real self-fulfillment of that which is in and for itself rational and true [*des an und für sich Vernünftigen und Wirklichen*]."[48] As vehicles of this rationality and truth, the heroes of tragedy are dramatic counterparts of the world-historical persons whose actions form the stuff of which Hegel's *philosophische Geschichte* is made. Thus tragedy, too, by making conflict a structuring unit in a dialectical process moving to resolution, finds its principle of order in the experience that at first threatens to dissolve it. Both philosophical history and dramatic art are ra-

---

[48] *VA*, vol. 14, p. 486.

tional not because they dispose of conflict, but because they mediate it in the interests of a higher unity.

This essential similarity between the philosopher and tragedian should not obscure the fact that the dramatic artist holds the humblest place in Hegel's system of absolute spirit. The three modes of thought composing this system—art, religion, and philosophy—all have in common a superior dialectical vantage point from which the thinker, no longer enmeshed in the necessary partiality of action, can reflect on the stages of human development as the various ways in which *Geist* has embodied itself in the world.[49] Only from his position is the identity of Spirit and individual life forms, of object and subject, apparent. But art engages in this reflection through imagistic thought patterns whose truth only philosophical discourse can fully render. Thus tragedy, though the highest aesthetic embodiment of the movement of Spirit, is less adequate than the conceptual language that frees itself, according to Hegel, from a sensuous medium and from picture thinking.[50] This difference, however, is less important for our purposes than the parallel between the dramatic artist and his philosophical exemplar, both of whom have a privileged perspective on human activity as a manifestation and vehicle of the divine. The tragedian, too, verifies the maxim of the historical lectures that "whoever looks at the world rationally finds that the world in turn takes on a rational appearance."[51]

Some of Hegel's most influential and stimulating ideas about tragedy derive from his theory of history and the role of the thinking spectator. Of particular importance for the development of dramatic criticism is his concept of dialectical mediation, by means of which *Kollision* is rendered as a principle of order. Purged of its associations with dissolution and irrationality, conflict can be identified as the *logos* of drama, as a structural element that gives unity to the shape of dramatic

[49] See Plant, *Hegel*, pp. 233–43, and Taylor, *Hegel*, pp. 116–24, 465–68, 510–33.

[50] See Taylor, *Hegel*, pp. 465–79.

[51] *VPG*, p. 23.

events. This transformation of conflict into the "soul of trag-edy," to use a phrase from the *Poetics*, displaces Aristotle's emphasis on the imitation of an action concerned with a mid-dling agent who falls because of a great hamartia. But signifi-cantly, it also strengthens the Aristotelian insistence on or-ganic unity and teleological design. The sense of order and equilibrium so pervasive in Aristotle's view of tragedy is no less pervasive in Hegel's. It is likely that the continuing popu-larity of the ideas contained in the lectures on aesthetics owes a good deal to the conflation of classical notions of artistic form with the modern attention to the motivating role of con-flict in history and human affairs.

Although Hegel's theoretical framework has generated both provocative and formative insights into tragedy, it contains premises that are problematic in interpretation, because their effect is to produce a highly coherent sense in the plays, ac-cording to which conflicts are transformed and subdued into paradigmatic illustrations of a philosophical system. The next section examines in greater detail how the Hegelian notions of necessity, dialectical mediation, and the privileged spectator act as interpretive strategies in the *Vorlesungen über die Äs-thetik* designed to validate a rational order and dramatic clo-sure, which the plays themselves can be shown to subvert.

WE HAVE SEEN that the superior place of drama in Hegel's aesthetic system is a consequence of its embodying the most advanced form of spiritual *Bestimmtheit*. Epic and lyric po-etry is by nature less able to articulate the advanced stages of *Geist*'s emergence into the concrete world of human activity. In the opening remarks to the section on "Das Drama als poe-tisches Kunstwerk," these points are explained at greater length.[52] Defining the central element of dramatic poetry, He-gel argues that it is constituted through a mediation of the op-posed principles of epic and lyric. Drama combines the epic event or practical affair (*Thun, Geschehen*), seen essentially as

[52] *VA*, vol. 14, pp. 480–86.

an external phenomenon against the background of a complex national life, with the independent self-reflective consciousness of lyric. In this combination, simple externality (*Äusserlichkeit*) is blotted out and event is transformed into action, the product of the executed will, which has personal motives and particular ends. Drama, in short, does not focus exclusively either on the inner life of the soul (*ein lyrisches Inneres*) or on the outer world of deeds but presents an individual's private life of thought in its external realization.[53] The dialectical mediation in drama of the characteristics basic to the genres below it is, from another perspective, a source of its distinction. For only in this final aesthetic phase does action step forth as true action, as the intentional fulfillment of inner purposes and aims, with which the subject entirely identifies.

As a type of dramatic poetry, tragedy is defined even more particularly in terms of the specific aims of characters and the actions they pursue. In the Hegelian idiom, these are summarized as "ethical" or "substantive" (*sittliche* or *substantielle*), specialized expressions describing what we have already discussed as "the universal content [supplied by the divine] of that in human individuality which drives men to resolutions and actions."[54] The ethical marks the point at which *die Allgemeinheit der Mächte*, "the universality of spiritual forces," intersects *die Besonderheit des Individuums*, "the specificity of the individual," and creates a "pathos," an impulse or passion to carry out the universal content.[55] This content is varied, but Hegel says that for the most part it is found in the love of husband and wife, of parents, children, and kin, in the collective social life of communities, the patriotism of citizens, the will of those in power, and the religious commitments of individuals.[56] All these are "the essentially positive and substantive spiritual powers that must alone furnish the true con-

[53] *VA*, vol. 14, pp. 482–83.
[54] *VA*, vol. 12, p. 314.
[55] A full discussion of pathos is in *VA*, vol. 12, pp. 313–18. The term is also defined in the section of *PhG* entitled "Die sittliche Handlung," pp. 361–67.
[56] *VA*, vol. 14, pp. 527–28.

tent of ideal action."[57] Now *das Sittliche* is a peaceful totality only under the inactive condition of the gods in their blessedness—a condition, as we have seen, presented by architecture and sculpture. But when ethical rights are attached, as they are in tragedy, to the wills and actions of individuals and "are realized as the determinate aim of a human pathos which passes into action," their concordancy (*Einklang*) is cancelled and they collide in opposition.[58] A character acting on a substantive right, by virtue of his or her exclusiveness, will stimulate the wrath of another pathos and so enter into conflict.

According to the Hegelian reading, then, the *sittliche Handlung* of tragedy is: (1) necessitated by the inevitable movement of Spirit into the realm of human activity and pathic by virtue of this movement; (2) justified in realizing itself because of its origins in the divine; (3) nonetheless wrong insofar as it attempts to realize itself by violating another equally legitimate claim to ethical recognition; and (4) ultimately both negated and affirmed in a necessary final reconciliation, which shows ethical truth to lie in the unity of the opposing claims, not their exclusiveness. Crucial to this model is the notion that in ethical action "there is no caprice, and likewise no struggle, no indecision, since it has given up the legislating and testing of laws; the essential ethical principle is, for it, something immediate, unwavering, without contradiction."[59] Such agents are decisively on one side or another, and their actions are unequivocal implementations of their interests. The conflict, therefore, in which they are mired is always external, against antagonists who also claim absolute right.

In turning from these tenets of Hegel's theory of tragedy to his application of them, we can begin with his remarks on Sophocles' *Antigone*, which he admires for its dramatization of ethical conflict and resolution. He sees in the play an exemplification of a point that characterizes Greek tragedy in

[57] *VA*, vol. 12, p. 302.
[58] *VA*, vol. 14, p. 529.
[59] *PhG*, vol. 2, p. 354.

general: "It is not at all bad will, crime, worthlessness, or mere misfortune, stupidity, and the like, which act as an incentive to the collisions, but rather, as I have already frequently urged, the ethical right to a definite action."[60] More specifically, the principal source of collisions in the work of both Sophocles and Aeschylus is the body politic, the opposition "between the state, that is, ethical life in its spiritual universality, and the family as the natural basis of ethical relations."[61] In *Antigone*, for example, the heroine reveres the ties of blood and the gods of the underworld who protect them. Creon, on the other hand, holds duty to the commonwealth first and recognizes Zeus as the god of civic life. The conflict entailed by the implementation of their different claims involves a split between divine law, the unwritten precept existing forever and not made by man, and human law, the written, civic edicts of a people's communal life. Both of these laws are entitled to expression— their ethical legitimacy is equally balanced—but acting on them gives rise to the crisis in Sophocles' play: by implementing one precept, each character violates the other. If the conflict in the play grows out of this violation, the resolution, according to Hegel, is contained in the fact that "imminent in the life of both is the value each combats."[62] As daughter of a king and the affianced of Haemon, Antigone is obliged to render obedience to political authority. As husband and father, Creon is under obligation to respect the sacred ties of family. Both characters are destroyed by a bond implied in their very social existence. But the elimination of partial individuality in Sophocles' drama allows an assertion of the higher unity of state and family. "The one-sided mode is cancelled, and the undisturbed ideal harmony brings back again that condition of the chorus, which gives equal honor without reserve" to both sides.[63]

[60] *VA*, vol. 14, p. 550.
[61] *VA*, vol. 14, p. 551.
[62] *VA*, vol. 14, p. 556. For a fuller treatment of this reciprocity of state and family, see *PhG*, vol. 2, pp. 340–54.
[63] *VA*, vol. 14, p. 553.

Influential in several respects for later critical formulations of *Antigone*, this interpretation is especially notable for centering attention on the validity and essential reciprocity of each *sittliche pathos* in conflict. Hegel's focus is appealing: making way for a perceptive analysis of the conflict between family and state, it encourages sensitivity to the moral ambiguities of the play that forestall unequivocal attribution of blame and honor to the protagonists. This reading continues to be an attractive alternative to critical views that melodramatize the tragedy, by turning it into either an encomium of female rebellion and kinship bonds or a defense of political authority and governmental controls of individualistic extremism. But appealing as Hegel's framework may be, its assumptions are also problematic and involve exclusions characteristically found in later readings of the tragedy. The reasons for these exclusions have not yet been adequately explored and appreciated. My effort in the following pages is to fill this gap, by illuminating not only some of the limitations of Hegel's method but the tendencies of a more recent critical establishment, which has adopted and built on his interpretation.

Hegel understands the conflict in the play in pervasively binary terms: Antigone versus Creon, family versus state, female versus male, unwritten divine law versus written civic edicts. These structures of opposition have become quite familiar in criticism of the *Antigone*.[64] In Hegel's system they fulfill two related premises attached to the artistic embodiment of Spirit about which he speaks in the opening chapters of the *Vorlesungen über die Ästhetik*: that the ethical struggles in tragedy are a result of the movement of the Ideal into differentiation and that this movement must be carried only so far by the playwright that mediation is not threatened. The binarism central to Hegel's dialectical reading is an expression of the

[64] For a recent review of scholarship on the play that lists the major Hegelian critics, see D. A. Hester, "Sophocles the Unphilosophical: A Study in the *Antigone*," *Mnemosyne*, 4th ser., vol. 24, no. 1 (1971): 11–59.

Nothwendigkeit that he claims is a shaping force both in the struggles and reconciliations of tragedy. To put it another way, the necessity of a return to the Ideal acts as a kind of regulative principle, dictating an understanding of conflict as the violent opposition between thesis and antithesis, which is teleologically guided toward synthesis. The eminent coherence in this interpretation is achieved by controlling the terms of conflict, so that the conditions of harmony are not destabilized.[65] Dividedness, itself a controlled form of differentiation, is overcome because the elements that compose it are essentially united: "Imminent in both is the value each combats." It is important to recognize that this dividedness in the ethical substance produces an opposition between characters who are within themselves single in purpose and coherently organized around a unified right. For Hegel to insist that Creon and Antigone are both beholden to the values of the other, though they do not realize it, does not disturb his position about the homogeneity of their characters. This view of character and action, however, must be reevaluated in terms of evidence from Sophocles' drama that Hegel fails to take into account.

Generally, this evidence undermines the stability of binary structures posited in his reading. While the tragedy is arguably interested in presenting a struggle between two basic institutional bodies and the forces they bring into play, it also calls into question, in a variety of ways, the identity and coherence of the agents in conflict. If we do not assume a priori the identifiability of Creon and Antigone with the values of state and family, respectively, we can follow several developments in the drama that frustrate attempts at the kind of definition and moral decidability exemplified in a Hegelian reading. These developments make problematic the very terms Hegel implements in his interpretation and provide an insight into a side of Greek tragedy that we will examine repeatedly in the subsequent pages: its profoundly explorative and interrogative

---

[65] On the importance of coherence and synthesis in the Hegelian system, see Plant, *Hegel*, pp. 124–46, 199–203, and Taylor, *Hegel*, pp. 51–75.

orientation, which does not validate systematic expectations of order so much as complicate or subvert them. We may best approach an understanding of this orientation in the *Antigone* by noting how Hegel's theoretical model motivates a highly selective choice of evidence in his account of the work.

His method typically favors the long set speeches between the main antagonists, where views are laid out with a formality and position-taking posture made possible both by the conventions of this mode of dramatic presentation and by the temporary absence of interruption from other interlocutors. In the form of a *rhesis*, characters can gather together and sum up their stand in a relatively structured way, without distraction or interference. These are the discourses to which Hegel most commonly turns. He remains virtually oblivious, in his readings, to scenes of dialogue or heated stichomythia, where factors complicating an ostensible homogeneity of character are more in view. For example, Hegel's binarism leads to an emphasis on the confrontation between Creon and Antigone in the middle of the drama (450–525), in which, among other things, she justifies her act of burial by an appeal to the unwritten laws (ἄγραπτα νόμιμα), while Creon, defending the priority of civic obligations, construes her conduct as hubristic and criminal. By making the scene a fulcrum for his interpretation, Hegel establishes a prop for organizing meaning in the play: what is important to the drama can be subordinated to the struggle he finds developed in these lines, and what does not fit his framework falls out of consideration. As a result, aspects of the scene that unsettle Hegel's binary terms are passed over, as are other conflicts in the tragedy that disrupt rather than consolidate the oppositions between family and state, divine and human, supposedly represented in the confrontation of Antigone and Creon.

To take up a relatively simple point first, when Hegel defines the colliding laws (*nomoi*) in the play as divine and human, he misrepresents a matter to which he is elsewhere sensitive, namely, that Creon no less than Antigone envisages his laws as divinely based and hence religious in nature.[66] This is clear from the moment he first enters stage in his capacity as civic leader in Thebes and acknowledges the gods as those who have guided the city to its present standing. Throughout his inaugural address, it is apparent that behind the decrees of the polis and the well-being of the community are its divinities and the values they espouse. Thus the antinomy of divine and human law is problematic for it suggests a contrast between sources of authority that is belied by evidence in the play.[67] As with many Greek tragedies, the social collision here reflects metaphysical disorder; the gods, in whom value is traditionally invested, generate contradictions. Thus the collision of divine and human collapses into a more fundamental incoherence about moral action as a consistent vehicle of the gods' will. Although Hegel's notion of *Geist* could account for such an incoherence, his tendency toward binary structures in this case introduces an unfortunately skewed understanding of opposition.

Also problematic is the contrast between unwritten and written, which Hegel uses in depicting the characteristics of the two laws. The *agrapta nomima* to which Antigone makes reference in her self-defense before Creon are not balanced in the play against written edicts. The *kerugma*, or notice, that Creon issues is a public proclamation, announced by a herald in time of crisis, with the binding status of what we would call martial law.[68] It is not inscribed. Hegel may have responded to this lack of symmetry, had he been sensitive to it, as Victor Ehrenberg has, saying that "in opposing the unwritten laws to Creon's decree Sophocles made what could perhaps be called a logical mistake."[69] This may very well be the case, but even

[66] See, for example, his discussion of the ethical collision between family and state in the first part of chap. 6 of *PhG*.

[67] See Bernard Knox, *The Heroic Temper: Studies in Sophoclean Tragedy*, Sather Classical Lectures no. 35 (Berkeley: University of California Press, 1964), pp. 91–102.

[68] Knox, *The Heroic Temper*, pp. 94–97.

[69] Victor Ehrenberg, *Sophocles and Pericles* (Oxford: Basil Blackwell,

if so, it is testimony to an aspect of the text that we will have more occasion to observe later. Often the play develops in ways that are not in conformity with logical or systematic expectations of order. The tendency to see binary symmetry in *Antigone* amounts to a presupposition that can make over the text into a semblance of the critical model at hand, but a semblance wrought at the price of repressing or circumventing recalcitrant material.

The oppositions for which Hegel argues are undermined in other ways as well. Because his interpretation relies on the solidarity of ethical claims embodied by the antagonists, scenes that take apart the conditions in which this solidarity could emerge deserve scrutiny. Consider, for example, the consequences of Antigone's confrontations with Ismene for her so-called familial ethic. In the prologue, Antigone seems to invite Hegel's formulation of her as a defender of family rights, whose actions are aimed at revering the sacred bonds uniting kin. She initially aligns herself with her sister and deceased relatives as loved ones (φίλοι) and supplicates Ismene to share her labor and deed by aiding in the burial of Polyneices (41). By joining with each other in an act designed to restore honor (τιμή) to their abused brother, they will consolidate the family unit. But the solidarity of blood ties to which Antigone appeals is soon threatened by the position she adopts vis-à-vis her sister. The love (φιλία) motivating her request falters when Ismene, refusing to oppose kingly edict by participating in the burial, is spurned by her sister as an enemy (ἐχθρός): "If you say these things, you will be hated by me / And you will justly be subject to the enmity of the dead" (93–94). From Antigone's perspective, the circle of *philia* now narrows to include, explicitly, only herself and her dishonored brother—"I will rest a loved one with him, a loved one" (73)—though her

---

1954), p. 40. Aristotle's discussion of *nomoi* in *Rhetoric* 1.13, ed. John Sandys with comm. by Edward Cope (Cambridge: Cambridge University Press, 1877), has sometimes confused interpretation of the Sophoclean passage, for he differentiates between written and unwritten laws, quoting Antigone's famous lines.

other dead relatives are implicitly contained in this grouping. She excludes Ismene. Ismene, on the other hand, notwithstanding disapproval of her sister's decision, continues to affirm a more basic bond of love uniting them and bids her sister farewell: "Know this, / That although you go your way a fool, you are truly loved by your loved ones" (99). Implementing the terms that Antigone just has in eliminating her sister as a *phile*, Ismene affirms the solidarity of her kinship with Antigone. These divergent appropriations of language, typical of the play, reveal a breach in the notion of what establishes and validates *philia*, or familial love, among blood relations. While Antigone opts to serve the dead, Ismene strives to protect the living. Both support family, though Ismene is usually taken to be a sellout, more interested in expediency than kinship; and both deny family, though Antigone's rejection of her sister is often downplayed or ignored altogether. There is an insistent ambiguity here that Hegel and other critics, who expect uniform definability in tragic heroes, bypass.

Modern critics have commonly argued, for example, that the heroic purity of Antigone's commitment to kinship is confirmed in this scene through the veneration she shows the dead of her family and through her insistence on rendering them the honor that is their due.[70] Ismene is the one who disrespects this bond by uncourageously demurring from an act of outright defiance against the crown. Now the privilege accorded family members who have passed away may well be traditional, age-old, and, in the circumstances, heroically daring, as admirers of Antigone have remarked. But by adhering to it, she fractures the solidarity of blood ties by favoring her deceased kin over the living. One could urge against her an argument she uses in her own defense later. To give the highly controversial formulation (about which I will say more later)

---

[70] See R. P. Winnington-Ingram, *Sophocles: An Interpretation* (Cambridge: Cambridge University Press, 1980), pp. 128–36; despite his attempt to align Antigone with the preservation of *philia* in the family, he has a good discussion of the instability of the *philia / echthra* duality in the play; and Knox, *The Heroic Temper*, pp. 90–93.

a slightly different twist than she does: with both parents gone her sister is irreplaceable, and so she might very well choose to save and protect a live sibling rather than bury a dead one. In the Herodotean passage that Sophocles seems to be adapting, the argument of irreplaceability launched by the wife of Intaphernes is indeed made on behalf of a living brother.[71] Not only does Antigone reject her sister, but she refuses her the status of kin by calling her an *echthros*, while Ismene reaffirms the status and tries to preserve it regardless of the differences between them. This strident refusal to compromise begins the process of Antigone's tragic alienation, which recent critics have identified with the Sophoclean heroic temper and to which Hegel is sensitive. But it is an alienation depriving Antigone of the ethical unity, grounded in love of family, that such critics would also want to bestow on her.

In short, there is a split in this scene that destabilizes the ground for a Hegelian understanding of the conflict between Antigone and Creon as a collision of familial and civic obligations. While embracing an action that expresses loyalty to kin, Antigone simultaneously creates a rift between herself and the only other surviving member of her family. The act of burial, which Hegel and others read as an expression of a character whose ethical identity is completely tied to the preservation of family ties, is at once an affirmation and a devaluation of family. Consequently, the denigration of kin, which many attribute to the civic-minded Creon, is already played out in Antigone's initial confrontation with her sister. A Hegelian conflict between Antigone and Creon is decentered, since the opposition held to be between the antagonists is contained within one side of the binary structure. Hegel's reading is not unfounded. But no sooner does the tragedy present us with material to define a character, to set a limit and a term to her identity, than it jostles the interpretive desire for compartmentalization by introducing a logical disjunction, something

[71] Herodotus, *Historiae*, ed. C. Hude, 3d ed., 2 vols. (1927; reprint, Oxford: Clarendon Press, 1975), vol. 1, 3.119.

that does not fit the containing structure. The insufficiency of Hegel's ethical category for comprehending Antigone is the insufficiency of many critical categories that truncate the text, at the points it unpredictably ramifies, to produce an organically unified image of character.

Rather than being part of a dialectical pattern that admits of mediation, this fracture unsettles the terms of dialectic and eludes their structuring force. Within the economy of Hegel's system of interpretation, it is an example of recalcitrant material unassimilable to his formulation of the conflict. The pathos that Hegel calls one-sided and that he regards as coextensive with a deed is at least double. However, it is not double in the psychological sense: Antigone does not struggle inwardly about competing obligations or duties, weighing one against the other. Nor is it double in the sense implied by Hegel's view that imminent in her identity is the value she combats. For the destruction of family ties inherent in Antigone's conduct is not a value in the way that the civic laws, which Hegel says provide a ground for her action, are. Instead, in damaging the very bond that she would in another sense want to preserve, Antigone's interaction with Ismene fragments the unity of ethical identity posited by Hegelian critics. The negation of Antigone's commitment to family does not initially come from without, in Creon's denial of her moral priorities, but is contained within her actions from the outset. Thus her character disseminates in directions that are not consistent with or controlled by the moral claim to which Hegel maintains she adheres in burying her brother. This dissemination breaks up the solidarity of that claim at the very moment we first find evidence of it in the beginning of the play.

Additional qualifications of a Hegelian conflict in Sophocles' tragedy can be found in the second encounter between Antigone and Ismene, where the preservation of one sibling bond at the expense of another continues to upset the notion of pathic unity that is a precondition for the dialectic of family versus state. But there are other factors, too, that challenge Hegel's view of the coherence in Antigone's moral claim. The notorious interpretive crux revolving around her final appearance in the play concerns a speech in lines 905–12 that critics at least since Goethe have regarded as seriously flawed, because it threatens the integrity of Antigone's ethical identity.[72] The German poet wished that on some compelling philological basis scholars would find it spurious. His desire was the expression of a now common opinion that the intelligibility and nobility of Antigone's decision to bury her brother are grounded in the general principles to which she gives utterance in her self-defense before Creon.[73] Stating that no mortal can override the unwritten and unfailing laws of the gods, Antigone maintains that she would have to answer to divinity for breaking them. The justice that dwells with the gods below requires that rites should be paid the dead by the living: regardless of the political status of her brothers while on earth, "Hades nevertheless desires these laws" (519).[74] The context in which she makes this generalizing statement to a certain extent particularizes the claim, for Antigone is answering the charge of Creon that equal honor ought not be accorded a civic hero and a criminal traitor. In other words, the equality of treatment that Antigone would render the dead is especially applicable in the circumstances to her enemy brothers, irrespective of their deeds or accomplishments. But even this qualification of the general principle fails to minimize the initial impact of Antigone's later, death-bed justification of her act:

[72] Hester in "Sophocles the Unphilosophical" discusses the crux and various interpretations of it. See also more recently J. C. Kamerbeek's commentary on *Antigone* (Leiden: E. J. Brill, 1978), pp. 158–60.

[73] For an early scholarly statement of this position, see Sir Richard Jebb's edition and commentary of *Antigone* (Cambridge: Cambridge University Press, 1928), pp. 258–63. More recently, see Whitman, *Sophocles*, pp. 81–99, and Winnington-Ingram, *Sophocles*, pp. 145–46.

[74] With Jebb and Kamerbeek, I read "τοὺς νόμους τούτους" in the Greek text, which is what the manuscripts have. Pearson's adoption of the scholiast's variant "ἴσους" is unnecessary. As Jebb remarks, "the simple 'τούτους' is perfectly suitable—'these laws,' the laws of sepulture; and everything that 'ἴσους' would convey is already expressed by 'ὅμως' "(p. 101).

Neither if I were a mother of children
Nor if my husband were dead and moldering
Would I have chosen this labor in defiance of the
     citizens.
On account of what law do I say these things?
With one husband dead, I could have had another,
And I could have had a child from another man, if I lost
     the first.
But since my mother and father have been hidden away
     in Hades,
There is no brother who could be born for me ever
     again.

(905–12)[75]

The exclusive duty to her dead brother expressed in this passage does not easily square with the view Antigone has sanctioned earlier, namely, that the justice of the infernal gods demands equal laws for all the dead. And because the earlier view conforms best to a critical reading that presents Antigone as bound by a sacred and noble fidelity to blood ties in general, it is her death-bed speech that has been regarded as problematic, an awkward, ill-fitting piece of sophistry. In short, her attitude as she faces the Chorus in her last moments does not fit the bill of a dignified heroine whose whole purpose, even under great duress, is to honor familial bonds—at least not without a good deal of wrangling. It is worth making quite explicit how this critical dilemma has emerged: the enigma of Antigone's death-bed speech becomes one within an interpretive framework that homes in prematurely on one pattern or idea in the text that is friendly to its critical presuppositions about tragic heroism or conflict and then seeks to subordinate the remaining mass of literary material, even when it resists, to that select portion. Within such a framework, Antigone's

---

[75] Jebb's discussion of the textual difficulties in this passage is largely motivated by his opinion that the lines are spurious. For a less prejudiced view, see Kamberbeek's note, pp. 158–61.

heroism is marred unless it can be unified around an intelligible, consistent moral principle.

Various ways of establishing coherence and mitigating the disjunction have been proposed by critics.[76] Following the lead of Goethe, who found Antigone's argument about the irreplaceability of a brother *ganz schlecht*, "very bad indeed," Sir Richard Jebb justified a radical piece of surgery on the text, which ended up cutting not only the controversial lines 905–12, but lines 904 and 913–20, too, because the resulting configuration was more felicitous to his sense of logical development.[77] Jebb's response to the problems of Antigone's death speech gained quite a strong foothold in criticism during the years following publication of his texts and commentaries. Recent trends have reversed his direction of thought in favor of the genuineness of the passage, although there is hardly consensus now about whether or not the lines are Sophoclean. Bernard Knox has reminded us that the offending lines in *Antigone* were in the text "Aristotle read approximately a century after the first performance of the play, which means that our authority for this passage is better than what we have for the rest of the play—a manuscript written *fifteen* centuries after the performance . . . If [the lines are an interpolation], then we are forced to conclude that already in Aristotle's time, the text of the *Antigone* was so fundamentally corrupt in a crucial passage that there was no criterion, no record, no tradition by which it could be corrected. Such a presupposition deals a mortal blow to our confidence in the general soundness of the tragic texts."[78] It is indeed a bold and risky venture to go as far as Jebb and others have in rendering the text coherent by their standards. But such emendations testify to the sometimes astounding power of critical assumptions to make over literary material into a likeness of the interpreter's own premises.

[76] See Hester, "Sophocles the Unphilosophical," pp. 55–58.
[77] Jebb, *Antigone*, pp. 260–61.
[78] Knox, *The Heroic Temper*, p. 104.

To his credit, Hegel does not figure among the cut-and-paste group of scholars. In fact, he seems unbothered, at least overtly, by Antigone's argument in lines 905–12. This is because he regards the speech as a seamless part of the ethical whole that constitutes Antigone's dramatic character. For him, there is no disjunction between the general precept about burial with which she first defends herself before Creon and her later appeal to the unique irreplaceability of a brother. This view emerges most clearly in the chapter on *Sittlichkeit* in the *Phänomenologie*, where he draws out more fully than he does in the *Vorlesungen über die Ästhetik* the familial structure in which Antigone is implicated in Sophocles' tragedy.[79]

Arguing that the ethical component of family life involves the preservation of the individual members who constitute the group as a whole, Hegel stresses in typical fashion that it is not contingent individuality that the family, in its ethical perspective, protects but the idea of individuality, when it becomes freed from the accidents of life.[80] Ethical action "no longer concerns the living but the dead, one who, out of the long sequence of his broken and diversified existence, has gathered up his being into one completed embodiment, who has lifted himself out of the unrest of a life of chance and change into the peace of simple universality."[81] In its interment of relations who pass away, the family finds its true ethical function: imparting meaning to death by making it an action of Spirit. While this meaning is occasioned by the individual's abandonment of contingency, the deceased also

[79] *PhG*, vol. 2, pp. 340–354. Actually, Hegel's aim in this chapter is not to perform a literary analysis of the classical play, but to use it as a hermeneutic tool in elaborating the ethical phase of the embodiment of *Geist*. Though the drama, in this context, becomes an interpretive structure for understanding history, Hegel's appropriation of it nonetheless reveals how he reads Sophocles' play.

[80] See Jean Hyppolite, *Genesis and Structure of Hegel's Phenomenology of Spirit*, tr. Samuel Cherniak and John Heckman (Evanston, Ill.: Northwestern University Press, 1974), pp. 339–44.

[81] *PhG*, vol. 2, pp. 343–44.

falls prey to the elemental, physical earth that decomposes it and so is in danger of being negated as a spiritual entity. The duty of family is to embrace this physical aspect of death and transform it so that it does not remain "something irrational, but is the result of an action in which the rights of consciousness are asserted."[82] By uniting its member with the earth through interment and making him a *daimon* who dwells with the gods below, the family makes the action of nature its own. "This dishonoring of the dead by unconscious organic processes and abstract elements the family wards off, puts its own action in their place, and unites the deceased relative to the bosom of the earth. . . . In this way the family makes the dead part of a community, which prevails over and binds the powers of the particular material elements and the lower forms of life, which wanted to have their way against him and destroy him."[83] In this context, differences between kin are not recognized; spouses, parents, children, and siblings are accorded equal rites of burial.

At the same time as Hegel offers this reading of burial in Sophocles' play, he launches another argument about Antigone's death-bed justification of her act that eclipses any sign of discrepancy between the general ethical precept regarding burial and the heroine's later version of her motives. He claims that unlike the relationship between husband and wife or parent and child, that of brother and sister is unmixed and intransitive: "They are of the same blood, which, however, in them has entered into stability and equilibrium." They do not desire each other sexually, as spouses do, nor have they given to each other or received from each other the independence of individual being, as parents and offspring have. "They are free individualities with respect to each other." As a result, Hegel says, "the loss of a brother is irreparable to the sister and her duty toward him is the highest."[84]

[82] *PhG*, vol. 2, p. 344.
[83] *PhG*, vol. 2, p. 345.
[84] *PhG*, vol. 2, pp. 348–49.

Although Hegel offers an illuminating explanation of the significance of ancient burial, his account of Sophocles' play is problematic.[85] First, in situating burial obligations within the larger family structure, he says nothing of the relationship between sisters, which is so important to the tragedy and which could be characterized in the same terms of "unmixed intransitiveness" as he applies to Antigone and Polyneices. In other words, his reading does not account for the fact that Antigone privileges a brother at the expense of losing a sister. How does Ismene fit into his scheme, or is there no place for her? Is she not irreplaceable, too, on Hegel's argument, and hence as valuable as the brother on whom Antigone's attention instead centers? More problematical, Hegel's sense of the hierarchy of familial duties conforms to what may be called the sliding scale theory of values. According to such a theory, Antigone does not give up her original motive—religious obligation to bury kin. But she feels this duty has degrees, answering to degrees of kinship, with the case regarding a brother being the strongest. Although this theory mitigates a pressing discrepancy in the play, it is doubtful that such a sliding scale of values characterized the observance of religious duty among the Greeks.

Evidence from the ancient world is scanty, but it seems that the Greeks usually distinguished, in cases such as the one Antigone faces, between *thuraioi*, "strangers" or "outsiders," and *oikeioi*, "kinsmen" or "insiders."[86] A husband, child, or

[85] For a more recent discussion of ancient burial, see G. Rachel Levy, *The Gate of Horn: A Study of the Religious Conceptions of the Stone Age, and Their Influence upon European Thought* (London: Faber and Faber, 1948).

[86] See Jebb, *Antigone*, pp. 261–62, who argues against Bellerman's sliding scale theory of value, with a view to emphasizing the strangeness of Antigone's reasoning and hence the spuriousness of the passage. I think, like Jebb, that her rationale is unusual by standards of popular Greek morality, but that its peculiarity and incongruity with earlier statements of value in the play are not adequate to reject it as interpolated. For a discussion of the ancient evidence, see Johannes Kakridis, *Homeric Researches* (Lund: C.W.K. Gleerup, 1949), pp. 152–64, who argues the reverse of Jebb's view, but again on sparse classical sources, one of which is the Meleager legend. On the solidarity of

sister is on the same side of the line as a brother, no distinctions holding. If the dead had been a stranger and not related by blood or marriage, Antigone would not have been deemed *enages*, "cursed," for refusing to bury him. This perspective bears out the peculiarity of Antigone's argument, within a traditional framework that stresses the solidarity of familial bonds, and it is a peculiarity substantiated by the only two ancient responses that are extant on the *topos* of a brother's irreplaceability.

First, the Herodotean passage, from which most scholars think Sophocles is borrowing, presents Darius's reaction to the argument of Intaphernes' wife as one of amazement: he listens in wonder to her account, "θωμάσας τὸν λόγον."[87] Hers is a marvelous, paradoxical reasoning that has the mark of the surprising or improbable, and Herodotus was probably drawn to it for this reason. Second, Aristotle's attitude toward Antigone's argument, which he cites in the *Rhetoric*, is that it is *apiston*, "unbelievable."[88] In a context where he is talking about the importance of establishing moral character through the clarification of one's purpose, he warns against statements that would seem incredible to an audience. If such a statement is introduced, however, as in the case of Antigone's lines 911–12, he urges that a reason (*aitia*) for the strange explanation

---

family ties in ancient Greece, see E. R. Dodds, *The Greeks and the Irrational*, Sather Classical Lectures no. 25 (1951; reprint, Berkeley: University of California Press, 1971), pp. 33–34, 46–47.

[87] Herodotus, *Historiae*, vol. 1, 3.119. On Herodotus's fondness for wonders (*thomata*), see William Mure, *A Critical History of the Language and Literature of Ancient Greece*, 5 vols. (London: Longman, 1854), vol. 4, pp. 382–92; W. W. How and J. Wells, *A Commentary on Herodotus*, 2 vols. (Oxford: Clarendon Press, 1912), vol. 1, pp. 32–34, 44; T. R. Glover, *Herodotus*, Sather Classical Lectures no. 3 (Berkeley: University of California Press, 1924), pp. 26, 38, 266.

[88] Aristotle, *Rhetoric*, 3.l6.9. "Should a statement be unbelievable, then add a reason for it, in the way Sophocles constructs the argument of Antigone, that she cared more for a brother than for a husband or children. For others could be born, if these died, 'but since my mother and father have gone [βεβη-κότων] to Hades, / there is no brother who could be born for me ever again'."

be adduced to mitigate the element of incomprehensibility. What is important about Aristotle's comments is that they respond to a problem that Antigone's way of thinking poses for the intelligibility of her moral identity. While he also seems to think that her reference to the death of her father and mother explains something about Polyneices' irreplaceability, his discussion nonetheless intimates difficulties in the speech that appear to have been well known by his time.

Considering this evidence, I submit that the passage presents both an unconventional view of family moral obligations and a discrepancy with Antigone's earlier statements about the *agrapta nomima*. Her rationale seems designed to jar an audience's sense of traditional religious practice, and the assault is all the more unsettling given her apparent sanction of those practices in previous scenes. The effect of Antigone's words on several centuries of scholars, who have tried hard to find a reconciling framework for the disjunctions, is ample testimony of the strength exerted by critical expectations of consistency and unity in dramatic character.

But the troublesome aspects of the scene press hard, and a Hegelian approach does not mitigate them. Not only does Antigone's basis of action shift in her death scene, but she calls the position about her brother on which she now stands a *nomos*. In a play that has invested this term with a remarkable variety of applications that reflect its instability in the cultural sphere, we are perhaps not surprised to find yet another implementation.[89] If, however, as Herodotus and Aristotle suggest, Antigone's argument has an air of surprise and unbelievability about it, in what does its status as a *nomos* reside? Is she appealing to a more primitive principle of blood relationship, strange perhaps to classical Greeks but of very ancient provenance? Or is it possible that she uses the term to describe a purely personal sense of commitment that does not extend beyond her private world and understanding? If the basis of

[89] See Jean-Pierre Vernant and Pierre Vidal-Naquet, *Mythe et tragédie en Grèce ancienne* (Paris: François Maspero, 1972), pp. 34–36.

her heroism is in the last resort individual, as some critics have suggested, is it not a disturbing turn that makes of *nomos*, which implies a generally sanctioned custom or ordinance, a personal law?[90] The play sends us scrambling—and not so much because we are missing crucial historical facts. Our difficulties emerge from the failure of moral definition.[91]

What we find, then, in this crux that has fixed the attention of critics and theatrical audiences alike is another manifestation of an instability that in different ways marks Antigone's status from the beginning of the play. Just as her encounters with Ismene unsettle the dialectic of family and state by decentering the terms of opposition, so does Antigone's final speech, in which the already fractured solidarity of blood ties is further broken by a peculiar formulation of *philia* that hinges on the unique irreplaceability of a brother. As the moral center shifts and Antigone unsuccessfully seeks a sound basis, a law, to validate her conduct, the play enacts a crisis of values that puts off critical efforts to fix ethical claims in stable categories. Antigone's words before she leaves stage for the last time echo the dilemma that this dislocation of values entails:

> Ill-fated, deprived of friends,
> Live I go to the graves of the dead.
> What divine justice have I transgressed?
> Why should I, wretched one, still look to the gods?

[90] For the theory that Antigone's *nomos* is of ancient provenance, see Kakrides, *Homeric Researches*, pp. 152–64. For a view that stresses the personal basis of Antigone's heroism, see Knox, *The Heroic Temper*, p. 106, who glosses over Antigone's use of *nomos* in her argument about a brother's irreplaceability.

[91] Various recent books discuss the nature and consequences of these interpretive expectations for coherence and unity. In connection with Hegel, see Plant, *Hegel*, pp. 199–202; in connection with tragedy, see Stephen Booth, *King Lear, Macbeth, Indefinition, and Tragedy* (New Haven: Yale University Press, 1983), pp. 79–118; in connection with biblical writings, see Frank Kermode, *The Genesis of Secrecy: On the Interpretation of Narrative* (Cambridge, Mass.: Harvard University Press, 1979).

Which one of them ought I call upon as my ally,
Since by acting piously I have incurred the charge of
   impiety?

(919–24)

The oxymoronic formulation in the last line is more than a
rhetorical flourish. It expresses the despair of a character
whose action is morally ambivalent and who has no framework within which to establish the ethical nature of her deed.

As the previous discussion tries to show, Hegel's interpretation of Antigone's role in the conflict brings into the foreground selective aspects of the tragic action that validate his
premises, while relegating others to the periphery. This exclu-
sivity of critical vision is apparent in yet another way in the
lectures on aesthetics, which I want to consider briefly. In ac-
counting for the operation of the Erinyes in Sophocles' play,
Hegel identifies these divinities with a determinate, hence partial, notion of right and justice.[92] They are the gods with
whom Antigone aligns herself in defending the interests of the
family, and their role, consequently, is to be understood as
affirmative of the love of kindred. By interring the dead,
Antigone satisfies, according to Hegel, the constraints of the
Furies, who would take revenge against abusers of blood ties.
Certainly, it can be argued that Antigone feels the imminent
weight of a curse that would fall on her if she fails to bury
Polyneices. Her first words in the prologue refer to the multiple evils in the house of Oedipus and express a desire to avert
further disaster by giving her deceased brother proper burial
services. The guard in the first episode, before Antigone has
been caught, relates how a light coating of dust was sprinkled
over the corpse to avert a curse—"ἄγος φεύγοντος" (256). In
her self-defense before Creon, Antigone says she would have
suffered distress had she not respected *Dike*, who dwells with
the gods below, but that now she has no cause to grieve.

Such evidence could be cited in support of Hegel's view of
the Erinyes as deities whose curse Antigone seeks to divert by

---

[92] *VA*, vol. 13, pp. 49–52.

respecting Polyneices' right to burial. However, the same Furies who defend the primacy of family ties have destroyed the house of Labdacus, as the second stasimon of the play makes abundantly clear. Though this ode, with its typical lack of specific reference, is resonant with associations, one of the matters to which it responds is the previous episode, where Antigone has freely admitted and proudly defended to Creon her defiance of the kingly edict. For the chorus, who has witnessed this scene, the perpetuation of the curse in Labdacus's line is being worked out in his granddaughter, who will be the latest casualty of the *ate*, the "ruin" or "curse," rooted in the family.

> For now the light has stretched beyond
> The last scions of the house of Oedipus.
> Again the bloody knife of the infernal gods cuts them
>   down—
> Folly and a Fury of the mind [φρενῶν ἐρινύς].[93]
>
>   (599–603)

Thus we encounter the paradox that Antigone, by obeying the infernal gods who protect bonds of kinship, is simultaneously, through the act of burial, fulfilling the destruction to which they have doomed her and her relatives. She is at once, in the same act, the vehicle of the Furies' revenge and the agent who seeks to avert their revenge. Rather than being identifiable with the integrity of Antigone's pathos, as Hegel understands it, the Furies participate in the ambivalence that pervades her action and that undercuts the basis for a binary model of conflict in the play.

So far, I have concentrated on the ways in which Sophocles' text disrupts the solidarity of Antigone's identity as a defender of family rights. A similar case could be made regarding Creon, whose status as patriotic ruler with priorities accorded to the polis is complicated by factors that disseminate this

---

[93] The lines quoted contain a number of textual problems. For a recent commentary, see Kamerbeek's edition, pp. 119–21. I read κοπίς, not κόνις, in l. 602, Pearson's reading following Jortin's conjecture; in l. 601, I take νιν as referring to ῥίζας; in l. 603, λόγου τ' ἄνοια καὶ φρενῶν ἐρινύς is in apposition to κοπίς.

unity bestowed on him by the Hegelian interpreter. The civic-mindedness of his edict seems to be questioned, though only subtly and indirectly, early in the play after he makes his first public announcement before the Thebans. In response to this speech, which concludes, "He who is loyal to the city in death / And life alike will be honored by me" (209–10), the chorus says coolly and without affirmation of his principles, "These things it pleases you to do, son of Menoecus / To the traitor and the patriot. / And it is possible for you to implement any law / About the dead and the living" (211–14). Moreover, it declines the task of being watchguards over Creon's decree and requests that he find younger men to fulfill this function. Though nothing explicit is said here in qualification of Creon's patriotism, the chorus has expressed an implicit reservation that is picked up and developed later in the play. Antigone's judgment about this matter is bound to be partial, but her contention, that the chorus sees things her way yet out of fear keeps silent, is strengthened in Haemon's confrontation with his father. Echoing Antigone's charge, Creon's son says, in lines unfortunately damaged by a lacuna but whose sense is intelligible, that the common man in Thebes is afraid to utter things Creon does not want to hear—a point the audience has already seen vividly confirmed in the king's dealings with the guard. The reservations of the citizens are then played out in some detail by Haemon.

> I can hear these things in the darkness,
> How the city grieves for this maiden,
> That she, the least deserving of all women,
> Perishes so unfairly for her most glorious deeds;
> She who did not permit her own brother,
> When he fell in bloody struggle unburied,
> To be destroyed either by flesh-eating dogs or by any
>   bird.
> Does she not deserve to win the prize of golden honor?
> Such is the dark rumor that spreads silently.
>   (692–700)

That the polis not only sympathizes with Antigone but regards her as worthy of honor for having saved her brother from the ignoble fate of being eaten by dogs is evidence that the ruler's civic action is also uncivilized and politically hazardous. Creon's edict, designed to enlarge the state, arouses opposition from the citizens it is aimed at placating. Attempting to consolidate his power through a deed that reveals the primacy of his allegiance to the polis, Creon actually undermines the integrity of his civic commitment and initiates a breach between himself and the community from which he draws his political identity. Like Antigone, he divides himself through his action from the very people and the very ethical sphere with which he perceives himself to be tied. Whereas Hegel gives us a framework for understanding the collision between Antigone and Creon, which stems from their mutually violating actions, he does not give us a way of understanding what might be called the self-violation of their pathe. Each pathos already contains within itself its own negation.

Compelling support for this point comes from the harsh condemnation of Creon's edict by Teiresias. Describing the frightful consequences of the king's decision to expose Polyneices' corpse, Teiresias lays responsibility for the sickness in the state directly at Creon's feet: "The city suffers this disease because of your counsel" (1015). The leader who has prided himself on steering the ship of state on the right course with his edict has made it founder. It is not Antigone who threatens to destabilize the welfare of the community but Creon himself. He is the enemy he would fight.

If Creon's actions taint the purity of the civic commitment to which he lays claim, so do other features of his character that emerge in the play. Teiresias accuses the king of being, like the entire tribe of tyrants, money-hungry, more interested in profit (*kerdos*) than the well-being of the country. This is a commonplace in tragedy of the fifth century. But notwithstanding its conventional nature, the idea that Creon has personal motives directing his conduct, motives that are not civic, is suggested in other ways as well. When he faces Antigone earlier in the play, he opposes her several times not by an appeal to the state's health or to the superior validity of his ethical position but through an incensed indignation at being overpowered by a woman: "For now I am not a man, but she is / If this dominance remains hers without penalty" (484–85).[94] The virulence of this sentiment becomes especially apparent in Creon's conversation with Haemon, where the initially rational exchange between father and son degenerates into angry stichomythic repartée, in which Creon abandons arguments for the political soundness of his edict and resorts to contemptuous mockeries of Haemon for being a woman's slave. I do not mean to suggest that Creon is showing his true colors when he lets it fly at moments like these, but that the solidarity of his character as a statesman first and last is considerably complicated by such personal fears, which are difficult to reconcile with his status as defender of the community. Haemon himself responds to his father's remarks as if concern for the general welfare is absent from Creon's thinking. Had Hegel taken these factors, and others discussed earlier, into consideration, he would have found it hard to sustain the terms in which he presents the opposition of family versus state in Sophocles' *Antigone*.

In challenging a Hegelian reading of conflict by presenting evidence for the dislocation of binary oppositions in the play, I wanted to show that the principle of *Nothwendigkeit*, which Hegel takes to be inherent in the artistic design as a force organizing and controlling differentiation, is rather a premise of his critical method. By implementing the principle, he can extract a meaning from the tragedy that conforms to his notion of the embodied Ideal as an antagonistic meeting of two opposing ethical values, which are actually integral. But such a reading succeeds only through a highly selective appropriation of the text. Sophocles' play challenges the validity of identities and definitions that Hegel's method posits.

It seems that the notion of an ethical claim, as Hegel con-

---

[94] See also *Antigone*, ll. 525, 578–79, 740–41, 746, 756.

ceives of it, is too narrowly dictated by systematic interests and by anachronistic legal ideas to do justice to the Greek tragedy. In a study that provides a valuable corrective to some excesses in Hegel's views, Louis Gernet argues convincingly that ancient Greece simply did not have a philosophy of law that recognized the notion of an ethical individual with rights whose legitimacy was grounded in an anterior, universally respected precept.[95] Instead, the Greeks developed a philosophy of justice, founded on a broad sense of equilibrium, whose stability could be shaken by rival claims but restored through a process of mediation, geared toward establishing preference or relative merit, not absolute value or a synthesis of absolute values, such as Hegel envisions. The highly flexible, shifting nature of value, which Hegel's dialectic controls to guarantee systematic resolution, partly accounts for the instability of concepts such as *nomos* in the *Antigone*. But unlike the developing legal thought in the fifth century, whose efforts to articulate criteria for deciding crises and implementing workable judgments are the focus of Gernet's work, tragedy explores the forces that fragment identity and make moral decidability problematic; its orientation toward the social context is interrogative and even adversarial, for it holds us in the grip of conflicts that various mechanisms of the culture aim to neutralize and dissipate. Critical theory, especially Hegel's ethical brand, is rather like the law in this respect: it formulates strategies to subdue the complexities and recalcitrant moral ambivalences dramatized in the struggles of tragedy.

If Hegel's notion of *sittliche pathos* is anachronistic in importing into the *Antigone* broadly legal assumptions derived from more modern times, it is also challenged by aspects of the play that simply elude formulation in ethical terms. The themes of youthfulness and old age, for example, which have little if anything to do with ethics in the Hegelian sense, are worked out differently in the interactions between Antigone,

[95] Louis Gernet, *Droit et société dans la Grèce ancienne* (Paris: Sirey, 1955), pp. 61–81.

Creon, Haemon, and the chorus. Similarly, the relation between action and temperamental traits such as pettiness, rigid-
ity, and suspicion is probed through a series of developments
involving now Ismene, then Antigone, later Creon, with a continuous change of the dramatic constellation and emphasis
from scene to scene. The *eros* about which the chorus sings in
the third stasimon is not identifiable with the *philia* among kin
that Hegel focuses on; nor is its relevance for the play satisfactorily described in Hegelian terms. One critic has remarked in
considering this rich multiplicity in Sophocles' play: "In the
face of such a variety of themes it is understandable that . . .
what appears to us diverse should perhaps be traced back to
some unity, some single idea, in fact to a clash of ideas—
traced back to a conflict of two principles each justified in itself."[96] This observation reflects an appreciation of the ways
in which the unsystematic heterogeneity and ethical elusiveness of the tragedy have stimulated the search for critical categories that can provide determinate readings and moral certainty.

If the binary dividedness attributed by Hegel to the playwright's control of *Differenz* is instead a product of interpretive control and if the text is more highly differentiated than
the theoretical framework allows, then a basis in the tragedy
for a synthetic reconciliation of opposites is undone. Or such
a basis may be erected only on partial ground, which is precisely what Hegel does. He sees in the play a "cancellation of
the one-sided mode" and a return to a condition of harmony,
in which both opposed values are affirmed in their essential
unity. This harmony resides, he maintains, in the chorus. In its
point of view lies the spiritual truth that Sophocles is affirming: "Imminent in both [Creon and Antigone] is the value each
combats." Such an interpretation implies a unity of several
privileged perspectives: those of the chorus, the playwright,
and the philosophical spectator/interpreter, whose visions

[96] Karl Reinhardt, *Sophocles*, tr. Hazel Harvey and David Harvey (Oxford:
Basil Blackwell, 1979), p. 65.

unite in a dialectically mediated appreciation of the ethical totality in the play.

Even were we to bypass evidence raised earlier that an ethical view of the play is partial and concentrate, for the sake of
argument, on the opposition of family versus state, Hegel's
view of resolution is difficult. It relies, as we have seen, on the
integrity of the antagonistic elements and on external opposition. But if the so-called pathe in the play are themselves fractured, if they both affirm and undermine the value to which
they supposedly lay claim, then the moral center of each
breaks down and so does the consistency of ethical conduct.
The negation of an ethical position is contained within its implementation. Only by excluding evidence of this point and by
retreating to the chorus can Hegel find dialectical resolution
in the play.

This choral point of view is itself problematic and can
hardly be identified with the playwright. While the Theban
elders at various moments, in their typical middle-of-the-road
fashion, accord honor to both Antigone and Creon, there is
no evidence that they find imminent in both antagonists the
value each combats. Moreover, the words they do utter about
the final state of affairs are moral platitudes that fall especially
flat because they are obviously inadequate to the experience
of the play.

> Wisdom is by far the first part of happiness.
> One must in no way dishonor the gods.
> Great words by overweening people,
> Bringing great blows upon them,
> Teach wisdom to old age.
>
> (1348–53)

The elders do not express a satisfactory solution to the moral
dilemmas they have witnessed but retreat to a conventional
reliance on the efficacy of wisdom (τὸ φρονεῖν) and the punishment of hubris that the tragic action has tested and questioned in a variety of ways. It is hard to imagine that Hegel's
choral resolution is anything but the expression of a desire to

find moral coherence affirmed in a way that makes systematic sense. In any case, he is left hanging fire, once he has identified himself, the philosophical spectator, with the voice of traditional moral conservatism.

IN TRACING, through his reading of *Antigone*, some of the limitations in Hegel's theory of tragedy, I wanted to show how a larger systematic framework structures his ideas about drama in ways that can go against the grain of the plays themselves. In the process, I hope it has become apparent that tenets of Hegelian philosophy, such as the notion of embodied *Geist*, which appear highly technical in the abstract, have applications that enjoy considerable popularity in contemporary criticism. The shortcomings of Hegel's orientation, then, are not unique to him but characterize less philosophical approaches that have incorporated his ideas, if only indirectly. From the perspective offered in the previous pages, these shortcomings may be seen as the product of interpretive controls that allow Hegel to scrutinize dramatic conflict without endangering the traditional expectation of rationality and moral coherence in tragedy. By imposing an orderly teleology on the collisions and contradictions of the play, he can guarantee a mediation that secures the ultimate unity sought by critics of tragedy from the time of Aristotle. But the insistence on unity leads away from an appreciation of the strategies in tragedy that disrupt our categories of understanding, expose the inconsistencies of moral standards, and undermine the stability of such ideas as "knowledge" or "wisdom" by means of which we order our sense of truth.

The positive side of Hegel's theory is that it opens the way for a distinct departure from classical and neoclassical approaches. Not only does he provide a context for discussing the collisions in drama, which earlier criticism largely bypassed, but he argues that an exemplary tragic struggle is between two equally weighted rights. Historically, this formulation helped criticism move away from a sense of the classical plays as morality dramas, clearly differentiating right from wrong in an effort to expound a didactic imperative about how we ought to live our lives. A deeper appreciation of the crises presented in tragedy can emerge in a framework that is sensitive to ruptures in a social order, whose consistency is brought to a serious straining point, where justice collides with justice. Moreover, the Hegelian dialectic makes way for a critical approach to the problem of ethical and interpretive indeterminacy in tragedy. For it invites us to formulate the crisis of the play in terms of the undecidability of criteria for absolute judgment. It also localizes or restricts this undecidability to the experience of characters within the play, at the same time that it labels this experience blind. The lack of clear vision, which Hegel deems an integral part of tragic suffering, is the nondialectical or nonmediated form of what becomes absolute knowledge, at the level of philosophical observation. The high valuation put on critical spectatorship by Hegel takes place within a system whose engineer is unusually self-conscious of the methodological strategy he adopts for fixing meaning. Indeed, such self-consciousness is inseparable from philosophical activity. Later Hegelian approaches have implemented similar hermeneutic strategies, but with less awareness of how they posit criteria for halting the deferral of interpretive judgment. If the attractiveness of Hegel's readings lies partly in this impressive surveillance of the philosophical moves he engages, it also lies, as I already noted, in securing the longstanding critical norms of order, closure, and equilibrium in tragedy. The power of his insight into tragic conflict is tempered by the reliance on systematic controls, which in many ways continue to be the controls governing more recent readings of tragedy.

It is true that only some Greek plays lend themselves to the approach exemplified in Hegel's treatment of *Antigone*. Aeschylus's *Oresteia* arguably presents a double bind in which the claims of the gods from the upper and lower worlds are so evenly balanced that the agent, who must act, transgresses whichever way he goes. However, other dramatic versions of the Orestes legend, such as Sophocles' *Electra* and Euripides'

Electra and *Orestes*, seem to contain less evidence than the Aeschylean version does for the symmetries of tragic conflict. Sophocles' presentation offers a puzzlingly archaic view of the simple justice in revenge, with no sanctions mobilized against the avengers. But his main character, Electra, lacks a compelling ethical identity and seems more driven by hate and the vindictiveness born of private misery than by any moral claims. Similarly, Euripides depicts the disturbing perversity and degeneration in characters who seek out a revenge that is justified by the gods, but gods who are incompetent, distasteful, and barely able to elude the cross-fire of other deities. These renditions of revenge in the house of Atreus are especially open to the kind of critique already argued in the case of Sophocles' *Antigone*. In their persistent undermining of a stable moral perspective from which an audience or an interpreter could judge the question of right action, they offer considerable challenge to a Hegelian reading of tragedy as a collision of ethical claims whose ultimate mediation is apparent to the privileged spectator.

One could cite a host of other Greek plays that elude the terms in which Hegel talks about *Antigone*. But we would do well to recall at this point that the view of tragedy exemplified by Sophocles' drama represents only a part of Hegel's wider account of the classical form. His lectures delineate a second type of tragedy, which explores the moral dilemma of responsibility for deeds committed in fact but not with conscious intent by a person acting under the direction of the gods. In *Oedipus Tyrannus*, a prime example of this type, the hero "has killed his father, married his mother, has begotten children in this incestuous alliance, and nevertheless is involved in these most terrible of crimes without will or knowledge."[97] Here the conflict is not social but individual: it involves a split between subjective and objective fact. Oedipus is not in a state of emotional vacillation, but he incurs blame for deeds performed unintentionally. What he has done is not an expres-

[97] *VA*, vol. 14, pp. 551–52.

sion of his ethical identity; if it were, he would be a deranged freak. In this qualified sense, he is not one with his acts, as Antigone is supposed to be. But he does not, on the other hand, disclaim them as alien.

He does not do so, Hegel says, because the ancient Greek, unlike the modern person, adheres to the bare fact that an individual has achieved and refuses to recognize the difference between crimes attributable to personal knowledge or volition and inadvertent mistakes. The case is somewhat overstated, for we know that Athenian courts took account of intention in distinguishing between murder and accidental homicide or homicide committed in self-defense. But Hegel is nonetheless right to argue that in the case of a play such as *Oedipus Tyrannus*, we must dispense with the mistaken notions of guilt and innocence, since the hero is as much under one category as another. "If the idea is valid, that a man is guilty only in the case that a choice lay open to him, and he decided freely [*mit Willkür*] on what he carried out, then the ancient dramatic figures are guiltless."[98] On the other hand, the objective fact of their action carries blame—what the ancients called *miasma*, which inhered in the act itself, irrespective of motive—and this blame they in no way avoid. Their greatness is to have done what they have done. "About such a hero one could say nothing worse than that he has acted without guilt."[99] This interpretation is one that E. R. Dodds found necessary to reiterate, in somewhat different terms, just twenty years ago to critics who continue to apply modern notions of guilt, with their insistence on the supreme importance of personal knowledge and will, to plays that do not accommodate them.[100]

One of the reasons Hegel launches this argument in the *Vorlesungen über die Ästhetik* is to differentiate classical plays

[98] *VA*, vol. 14, p. 552.
[99] *VA*, vol. 14, p. 553.
[100] E. R. Dodds, "On Misunderstanding *Oedipus Rex*," *Greece and Rome* 13 (1966): 37–49. Also see Dodds, *The Greeks and the Irrational*, pp. 35–37.

from modern ones (by which he means Renaissance and Romantic), whose interest often lies in probing the hero's battles of the soul in laying claim to an action. He is eager, in short, to dispel the notion that Greek tragedy is primarily psychological, oriented toward the inner life of a personality mired in the moral complexities of responsibility and decision making. His point is well taken and serves to remind us of how spare ancient drama is in its depictions of the mental processes involved in the tragic dilemma.[101] Nonetheless, the consequences of Hegel's recognition that a character such as Oedipus is what he does, regardless of intention, are more far-reaching than he acknowledges and at odds with several tenets of his theory of tragedy.

Although Sophocles in *Oedipus Tyrannus* does not focus on the internal waverings and indecisions of the main character, Oedipus, who remains psychologically the same from beginning to end in the drama, he presents us with a figure who is, in another sense, pervasively double. The play enacts the process of inquiry and recognition through which Oedipus comes to see the contradiction he has been all along. The reversal or *peripeteia* in the play is not one in which Oedipus, formerly one sort of person, suddenly becomes another. To separate out the opposing aspects of his character in this fashion and render them as temporally successive is to dissipate the disturbing enigma that the tragedy sets before us of someone who cannot be defined in accordance with notions of identity and noncontradiction.[102] Oedipus is simultaneously a noble ruler and a criminal contaminated with *miasma*; the savior of the city of Thebes and its curse; the first among men and the most diseased; the solver of riddles and himself a riddle he cannot solve; a man of keen intellect and a victim of his own mental blindness; the hunter and the quarry. He is both what he appears to be and what he does not appear to be.

[101] See T. G. Rosenmeyer, "Wahlakt und Entscheidungsprozess in der antiken Tragödie," *Poetica*, vol. 10, no. 1 (1978): 1–24.

[102] See Vernant and Vidal-Naquet, *Mythe et tragédie en Grèce ancienne*, pp. 101–16.

This meeting of irreconcilable traits cannot be satisfactorily described as a harmony of opposites (*concordia discors*), possessed of its own logical unity in which now one element and now another is dominant or in play within a larger congruous pattern of wholeness. Such a structure may well correspond to the pre-Socratic logic of opposition, which Hegel adapted to his own teleological dialectic.[103] But what we find in Sophocles' play is something more radical. Oedipus is a being that no logic can embrace in a self-consistent definition. As a mixture of heterogeneous elements that, according to systematic notions of identity, ought to be exclusive of each other, he cannot be encompassed in a uniform category. He is at once both the positive term of an opposition and the negative.[104]

Some have seen in these unmediated ambivalences the mark of a ritual scapegoat (*pharmakos*), and compelling arguments, for example by René Girard, Jean-Pierre Vernant, and Pierre Vidal-Naquet, have recently carried this line of interpretation significantly beyond the earlier research of the Cambridge ritualists.[105] Without engaging here the provocative conclusions such new works have reached, I want to suggest, in the interests of the present chapter, a problem that the issues raised here pose for a reading such as Hegel's. If we accept his insight into Greek tragic heroes as figures who are identifiable with their deeds and not separable from them on grounds of intentionality, then we cannot, for purposes of interpretive analysis, divide Oedipus into two different persons and align the

[103] On the pre-Socratic logic of opposition, see, for example, Charles Kahn, *Anaximander and the Origins of Greek Cosmology* (New York: Columbia University Press, 1960), pp. 119–65; Gregory Vlastos, "Equality and Justice in Early Greek Cosmology," *Studies in Presocratic Philosophy*, vol. 1, ed. David Furley and R. E. Allen (New York: Humanities Press, 1970), pp. 56–91.

[104] On this contradictory "nonlogic," see Jacques Derrida, *Dissemination*, tr. Barbara Johnson (Chicago: University of Chicago Press, 1981), pp. 95–119.

[105] Girard, *Violence and the Sacred*; Vernant and Vidal-Naquet, *Mythe et tragédie en Grèce ancienne*, pp. 117–31; also see Derrida, *Dissemination*, pp. 128–34.

"real man" with the noble, virtuous, efficient king who makes conscious decisions and acts on his knowledge of persons and circumstances. Certainly, neither Oedipus nor any other character in the tragedy reasons this way about the parricide and incest.[106] Their attention, rather, focuses on the unmitigated horror that the king and savior of Thebes is also its blight and curse. In other words, we cannot overcome the contradiction that Oedipus is by resolving, through a process of analysis, the differences he embodies, or by referring the good parts of his character to conscious agency and the criminal aspects to unconscious. Our modern frames of reference might motivate such an analysis, but the play does not, and it is to Hegel's credit that he recognizes this point. However, the consequences of this insight do not support his theory. Although Hegel thinks he is entitled, in light of his arguments about blame, to speak of Oedipus as a character unified around a pathos and thus single in his identity, he cannot do so. The reason for this lies in a duality that Hegel himself implies. Oedipus is not psychologically divided; rather, his "identity" (the word itself is problematic in this context) incorporates irreconcilable opposites in a way that makes it impossible to set a limiting term to his being.[107] Such radical heterogeneity disrupts the self-consistency fundamental to Hegel's sense of dramatic character.

In different ways, then, *Antigone* and *Oedipus Tyrannus*, plays representative of two types of classical tragedy in the Hegelian system, challenge the terms in which the German

---

[106] Although references are made by Oedipus and the chorus in ll. 1300 ff. to the *daimon* that drove him to blind himself, this is no evidence that Oedipus tries to exculpate himself of blame for the crimes of parricide and incest by witnessing the force of a divinity. As many critics have shown, terms such as *daimon* (lot, fortune), *ate* (ruin, curse), *moira* (portion, destiny), and others, far from separating out of a person's character the unwitting acts he or she commits, implicate divine and human agency in a way typically described as overdetermined. See Dodds, *The Greeks and the Irrational*, pp. 28–50, and Winnington-Ingram, *Sophocles*, pp. 173–78.

[107] See Vernant and Vidal-Naquet, *Mythe et tragédie en Grèce ancienne*, p. 107.

philosopher formulates conflict and mediation. *Antigone*, however, at least superficially, conforms better to the premises of the *Vorlesungen über die Ästhetik* because it can more easily be said to dramatize an external collision of characters with opposing ideas of ethical right. Repeatedly, we find in Hegel's lectures a ranking of plays in which the best tragedies appear as those whose actions are the willing accomplishment of an agent.[108] When physical conditions, such as illness or death, bring on struggles that otherwise would not arise, as in *Alcestis* or *Philoctetes*, for example, then the collision is less advanced. The same holds true of dramas like *Phoenissae* in which natural exigencies, such as birth rights, are the primary conditions instigating clashes.[109] But if a person "is incited to conflict against something that is in and for itself ethical, true, and venerable," then we find clashes that "justifiably appear as the truly interesting oppositions, insofar as they proceed from the specific and individual activity of man."[110] This scheme of classification motivates Hegel to put first among tragedies the plays that Aristotle put last—those involving hamartia committed with full knowledge of the deed.[111] We will return to this point in chapter 2. For now, I want to observe that Hegel's ranking, with its bias against psychological struggle, predisposes him to criticize much postclassical tragedy. He has to modulate his terms to accommodate the interests of such masters as Shakespeare. Let us turn next to his discussion of "romantic drama" (that is, drama of the Renaissance and later), and of Shakespeare, in particular, in order to test in a different area his interpretations of tragic conflict.

BECAUSE HE PRIVILEGES one particular kind of collision—the external battle between two characters whose pathe strive for supreme recognition—Hegel not only requires internal integrity in the tragic protagonist but seems to devalue struggles of

[108] *VA*, vol. 12, pp. 278–95, the section entitled "Die Kollision."
[109] *VA*, vol. 12, pp. 280–83.
[110] *VA*, vol. 12, pp. 291, 280.
[111] See *Poetics*, chap. 9.

the heart between vying claims. A. C. Bradley consequently observes in his Oxford lecture on Hegel that the German philosopher leaves "rightly or wrongly the impression that to his mind the principle of tragedy is more adequately realized in the best classical tragedies than in modern works."[112] Although it is true that the orientation toward deliberate action renders many plays of the Renaissance and the seventeenth and eighteenth centuries problematic for Hegel, it is no less true that his preference for Greek drama has been exaggerated and the full range of his comments on personal conflict in modern drama oversimplified. I therefore examine in greater detail what Hegel says about psychological turmoil in tragedy and how he tries to reconcile an apparent incongruity between his principle of active collision and the interest of postclassical plays in one's internal life.

Bradley draws his observation from passages in which Hegel overtly censures the spiritual vacillation and emotional inconstancy of modern tragic characters. "Even though the tragic action must depend on collision, yet the incorporation of division in one and the same individual is always a risky business. For the fragmentation into opposed interests has its ground partly in an obscurity and dullness of spirit and partly in weakness and immaturity."[113] And again, "character must unite its particularity with its spiritual substance; it must be a determinate type [*eine bestimmte Gestalt*] and in this determinacy have the energy and solidity of a pathos remaining true to itself. . . . Solidity and decisiveness are an important rule for the ideal representation of character."[114] Don Rodrigue in *Le Cid* does not exemplify this desired feature of character, and Hegel criticizes Corneille for his handling of the emotional disturbance in his hero's career. Phèdre, too, is subject to censure, for Racine shows her pathos being ignobly overmastered by the persuasion of a subordinate character,

---

[112] Bradley, *Oxford Lectures on Poetry*, p. 76.
[113] *VA*, vol. 14, p. 570.
[114] *VA*, vol. 12, pp. 324–25.

Oenone. But the real object of Hegel's disapproval is the work of some of his own contemporaries, who are accused of cranking out an endless array of figures possessed of an intolerable "flatulence of emotion." Goethe's Werther is the classic example of this "lovely soul" (*schöne Seele*), "who is not open to the truly ethical interests and worthwhile aims of life, but spins a cocoon about itself and passes its life and weaves a web [*und lebt und webt*] only in the midst of its most personal religious and moral fabrications."[115]

Hegel's derisive comments reveal that internal conflict is discreditable because it prevents the emergence of a secure and stable individuality, which can direct its spiritual energy toward an action. And since tragedy, on the Hegelian reading, is nothing without action, this psychological distraction threatens to dismantle the core of the dramatic machinery. Thought does not crystallize in a deed but is continuously stymied by an obtuse mind lacking definition and consequently, also, a confident outward thrust, such as Greek tragic heroes possess. It is the distrust of emotional vacillation in dramatic protagonists that motivates Hegel's critique of the theory of irony, popular in his day. This theory prizes both a wide diversity of qualities in character and the inversion into its opposite of a trait or tendency first put before the audience: "The character is presented as nothing other than the negation of its determinate form and its very self."[116]

But Hegel's frequent judgments against psychological indecision are not his last words on the subject. He introduces an important distinction, not commonly noted, between internal conflict as an intrinsic, pathological condition of a weak human psyche and vacillation in an otherwise stable character, who is under the necessity of choosing one way or another.[117] In the latter case, the struggle is a momentary one from which the individual recovers. Furthermore, it is an essential one,

115 *VA*, vol. 12, p. 326.
116 *VA*, vol. 12, p. 328.
117 *VA*, vol. 14, p. 571.

brought about by a moral dilemma that demands testing, weighing, and doubt. Shakespeare, according to Hegel, is a master of this kind of psychological portrayal, which to the modern sensibility is more satisfying than the "objective" treatment of character by ancient writers.

This expression of admiration for plays featuring the necessity of self-mistrust in a problematic moral universe is not restricted to a few remarks in the *Vorlesungen über die Ästhetik*. Earlier, in the *Phänomenologie*, Hegel evaluates the achievements of ancient and modern tragedy and reaches a similar judgment. His discussion, found in the section "The Spiritual Work of Art" in chapter 7, is particularly provocative for our purposes. In it he explains that a split in the "ethical substance," a consequence of one-sided action with which the agent completely identifies himself, can be anticipated and forestalled by a hero with a less naive moral consciousness than classical dramatic characters typically possess. Such a hero can in effect function as a sort of internal spectator, to use a term Hegel favors, one who recognizes, like the tragedian or philosopher, that "truth" is complex and the channels through which it is revealed potentially deceptive.[118] Deferring the retaliation of another, opposing claim to truth by putting off action, this more sensitive mind engages in a testing of the vehicles through which Spirit expresses itself. According to Hegel's underlying philosophical assumptions, rationality is inherent in this awareness of ethical totality, which is the lot of the thinking rather than the acting dramatic character. But this mode of rationality seems to render action finally impossible, for it implicates the potential agent in a range of understanding that precludes identification with a single point of view. Let us look more carefully at this issue and its consequences.

In the section on *Sittlichkeit* in the *Phänomenologie*, the nobility of an acting individual is constituted, as it is later in the aesthetic lectures, by the person's certainty that he or she pur-

---

[118] *PhG*, vol. 2, pp. 553–69.

sues an ethical right deserving to be realized. Such certainty, however, as we have seen, blinds the person to the power of the opposition. It is this blindness that Hegel emphasizes when, in a subsequent passage of the *Phänomenologie* on the languages of tragedy, he treats the ethical "truth" on which classical characters act as a sign of ignorance. The second evaluation is based on a problem we have already had the occasion of discussing, though in different terms: the agent convinced of his rightfulness in acting answers the call of a divine power whom he believes speaks unequivocally, but the commands of this truth-speaking god are deceptive.[119] Oedipus and Orestes exemplify these agents, who are destroyed for putting their trust in an oracular utterance whose truth is not in its manifest and obvious meaning, but in the totality of that meaning and what remains concealed. This formulation is a more oblique rendering of a point discussed earlier: the substantive whole (*das Substantielle*) is composed of laws that split into separate sides when they enter the realm of human activity; an agent recognizes only one side as right and is blind to the equally valid claim of the opposition. So, for example, hidden in Apollo's behest to the confident Orestes is the truth of the Furies, who are provoked when transgressed and press their own right. Action, in other words, reveals the deceptiveness of what passes as knowledge; it arouses an opposing power in the substantive whole and thus shows truth to be double.

According to Hegel, however, there is another consciousness, more prudent and thorough than the latter, which approaches the priestess and the beautiful god, Apollo, with "childlike confidence." This consciousness, "with regard to the revelation made by the spirit of his father about the crime that murdered him, hesitates about revenge and contrives yet other proofs—for the reason that this revealing spirit could also be the devil."[120] This is the mistrust of Hamlet, and it has

[119] *PhG*, vol. 2, p. 561.
[120] *PhG*, vol. 2, p. 562.

good grounds because it is founded on the realization that "certain knowledge," such as Oedipus and Orestes have, is only partial and that to act on the revealed command of revenge is to seize hold of merely one part of the ethical substance, whose opposite—duty to king and blood relative—is equally valid.

Later imported into his lectures on art, Hegel's comments offer a reading of *Hamlet* that is perceptively attuned to the crisis in the play. Inaction is not a consequence of weakness but instead the refusal of a spiritually sensitive and alert character to incur guilt by accepting and putting into effect a revelation that may be illusory and partial.[121] Recognizing the deceptiveness of language in the play, which casts doubt on the commands of the ghost, Hegel also postulates that Hamlet cannot eagerly embrace action, in the manner of his classical counterpart, Orestes, because the hero senses that its one-sidedness violates the complexity of truth. Although Hegel does not elaborate this reading, it is nonetheless apparent that some of his insights are well ahead of their time in articulating how illusion and mystery so pervade the world of the play, and especially its language, that the context for acting becomes increasingly problematic.[122] There is no univocal voice of truth with which the potential agent can identify. Moreover, by probing as he does the equivocations in his world, Hamlet's dilemma deepens rather than simplifies, for he becomes more enmeshed in the dialectical complementarities that thought can span but that action cannot encompass.[123]

Were we to follow the line of inquiry opened by Hegel several steps farther than he does, we would be lead to conclude

---

[121] *VA*, vol. 12, pp. 312–13.

[122] See, for example, Maynard Mack, "The World of *Hamlet*," *The Yale Review* 41 (1952): 502–33; Harry Levin, *The Question of Hamlet* (New York: Oxford University Press, 1959); Bernard McElroy, *Shakespeare's Mature Tragedies* (Princeton: Princeton University Press, 1973), pp. 29–88.

[123] See Norman Rabkin, *Shakespeare and the Common Understanding* (New York: Free Press, 1967), who adopts from quantum mechanics the concept of complementarity set forth by Robert Oppenheimer and Niels Bohr.

that what drama strives for according to the explicit precept of the aesthetic lectures, namely, a deliberate deed, is undermined in Shakespeare's play, which may be characterized in one sense as a dramatic critique of the conditions enabling action in a conventional tragic context. The play repeatedly assaults traditional modes of validating experience and right conduct, in ways that are more far-reaching than Hegel suggests.[124] The various sensory tools by means of which the world is apprehended are marshaled into performance in the opening of the play. The apparition first seen by Bernardo and Marcellus claims their fearful credulity but is discredited as a fantasy by Horatio, who requires the "sensible and true avouch of mine own eyes" for belief (1.1.56–57). Having seen, however, Horatio bombards the ghost with a cry that echoes repeatedly throughout the first scene: "Stay! Speak, speak. I charge thee, speak" (1.1.51). Eyes, instruments on which Horatio depends for validating a reported appearance, are inadequate gauges of reality. Unsure of what he beholds, Horatio expresses an implicit faith in the revelatory power of language to dispel doubt.

> Stay, illusion.
> If thou hast any sound or use of voice,
> Speak to me.
> If there be any good thing to be done
> That may to thee do ease and grace to me,
> Speak to me.
> If thou art privy to thy country's fate,
> Which happily foreknowing may avoid,
> O, speak!
> (1.1.127–35)

Hamlet, not Horatio, is finally addressed by the elusive ghost, but no sooner does the spirit reveal at length who he is and

[124] See Stephen Booth, "On the Value of *Hamlet*," in *Reinterpretations of Elizabethan Drama*, ed. Norman Rabkin (New York: Columbia University Press, 1969), pp. 137–76, on Shakespeare's multiple strategies in the play for unsettling an audience's expectations and disrupting categories of understanding.

why he has come than the initially believing Hamlet begins to
question what he has heard, requiring grounds more relative
than the appearance and language of a spirit to confirm the
guilt of the king (2.2.615–18).

In this sequence of events that opens the tragedy, the uncertainty and ambiguity surrounding two traditional ways of validating truth not only forestall Hamlet's ability to act decisively, but dramatize epistemological doubts that turn up
anywhere one looks in the play. Just as the ghost's language
and appearance are equivocal, so are Claudius's and Gertrude's. Neither the display the king puts on in act 1 nor the
words he utters are revelatory and productive of knowledge
about him. Rather, his slick oxymoronic style and cosmetic
rhetoric dissemble, and this dissembling calls for interpretation about the truth "hid within the centre." While Hamlet,
spurred by the ghost, sets his hermeneutic skills to work, his
antic disposition makes him in turn an object of others'
doubts, and they resort no less than he does to indirections to
find directions out. The figure who claims he knows not
"seem" ends up staging a baffling, enigmatic performance that
has the characters in the play and the audience alike looking
to "pluck out the heart of [his] mystery" (3.2.372–73). Soon
everyone in the drama is involved somehow in an elaborate
network of spying whose aim is, with the bait of falsehood, to
take the carp of truth (2.1.63). Hamlet spies on Claudius who
spies on Hamlet who spies on (and is spied on by) Polonius
who spies on Laertes. Each scurries to find an angle from
which appearances will deliver up their truth.

But such surreptitious, hidden posings do not produce the
certain knowledge that Polonius, in his homely fishing metaphor, is sure will come up. "Seeing unseen" does not guarantee the beholder that he can "frankly judge," and that is why
many of the supposed discoveries in the play turn out to be
red herrings, not carps of truth. In short, the divinatory power
that could emerge from a privileged position collapses in the
play. For what is beheld from the vantage point of spying requires no less interpretive ability to fathom than what is beheld openly. In both cases, the evidence is sufficiently ambig-

uous to intensify the uncertainty that is supposed to be discharged. In this series of developments, Hamlet becomes both doubting spectator and doubted spectacle, implicated like his "mighty opposite" in the double role generated by being part of a world whose truth is elusive.

The epistemological crisis at the heart of the various efforts at interpretation in the play operates partially as a metadramatic commentary on a crisis at another level—that of an audience of Shakespeare's tragedy.[125] In the continual dislocations of knowledge engendered by the search for accurate facts and certain senses, the play disrupts our categories for validating truth just as it does those of its dramatic characters. We, too, grope for a sandbank on which we can shore up our failed structures of understanding and our misjudged hypotheses but find each new promising retreat another quicksand of illusion. As external spectators, we are in no better position to espy the truth about the ghost, or Claudius, or Gertrude than is the master internal spectator, Hamlet himself. Like him, we are given enough clues to form hunches, but the definitive evidence we strain for comes slowly if at all. Hamlet's dilemmas of interpretation become ours, as we discover that the different contexts within which the question of right action might be put yield nothing like certain knowledge. With every slippage of language and appearance in the play, our systems for guaranteeing coherence are challenged and we have to retrench.

If Hegel does not follow out such consequences of his remarks on the language of *Hamlet*, it is probably because several tenets crucial to his theory of tragedy are jeopardized by his insights. First of all, action, the sine qua non of his definition of tragedy, is invalidated by the enigmas of knowledge in Shakespeare's play. Moreover, as I have argued, the interpreter is ineluctably drawn into the play's indeterminacy and

---

[125] See James L. Calderwood, *To Be and Not To Be: Negation and Metadrama in Hamlet* (New York: Columbia University Press, 1983), who addresses various aspects of metadrama in the play.

thus loses the privileged vantage point from which Hegel's insistence on dialectical coherence is secured. This is not to say that the play flies apart, but that it never quite comes together in the ways he expects it to. Or when it seems to meet his expectations, it suddenly goes veering off again in another unsettling direction, as we will see, frustrating the desire for conclusive answers.

It may be these tendencies of Shakespeare's play that tempt Hegel into several other, divergent critical responses to the tragedy, none of them as perceptive or as sympathetic as those recorded earlier. These alternative views stem more directly from his systematic interests in the *Vorlesungen über die Ästhetik* and seem designed to secure their cogency. One strain of comments relegates *Hamlet* to the class of flatulent dramas that Hegel scorns, those concerned to demonstrate that no character is firmly rooted and self-assured. This evaluation is derived largely from what Goethe said about it, though Goethe does not place the negative evaluation on inaction that Hegel does at such moments. According to this view, Hamlet is one of the "beautiful souls" (the *schöne Seele* are a disreputable bevy in the aesthetic lectures), whose finely strung, impractical nature is not steeled for the task imposed upon him. Bandied by his lack of backbone from pillar to post, he finally meets his doom through his own procrastination and through the external, contingent course of events.[126] As is apparent, this alternative interpretation to which Hegel sometimes subscribes is not sensitive to the epistemological crisis dramatized in Shakespeare's play but finds fault with the hero for a temperament unsuited to an action that a heartier soul would be able to carry out. In short, this line of approach, far from singling out *Hamlet* as a drama in which a superior consciousness of truth operates, demotes it to an inferior group because it languishes in doubt.

At other times, however, Hegel suggests that Shakespeare's hero is caught only in a momentary stasis, from which he fi-

---

[126] *VA*, vol. 12, pp. 312–13; *VA*, vol. 14, p. 506.

nally extirpates himself. Hamlet, he admits, is a case of mental indecision, but the hero agonizes only about the way he shall carry out his purpose, not about what has to be done.[127] This is hardly a convincing argument for the character we encounter through act 3, whose purpose no sooner crystallizes than it is "sicklied o'er with the pale cast of thought" so that "enterprises of great pitch and moment, / With this regard their currents turn awry, / And lose the name of action" (3.1.84–88). The obstacles in the way of forming purpose are much more in view than purpose itself. The player king's speech in "The Mousetrap" is a sort of compendium of these obstacles, cataloguing why "what we do determine oft we break" (3.2.193). But perhaps Hegel is drawing our attention to the Hamlet we meet after the play within the play, the Hamlet who appears to have broken the hold that doubt has on him, since he believes he has caught the conscience of the king.

It is typical of Shakespeare's tragedy that the expectation of decisive action in the hero that an audience is allowed to indulge after Claudius has been found out is cut short. Finding the king at prayer, Hamlet is in a good position to avenge the villain who has killed his father; he decides instead not to take him purging his soul but "about some act / That has no relish of salvation in 't" (3.3.92). It is more than an irony that Claudius, rather than repenting in this scene, as Hamlet thinks he does, lets his "words fly up" to heaven while his "thoughts remain below" (3.3.97–98). Thought and action are still disjoint, in Claudius no less than in Hamlet, whose performance is once more deferred, not by a frank judgment, but by a frank misjudgment. The ready avenger, who has just told us, "Now could I drink hot blood" (3.2.398), misses his chance. And the play makes our anticipations falter once again.

Increasingly, our attention is riveted on a mystery with which the play has already confronted us, a mystery Hamlet himself acknowledges as he gets ready to depart for England under Claudius's orders: "I do not know / Why yet I live to

[127] *VA*, vol. 12, pp. 328–29.

say, 'This thing's to do,' / Sith I have cause, and will, and strength, and means / To do't" (4.4.43–46). Having entrapped the conscience of the king and found a ready opportunity for revenge but the occasion unsuitable, Hamlet assures himself, "O, from this time forth, / My thoughts be bloody, or be nothing worth!" (4.4.65–66). But he utters this resolution as he is leaving Denmark. What does he have in mind? While the epistemological dilemmas dramatized in the first three acts seem less pressing at this juncture, another problem forces its way into the audience's already shaken sensibilities: the inscrutability of Hamlet's motives. What our understanding wants to grasp, and what Hegel's critical approach requires, namely, a comprehensible, unitary basis for defining his conduct, recedes behind the vague, halting possibilities that meet our queries. This inscrutability is sustained through the very end of the play. Why does the master spy, Hamlet, who has spent a good deal of time in the play sniffing out rats, go off to the duel with Laertes unsuspicious of intrigue? And is his murder of Claudius more than the accident it appears to be? Is it an expression of a deliberate purpose that he has sometimes announced, even vehemently, but just as often set aside?

Rather than bringing us to a resolution in which the ends are tied up in the fashion of revenge tragedy, Shakespeare's play keeps us wondering. Because we are unsettled by this doubt, which we expect the conclusion to dispel, we can appreciate the perspective from which Hegel delivers his more determinate dicta about the play. His perspective, at least in its more conservative form, articulates the certainty and stability that we want to find in the drama *Hamlet*. By turning Shakespeare's enigmatic hero into an example of a "prudent and solid consciousness" (*besonnenes und gründliches Bewusstsein*) whose hesitation is passing, he provides critical controls that mediate and unify the disparate conflicts and the unresolved contradictions in the tragedy. Admitting that Hamlet is a case of mental indecision, he also claims that the uncertainty is overcome and that a stable ground for action is ultimately uncovered in the play. But this "closed reading," which

tries to accommodate a great masterpiece of Western literature to a theoretical account of tragedy oriented toward deliberate action, is not Hegel's most provocative. It is a testimony
to his often keen literary insight that he can approach the play
in a way that goes against his critical grain, by opening to our
view its conception of the problematic nature of moral truth
and its critique of "naive action."

I have spent some time on Hegel's various responses to
Hamlet because they demonstrate a range of sensitivity to
problems in the play unmatched by his remarks on other
pieces of modern tragedy. One of the points that emerges from
this analysis is that Hegel has greater tolerance for dramatizations of psychological struggle or mental uncertainty in
tragedy than some of his more frequently quoted comments
suggest. Moreover, in contexts such as the discussion of literary languages in the *Phänomenologie*, where the focus is on
the dialectical complementarities that thinking can embrace,
the dilemma of Hamlet can be treated quite sympathetically.
For here the acting individual, with his one-sided attachment
to truth, takes an inferior place to a purely thinking consciousness. Even in this more sensitive reading, Hegel has a tendency, already noted in his treatment of *Antigone*, to pose the
conflict of *Hamlet* in binary terms, which flatten the denser,
uneven tensions dramatized in Shakespeare's play. Nonetheless, his insight into the dramatic relationship between
thought and action is intriguing and anticipates some of the
more productive trends in recent criticism.

This insight plays a lesser role in the *Vorlesungen über die
Ästhetik*, where the theoretical orientation to treat action as
the core of drama produces a more critical view of *Hamlet*.
From the perspective of the generic demands of tragedy, doing
is superior to thinking; the direction of analysis is here the
reverse of what we find in the *Phänomenologie*, and consequently the approach to Shakespeare's tragedy is somewhat
different. Were we to follow up Hegel's statements on other
Shakespearean tragedies in the aesthetic lectures, we would
find a similar emphasis on the key importance of unifying

character through gestural performance. For example, Macbeth and Othello are offered as illustrations of "essentially stable and consequential characters, who go to their destruction precisely because of the distinctive hold upon themselves and their ends."[128] Hegel rightly points to a pathos, albeit in these cases a nonethical one, that drives these figures—ambition in Macbeth and jealousy in Othello. But Shakespeare takes apart the idea that through action characters can effectively focus their inner lives, concentrate their energies, and so abandon doubts that come from thinking too precisely about their ends.

It is true that Macbeth and Othello in different ways try to mediate internal conflicts and unify their souls around a univocal purpose. But to do so, they must reduce the complexity of vying truths and desires. They must, in a sense, do what Hamlet cannot—artificialize the reality paralyzing them and deny part of it. In short, they must create, through a violent wrenching into focus of their aims, the confidence of an Orestes that allows directed action. Macbeth has to "bend up / Each corporal agent" to the terrible task of murdering Duncan and make "a false face . . . hide what a false heart doth know" (1.7.79–82). Othello is driven to summon up the powers of hell in order to quash his love for Desdemona and make his "just revenge" as compulsive as the course that "keeps due on / To the Propontic and the Hellespont" (3.3.453–56). But what do such wrenchings of the self out of uncertainty uncover in the end? The illusoriness of a unity which both characters crave—and which Hegel maintains they achieve. Screwing one's courage to the sticking place does not soothe mental anguish, and delivering the blow is not a be-all and an end-all. Both Macbeth and Othello continue to experience an internal distraction, verging on hysteria and madness, that they hoped decisive action would obliterate.

Hegel's desire to see in Shakespeare's tragic heroes a firmness and unwavering determination similar to that of Greek protagonists is founded on his conviction that only in such

[128] *VA*, vol. 14, p. 571.

unity of the self, such pathos, can the full course of "ideal action" be realized. For it is through the implementation of one-sided claims, which together compose the totality of ethical truth, that the "ideal" in art is asserted. But if this symmetry is broken up, if action does not express a right or passion with which the subject fully identifies himself and in which he finds his rationale for being, if the unity of pathos fragments and doubt becomes an irreducible truth, then the foundation of Hegel's theory of tragedy gives way and with it the manifestation of *Vernunft* in human affairs. *Hamlet* strikes the greatest blow to this theory, not simply because it dramatizes how action, the sine qua non of tragedy, can become impossible as an expression of directed purpose, but because this impossibility is grounded in a consciousness of the endless elusiveness of truth, into which the audience is drawn. A dialectically superior position is eroded throughout the play.

THOUGH THE REMARKS on modern, particularly Shakespearean, tragedy in the *Vorlesungen über die Ästhetik* and the analysis of *Hamlet* in the *Phänomenologie* suggest that Hegel values the introspective penetration of postclassical drama, they do not change the fact that his dramatic theory centers squarely on social and ethical conflict. Thus, although it is oversimplified to say, as some have, that the German philosopher has a low estimate of sixteenth- to eighteenth-century plays, it remains true that the bulk of his critical statements account best for Greek tragedy, especially the variety featuring crises in *Sittlichkeit*.

The bias is understandable in two ways. First, Hegel's thoughts on tragedy develop under the influence of his dialectical view of history, which stresses what people do rather than what they think. Tragic drama, therefore, tends to be assimilated to the historical premise that there is no difference between inner purposes and acts; one is the sum total of one's deeds, for deeds represent the ends one pursues. Furthermore, these ends are seen in terms of a process of conflict and resolution, which is supposed to carry out the rational project of

Geist. It is through the life of action that Spirit manifests itself in the world. Hegel's aesthetic system is predisposed from the beginning, then, to favor action—a point corroborated, as we have observed, by the organization of his introductory comments on the Ideal. These comments clarify why he has difficulty handling plays that make the relation between inner nature and deeds problematic, that show one is not the sum total of what one does and that action can misrepresent consciousness.

My effort in this chapter to explore the conditions enabling an agonistic treatment of tragedy has had a double focus: the insight into drama made possible by Hegel's dialectical understanding of history and the simultaneous exclusions entailed by the insight. This complexity of approach has necessitated an equivocal posture toward the breakthrough in literary studies initiated by Hegel's theory. Thus the appreciation of his contribution, which I hope to have advanced, has been consistently tempered and probably, at times, even diffused by an analysis of the limitations of his readings. This double assessment has perhaps strengthened a point to which I have often reverted: the radical potential in Hegel's approach is brought up short repeatedly in his discussions of plays, by critical controls that turn out to be new versions of traditional forms of closure, harmony, and order. So implicated in these conventional literary norms is the Hegelian approach to drama that it is not hard to see why his distinct innovations have been only partially understood. As we move, however, in the next chapers to consider Aristotle and his legacy, it will become increasingly clear how much of a departure from tradition Hegel makes in elevating into a principle of dramatic art an experience that remained up to his time outside the preserve of criticism. First, it is necessary to explore the ways in which the persistent associations of strife with irrationality and disorder were enough to keep it from becoming a focal point in discussions of tragedy from Aristotle through the eighteenth century.

CHAPTER TWO

Aristotle: Conflict and Disorder

Perhaps you have not considered that disease and discord
are the same thing? Is that because you think that discord
is anything other than a disagreement of what is related
by nature, brought about through some kind of corruption?

—Plato, *Sophist*

AN INVESTIGATION of the factors shaping Aristotle's nonagonistic approach to tragedy can proceed most fruitfully in
acknowledgment of some fundamental similarities between
the *Poetics* and Hegel's lectures on drama. I briefly raised
these points of contact in the first chapter, but they bear repeating at this juncture. Perhaps the most important common
ground on which the two influential theories stand is their insistence on a set of ordering principles that structure drama
into a unified, contained whole. For Hegel, these principles are
largely ethical and emerge from an effort to align tragedy with
philosophical history. The play is understood as an embodiment of a crisis of values, whose resolution leads to—or at
least implies—a higher, mediated level of social and spiritual
perfection. Within a dramatic context, conflict assumes a
prominent organizing role, as it does in Hegel's rational history, for it is the experience that gives to the transitional crisis
a structuring force and a teleological direction. Seen dialectically, which is the way the dramatist intends, strife is not a
harbinger of chaos or disorder, though it may appear to be so
to a myopic, nonphilosophical spectator. The moral confusion
that conflict brings in its wake is merely a stage in a larger
process that discloses to the mind of reason the immanent
power of *Geist* in human struggles.

Aristotle also attempts to ground tragedy in a rational principle, a *logos*. But he has his sight predominantly on structural elements, and in particular on the rules of likelihood and necessity, which link the constituent parts of a *praxis* and render them comprehensible in relation to a character's *ethos*, or predisposition to action. The structural focus does not exclude attention to ethical matters, such as the quality or moral tenor of this predisposition, but subordinates them to the larger preoccupation with form. This subordination is an important factor setting the analytic tone of the *Poetics*. The concern with organizational issues, which creates a tendency to treat even the tragic agent as a function of the highest formal principle, namely, *muthos*, enables Aristotle to adopt a scientific language of definition, categories, and hierarchical order in the *Poetics*, which is apparent from the very beginning in his introductory remarks: "Let us speak about poetry itself and its various kinds, about what effect each has and how the plots must be constructed, if the composition is going to be good; and, moreover, of how many and what kinds of parts a poem is composed; and similarly about as many other things as pertain to the same inquiry, beginning, according to nature, from first principles."[1] Behind the veneer of stable, containing formal properties, which can be specified, enumerated, and analyzed, recede the unsettling dilemmas often explored by the tragedians. With the confident, matter-of-fact approach of a biologist who goes about dividing his subject matter into its natural categories in order to comprehend it, Aristotle takes on some of the most disturbing and challenging literary productions in the Greek tradition.

In the following pages, we will study the formal principles of Aristotle's theory of tragedy and the ethical issues they organize, in order to understand more fully the exclusionary biases of the *Poetics*, especially as they relate to conflict. In the process it will become apparent that although Aristotle's non-

---

[1] Aristotle, *Poetics*, ed. with comm. by D. W. Lucas (1968; reprint, Oxford: Clarendon Press, 1980), 1447a8–13.

agonistic orientation sets him apart from Hegel, its effect nonetheless is to order drama in a way similar to the teleological rationalizations of struggle characteristic of the *Vorlesungen über die Ästhetik*. Both philosophers subdue the challenges tragedy poses for social, moral, and metaphysical order by containing them within the limiting terms of a theoretical framework. Against this common background, let us proceed to examine some distinctive features of the influential classical account of tragic drama.

IT IS USEFUL at the outset to situate Aristotle's views in terms of Plato's critique of tragedy in the *Republic*, in order to appreciate the broader intellectual context and the terms of literary discussion within which the author of the *Poetics* most likely moved. From this perspective, we can begin to see the Aristotelian approach as a strategic reorientation of the lines of inquiry established earlier by Plato, who is never once mentioned in the *Poetics*, but whose impact on that document can scarcely be doubted.[2] In isolating the major arguments in the *Republic* against tragedy, we would do well to remember that Plato's remarks are tied to the larger concerns in the dialogue with the question of justice and with the normative principles for the establishment of a healthy state. At several levels, poetry in general and tragedy in particular are regarded as threats to stability and unity; they are subversive of the standards essential to the creation and maintenance of a good commonwealth. The fact that Plato is discussing an ideal construct rather than the social reality of his time should not mitigate the force of his critique, which reveals a disapproval of the arts as they were and had been pursued in Greece.

In books 2 and 3, we encounter an attack against poetry on pedagogical grounds that gradually narrows to a censure of dramatic poetry. At the heart of the discussion is the question,

---

[2] On the *Poetics* as a response to Plato, see Lucas's introduction to his edition, pp. xiv–xxii; Gerald Else, *Aristotle's Poetics: The Argument* (Cambridge, Mass.: Harvard University Press, 1963), pp. 21–23, 304–6, 433–35; Thomas Gould's review of Else's edition in *Gnomon* 34 (1962): 641–49.

what sort of education will direct people with a proper natural aptitude for guardianship to be good guardians? Entailed in this question is an analysis of *mousike*, "training in arts and music for the soul," and *gymnastike* "physical training," which is for the sake of the body as much as the soul. Both kinds of *paideia*, or education, are distinctly geared toward the production of psychological and social harmony—experiences crucial to the integrity not only of the guardians but of the republic they will govern.[3] Within this framework, Plato confronts the problem of a future for poetry in a populace whose traditional values had been collected and transmitted via the poets.[4] What, if any, strictures ought to be put upon the exposure of the guardians to Homer, Hesiod, and the tragedians? Plato's response singles out for disapproval aspects of epic and dramatic literature that promote discord within and among individuals. At the top of his list of objectionable content is the portrayal of struggles among the gods. Homer is the major culprit in this discussion, but because he was the "teacher of the tragic poets," they too are implicated in Plato's censure. His point is that the future guardians of the state should regard the habit of quarreling and opposing each other as the basest of all things. Thus they should not be exposed to poetry in which strife is featured, especially divine strife, for if they are, they will follow the example of superiors and fall into the ways of the characters depicted.[5] This argument combines, in a way typical of Plato, a critique of the artist's mimesis—his representations of the gods are false, since gods do not fight—with words of warning about the audience's mi-

[3] For a fuller discussion of harmony as a normative value in the *Republic*, see, for example, Nicholas P. White, *A Companion to Plato's Republic* (Indianapolis: Hackett, 1979), pp. 17–20, 26, 39–43, and Julia Annas, *An Introduction to Plato's Republic* (Oxford: Clarendon Press, 1981), pp. 103–5, 118–56, 178–81.

[4] Eric Havelock discusses this issue at length in *Preface to Plato* (1963; reprint, Cambridge, Mass.: Harvard University Press, 1982), part 1.

[5] Plato, *Republic*, ed. John Burnet (1903; reprint, Oxford: Clarendon Press, 1965), 378c.

mesis—their imitation of bad examples (*paradeigmata*) breeds social conflict.

The dangers of mimetic behavior apparent in the discussion of poetic content in book 2 are rendered more explicitly at the beginning of book 3. Differentiating three modes of speech in poetry—narrative, dramatic or mimetic, and mixed—Plato treats the second form as especially dangerous. We do not want our guardians to be mimetic, he argues, because the impersonation of many types fragments the singularity and unity of *ethos* essential to the natural division of labor in the state, according to which each person performs the activity that most suits him by temperament and training.[6] The mimesis debunked in this passage is the traditional Greek educational practice of reciting and memorizing the poets by throwing oneself into a part like an actor or a rhapsode. Impersonation as a pedagogical experience can foster a personal style of conduct. This is the issue of concern to Plato. A man who regularly adopts the imitative mode will actually be "two or more persons at once" (διπλοῦς καὶ πολλαπλοῦς), unless he imitates a good type exactly like himself, a case that Plato does not disparage. In the instance of a guardian, ⌈diversified mimesis leads to a division of the person against himself in a way that gradually erodes the integrity of his identity.⌉ His self-control and braveness—attributes central to his role—will be overcome in the process of impersonating "foreign" types. "Have you not perceived," Plato's Socrates observes, "that mimetic forms of behavior, if pursued from youth up, turn into habit and nature both in the body and the tones of voice and the way of thinking?"[7] One is better off avoiding such reproduction altogether and adopting the narrative style; the danger of losing one's sense of selfhood is less when one does not enter into other roles and instead keeps a distance from the object being represented. But it is not only unity of character that is endangered by miming different types. Social order is also

[6] *Republic*, 394e-395a.
[7] *Republic*, 395d.

shaken by such mimesis, which destroys the principle of differentiation essential to the hierarchy of the state.

> Suppose, for instance, that a man who is an artisan or some other tradesperson by nature, being stirred up by wealth or a faction or physical strength or some similar thing, tries to enter the fighting class; or someone from the fighting class, who is unworthy, tries to enter the class of counsellors or guardians and these men lay claim to each other's tools and prerogatives; or consider a man who tries to do all these things at once. In such a situation, as you and I see it, the variability of these men and their meddlesomeness are destructive to the city . . . and could rightly be called the worst kind of wrong-doing.[8]

Only if a person unwaveringly pursues the one thing that best conforms to his disposition and skill can the division of labor be stabilized and protected from the dissension that arises from crossing natural boundaries. Although comedy and the dramatic portions of epic are included in this critique of mimesis as impersonation, many of Plato's examples suggest that he has tragedy chiefly in mind.

The social and psychological conflicts addressed in the attack on poetry in books 2 and 3 are developed even more fully in book 10.[9] Here, tragedy is definitely at the forefront of discussion; it epitomizes the worst dangers of poetry, since it is purely mimetic in form and since its content is almost always morally and socially subversive. Plato's objections at this

[8] *Republic*, 434b-c.

[9] The relationship between the arguments on poetry in books 2–3 and book 10 is still a subject of scholarly controversy, as is the dating of the latter. That different conceptions of mimesis emerge in these books is clear, but whether or not the conceptions may be reconciled is another question. Some of the more pressing disjunctions are mitigated, I believe, by recognizing that Plato is dealing with different issues in the earlier and later books; see White, *Companion to Plato's Republic*, pp. 246–64. Nonetheless, I think that the different arguments reveal a deep and unmediated ambivalence in Plato's evaluations of the nature and value of poetry; see Annas, *An Introduction to Plato's Republic*, pp. 335–44.

point in the argument of the *Republic* gain force from the discussion of the tripartite division of the soul in book 4, where the principle of hierarchical unity under the controlling power of *logos* is established as a criterion of psychological life.[10] In book 10, these earlier insights are brought to bear particularly on the characters of tragedy, whose threats to morality and society are probed in some detail.

The mimetic art, according to Plato, does not originate in or appeal to the highest part in the soul, the logical faculty (*to logismon*). It draws its subject matter from an inferior class of men, those with a fretful, complaining temper that is not law-abiding and prepared to listen to the authority of reason, which counsels equanimity and unity of mind. Such a temper, instead, is at war with itself, indulging its sorrow for losses that it knows should be borne without struggle. If the weaker-minded person provides the material for tragedy, that is because "the prudent and temperate disposition, being always at one with itself, is not easy to imitate nor when it is imitated is it easy to understand, especially by a large assembly and the motley crowd gathered in the theatre. For the imitation is of a state foreign to them."[11] Not only does the philosophical temper resist mimetic presentation, but it does not attract the dramatic poet, who must take as his subject the unstable types, if he is to have popular success. No audience would find the portrayal of a soul both constant and self-consistent an intriguing spectacle. Mutability, distemper, and conflict are staples of the stage because they have the greatest mass appeal.

The formal and thematic dangers of traditional poetry introduced in book 2 are filled out in this discussion through an analysis of typical features of tragic characters. The fact that such agents are fitful, self-contradictory, and without rational control makes it all the more deleterious for an audience to enter into their plights and weep or moan in sympathy for them. Anticipating an argument that Aristotle would later ma-

[10] *Republic*, 435c-442d.
[11] *Republic*, 604e.

nipulate with an important difference, Plato says that this spectatorly pity, which tragedy elicits, feeds and waters the passions and encourages people to become like the misdirected characters they behold on stage. In the words of Socrates, "Few, I believe, are able to infer that enjoying another's feelings necessarily affects our own, for once pity has grown strong through others' sufferings, it is not easy to restrain our own."[12] Tragedy, in short, breeds psychological conflict by endangering the rational harmony of the soul and accustoming spectators to the experience of emotional self-indulgence. In this argument, we discover that Plato's distrust of tragic mimesis extends beyond the fear of fragmentation produced by impersonating multiple types; the types themselves are examples of bad people who are torn by strife and who buck against the goad of reason in their souls.

Thus at various levels—psychological, moral, and social—Plato condemns tragedy, regarding the conflicts that it dramatizes and disseminates as subversions of normative reason. Rather than stabilizing and validating order in the soul and the state, tragedy promotes discord by unhinging the balance of power. Its mimetic form and degenerate subject matter combine to make it an especially insidious force of dissolution. If the tone of urgency and the degree of censure in Plato's discussion strike us as exaggerated, we should remember that he is addressing a body of literature that had not only great popular appeal but an official place of honor in the civic practices of classical Greece. The tragedy that Plato condemns was subsidized by state funds, judged by a committee of state officials, and performed at the theater of Dionysus during state-declared holidays, when multitudes showed up for the performances. Only in this perspective can we appreciate the often vehement force of the Platonic attack on tragic drama, whose danger seems to be perceived in proportion to the respect and admiration in which it was held.

The connection of tragedy with *stasis*, or discord, is remark-

[12] *Republic*, 606b.

ably consistent in the *Republic*. But unlike Hegel, who regards strife as a pivotal force directing cultural change, Plato treats it as a harbinger of chaos and anarchy; thus he takes a hard line on the dramatic productions of the fifth century. In his less condemnatory moments he regards them as forms of undignified, useless play (*paidia*), but more often he treats them as if they were bearers of contagious diseases that threaten to contaminate the entire community.[13] It is against this background that we can now set Aristotle's views. Departing from his predecessor's evaluation of mimetic art, he seeks to realign drama with principles that in many cases reverse those set forth in the *Republic*. For example, he grounds tragedy in the safety of a *spoudaia praxis*, "a good and serious action," thus opposing Plato's notion of *paidia* with tragic *spoude*.[14] Against the notion that dramatic characters are bad examples, he sets up the idea of a tragic agent who is basically a good and pitiable person foiled by an unwitting error. Finally, he argues for the tragedian's philosophical use of universals and focuses on elements of the tragic event that affirm the rule of formal order. The Platonic specter of psychological and social dissolution is glossed over by the reassuring containing structures and ethically nonthreatening terms that Aristotle adopts in his discussion. Similarly, the air of moral urgency in the *Republic* gives way to a scientifically neutral tone in the *Poetics*, which responds to the subject matter as if it were an interesting form of plant life that could be comprehended by "following the order of nature" and, beginning with the principles that come first, divided into genus and species. Aristotle's move is not to engage Plato directly, but to supersede his approach by proceeding as if the material simply invited the line of inquiry he adopts.

[13] For a recent treatment of these issues in Plato, see Jonas Barish, *The Antitheatrical Prejudice* (Berkeley: University of California Press, 1981), pp. 5–37.

[14] For Plato's use of the distinction between *paidia* and *spoude* in his discussion of poetry, see *Republic*, 602b6–10. For Aristotle's very different manipulation of this contrast, see *Poetics*, chap. 9.

While Aristotle breaks with Plato's views of tragedy, we might still wonder why he does not openly take up and reinterpret the problem of conflict. Once again, we seem to be dealing with a systematically motivated exclusion. As the subsequent study will show, Aristotle, notwithstanding his departure from Plato's literary evaluations, continues to think about *stasis* in the same formal and ethical terms as his predecessor does. Consequently, this aspect of tragic drama assumes a problematic status for the kind of rationalizing project he launches in the *Poetics*. His argument, which is partly designed to bring tragedy within safe cultural bounds and give it a place of honor among the arts, is predisposed not to include in its definitions a topic with strong ties to irrationality and disorder. Only if these ties could have been effectively broken by appeal to a model of conflict that dismantled its threats to reason might the topic of tragic *stasis* have found a prominent role in Aristotle's views. But as the *Poetics* stands, its orientation circumscribes a field of analysis from which strife is implicitly debarred. With these points in mind, let us now turn to more substantial evidence of a nonagonistic bias in the document.

I will first concentrate on passages from the *Metaphysics* and the *Prior* and *Posterior Analytics* to draw out the implications of the distinction between *poiesis*, "poetry," and *historie*, "history," in *Poetics*, chapter 9. One of the effects of this distinction is to cut off from Aristotle's view of the dramatic universe actions that occur without predictability or an explanatory cause attributable to character and an initial configuration of events. Not infrequently in Greek tragedy, collisions between the divine and human order operate in an indeterminate manner and so fall outside the standards of tragic plausibility established in the *Poetics*. Thus, on the basis of the principles he adopts in defining dramatic *muthos*, Aristotle is enabled to circumvent a class of tragic actions that Plato overtly censured—[conflicts precipitated by the indeterminate maleficence of deity and not motivated by an intelligible cause within the realm of human design and action]. With

the insights into dramatic form derived from this initial discussion, I will next turn to a more consequential issue with
wide-ranging effects for the concept of tragedy in the *Poetics*.
This issue concerns the nature of the *spoudaios* or *epieikes*,
the "good and worthy person," whom Aristotle makes his
tragic agent. Through a study of discussions in the *Politics* and
Nicomachean Ethics, where this figure is defined more elaborately than in the *Poetics*, we find that he is by nature resistant
to, if not completely removed from, conflict in thought and
action. In establishing the significance of this point for Aristotle's dramatic theory, we will have to consider the middling
status of the tragic *spoudaios*, as an agent who falls between
the two extremes of perfect virtue and malicious vice. But in
the end, I hope to show that the importation of *spoudaiotes*
into the *Poetics* discourages a view of the tragic action as a
representation of internal battles of the soul, of intense social
rivalries between individuals with competing ethical claims, or
of clashes between mortals and gods. Plato's critique of *stasis*
in tragedy is bypassed in Aristotle's definition of character and
plot. Finally, in order to illustrate the predominance of a nonagonistic bias in Aristotle's approach to fields closely related
to poetics, I will turn to the *Rhetoric*. While the very nature of
the subject matter treated in this work seems to be inseparable
from the experience of struggle and contestatory debate, the
method adopted by Aristotle involves an unmistakable effort
to generate controls that can subdue, defer, or mediate conflict. An understanding of this point can provide an important
perspective on a tendency that I take to be characteristic of
Aristotle's arguments on behalf of rhetoric as a *techne*.

THE CONCEPTION of tragic action in the *Poetics* relies implicitly on claims that Aristotle makes about action in various
other treatises, especially the *Nicomachean Ethics, De Motu
Animalium*, and *De Anima*.[15] It would be useful, in order to

---

[15] See especially *Nicomachean Ethics*, ed. J. Bywater (1894; reprint, Oxford: Clarendon Press, 1959), 6.2; abbreviated hereafter as *NE*. Also see Har-

get an overview of the nonagonistic form this conception takes at the most general level, to examine briefly the schema elaborated for a *praxis* in his system. Although there continues to be scholarly debate about various aspects of the schema, especially regarding the nature and role of the practical syllogisms commonly supposed to be included in it, we can for purposes of the present discussion avoid these more controversial questions and concentrate on broadly agreed on features.[16] As the subsequent model makes clear, a single agent and the psychological apparatus initiating action inform Aristotle's conceptual framework.[17]

Desire	I desire A.
Deliberation	B contributes to getting A.
	C contributes to getting B.
	....
	N contributes to getting M.
Perception	N is something I can do now.
Choice	I choose N.
Act	I do N.

This systematic account of action takes as its object not just a single agent but a rational one, whose decision making and choice are necessary preliminaries to the performance of a

die's discussion of other evidence in the *Ethics* in *Aristotle's Ethical Theory*, 2d ed. (Oxford: Clarendon Press, 1980), pp. 241–45; *De Motu Animalium*, ed. with trans. and comm. by Martha Craven Nussbaum (Princeton: Princeton University Press, 1978), 701a8–33; and *De Anima*, ed. with comm. by W. D. Ross (Oxford: Clarendon Press, 1961), G 10 and 11.

[16] On this controversy over the practical syllogism, see Hardie, *Aristotle's Ethical Theory*, pp. 240–57; Nussbaum, *Aristotle's De Motu Animalium*, pp. 165–220; and John M. Cooper, *Reason and the Human Good in Aristotle* (Cambridge, Mass.: Cambridge University Press, 1975), pp. 46–58.

[17] The diagram is a modification of the one produced by W. D. Ross, *Aristotle*, 5th ed., rev. (1949; reprint, New York: Barnes and Noble, 1964), p. 199. The modification includes a deletion of the phrase "the means to" and a substitution of "contributes to getting." For discussions of *ta pros to telos* as (a) causal conditions, (b) constituent parts, and (c) the results defining what something consists in, see Cooper, *Reason and Human Good in Aristotle*, pp. 10–22 and Nussbaum, *Aristotle's De Motu Animalium*, p. 170.

deed. Now it is typical of Aristotle's manipulation of this scheme in the *Poetics* that the individualistic or agent-oriented conception of *praxis* often slides over into a broader conception of the entire drama as an "action." What is suggested by this essential unity between individual agency and larger dramatic performance is a sense that the coherence of the whole play resides in how the deeds it represents—and drama is fundamentally doing *(dran)*—can be linked causally back to the rational deliberations and choices of characters ready to act. In tragedy, however, the first three steps in the schema outlined here are only implicit in an action and not overtly dramatized; the decision-making process that they compose is not presented to the audience. [Aristotle tells us that *prohairesis*, "deliberative choice," and *praxis*, "action," are the components of a tragic performance, and thus suggests that the psychological aspect of choosing, the deliberative activity, is not proper to the stage.[18] The significance of this point will be taken up later.

What concerns us in the present discussion is the aspect of necessity or inevitability that operates in this conception of *praxis*: when desire combines with deliberation and perception to form choice, the person selects a specific action, which he typically performs at once, although he may carry it out somewhat later. But in either case, he does what he has decided to do. *Prohairesis* and *praxis*, in short, are integral; the one entails the other.[19] Now, the simple teleology of action in the *Ethics*, according to which a person chooses something for the sake of an end and then does that something, thoroughly

---

[18] Aristotle, *Poetics*, chap. 6, particularly 1449b36–1450a29. For a full discussion of the "external" nature of character and action in the *Poetics*, see Jones, *On Aristotle and Greek Tragedy* (New York: Oxford University Press, 1962), pp. 11–62. Also see Thomas G. Rosenmeyer, "Wahlakt und Entscheidungsprozess in der antiken Tragödie," *Poetica*, vol. 10, no. 1 (1978).

[19] Aristotle, *NE*, 1147a26–28; *De Motu Animalium*, 701a7–701b1; *Metaphysics*, ed. with comm. by W. D. Ross, 2 vols. (1924; reprint, Oxford: Clarendon Press, 1958), 1048a12–24. Also see Cooper, *Reason and Human Good in Aristotle*, pp. 12–13, 23, 39. *Akrasia*, "incontinence," of course, presents a special case.

informs the idea of *praxis* in the *Poetics*. The tragic action is *teleia* and *hole*, "complete and whole," fulfilling the end set by the *arche* of *praxis, prohairesis*.[20] According to this formulation, the *prattontes*, "doers," are initiators of unified linear acts striving for realization. Acting singly, on their own motivation, and in a set direction, they do what they choose.

A peculiarity of Aristotle's schema is that its teleological focus on the aims of an individual agent tends to exclude consideration of a social context or "field" in which the prohairetic action of a *pratton* may be intruded on or obstructed. In the *Poetics*, action is typically not seen in terms of reaction or contrary force, for according to the basic model on which Aristotle relies, agents are not imagined in essential interaction with one another.[21] They tend to be rather like the individual organism of the biological treatises whose *ergon*, or function, is to reach an end in an orderly process of development, "should nothing stand in the way."[22] This qualifying phrase is significant, for it is found again in discussions of action in the *Nicomachean Ethics*, when Aristotle says that the act is necessary "for one having the ability and not being prevented."[23] The grounds for conflict between doers striving to realize an end would be contained, in all likelihood, in the prevention of one agent by a rival. Hegel's own formulation of the tragic event comes close to this line of reasoning; it is context-oriented and thus predisposed to consider the social field within which action can impinge on and violate other agents. But the issue of impeded purpose is not central to the understanding of dramatic action in the *Poetics*. Or to put this point more precisely, when the issue arises, it arises obliquely and is not

[20] Aristotle's use of *arche* in these discussions of action is flexible: he can speak of the *arche* of *praxis* as *prohairesis* and the *arche* of *prohairesis* as *boulesis*, "purpose." See *NE*, 6.2 and Hardie, *Aristotle's Ethical Theory*, p. 224.

[21] See Hardie, *Aristotle's Ethical Theory*, pp. 248–49.

[22] Aristotle, *On the Parts of Animals*, tr. A. L. Peck, Loeb Classical Library (Cambridge: Cambridge University Press, 1961), 641b24–26.

[23] *NE*, 1147a30–31.

handled with attention to the agonistic aspects of the situation. For example, in chapter 14 impeded purpose appears to be a constituent part of Aristotle's treatment of plots involving reversal and recognition.[24] In such *muthoi*, the deeds embarked on by tragic agents are either done or not done—and that either knowingly or unknowingly. Modern readers are apt to see a full-blown appreciation of conflict in such passages. But it is telling that Aristotle, despite the opening provided by his material and by some of the angles of his own discussion, does not organize his central defining categories around explicitly conflictual terms. If struggle and contention are discernible in his plots of reversal and recognition, it is all to the point that they are not foregrounded and elaborated. Aristotle's critical eye is instead focused on the major agent's state of mind or degree of awareness—on Medea's consciousness of her children's identity or on Oedipus's ignorance of his parents. Here again, the orientation of his theory is toward a single figure and the deliberative process as the origin of tragic *praxis*, a point further borne out by several Aristotelian ideas about the dramatic *muthos*, to which we will now turn.

After introducing in chapters 6 to 8 essential ideas about poetic order and structure, Aristotle proceeds to refine his claims and to bring certain points already raised into sharper focus. To this end, he employs a distinction between *poiesis* and *historie* in chapter 9 that differentiates between their proper ways of managing subject matter. The true criterion setting the poet apart from the historian is not his use of meter, Aristotle argues, but his portrayal of things that may happen (οἷα ἂν γένοιτο), namely, those that are possible according to likelihood or necessity (τὰ δυνατὰ κατὰ τὸ εἰκὸς ἢ τὸ ἀναγκαῖον). Because poetry tells more about universals (τὰ καθόλου), it is more philosophical than history, which is bound to report particulars, what actually has happened rather than what is possible. Aristotle rounds off this discussion with a few words describing what he has in mind by these terms.

[24] *Poetics*, 1453b26–39.

"Universal means the sorts of things a certain kind of person happens to do or say according to likelihood or necessity, which is what the poetic art strives for, adding on names later; particular is what Alcibiades did or had done to him."[25] On this basis, he reaffirms what he has already asserted earlier: the poet is a maker not of verses but of plots that are unified by virtue of the causal links they draw between character and event.

Although this passage is often read on its own as a critique of *historie*, whose attention to individual facts and fidelity to objective reporting prevents the attainment of organic unity and a desirable level of universal truth, it is more accurate to say that the distinction drawn implies a more fundamental similarity between historical writing and poetic art.[26] This similarity emerges from the fact that both are rooted in the particular, in what people did or had done to them, though Aristotle glosses over this common ground in order to distinguish how each form manipulates particulars.

To state their kinship more clearly, historical writing and poetic art are equally concerned with human lives and deeds, the practical sphere.[27] Unlike the theoretical science of metaphysics, which has the eternal and immutable (τὸ ἀίδιον καὶ τὸ ἀκίνητον) as its subject matter, they deal with actions, which are by nature contingent (κατὰ συμβεβηκός), not occur-

---

[25] *Poetics*, 1451b8–11.

[26] For the former view, see Lucas's edition of the *Poetics*, pp. 119–20; S. H. Butcher, *Aristotle's Theory of Poetry and Fine Art, with a Critical Text and Translation of the Poetics*, 4th ed. (New York: Dover, 1951), pp. 163–97; M. I. Finley, "Myth, Memory and History," in *History and Theory: Studies in the Philosophy of History*, vol. 4 (The Hague: Mouton, 1965), p. 282. On the essential similarities between *poiesis* and *historie*, see Kurt von Fritz, "Entstehung und Inhalt des neunten Kapitels von Aristoteles' *Poetik*," in *Antike und moderne Tragödie: Neun Abhandlungen* (Berlin: Walter de Gruyter, 1962), pp. 430–57, and G.E.M. de Ste. Croix, "Aristotle on History and Poetry (*Poetics* 9, 1451a36–b11)," in *The Ancient Historian and His Materials: Essays in Honour of C. E. Stevens on His Seventieth Birthday*, ed. Barbara Levick (Farnborough, England: Gregg International, 1975), pp. 45–58.

[27] See, for example, Else, *Aristotle's Poetics*, pp. 304–36.

ring always and in every case but admitting of being other than what they are.[28] According to this view, sketched out in various passages of the Aristotelian corpus, not only does the necessary fall outside the province of history and poetry, but the universal does too.[29] For necessity attaches to what cannot be otherwise and universality to what is "always and everywhere," pertaining per se, or καθ' αὐτό, to its subject.[30] Only the objects of metaphysics can be described in these terms. How, then, do we account for Aristotle's claim in the *Poetics* that poetry speaks more about universals than history does and that it incorporates necessity? An approach to the question—and to the relative superiority of *poiesis* to *historie*—is provided by Aristotle's attempts to differentiate between types of contingency and to allow for a third category of existing things that partakes of both the necessary and the contingent.

This trifold classification is laid out most explicitly, perhaps, in *Prior Analytics* 1.13, but it can also be found in the *Physics* and the *Metaphysics*.[31] The criterion for differentiation lies in Aristotle's definition of two types of contingency: the first describes what generally happens (τὸ ὡς ἐπὶ τὸ πολύ) but falls short of being strictly necessary, and the second describes the indeterminate (τὸ ἀόριστον), which can happen both in a given way or otherwise, indifferently and without predictability.[32] Thus between the necessary and the indeterminately contingent is what comes about "for the most part."

---

[28] *NE*, 3.3, 1112a17–1113a14.

[29] *Metaphysics*, 1025b1–1026a32; *Posterior Analytics*, ed. with comm. by W. D. Ross (1949; reprint, Oxford: Clarendon Press, 1965), 87b28–88a17; and *NE*, 1139b14–1140a23.

[30] *Posterior Analytics*, 73b25–29 and 87b31–33.

[31] *Physics*, ed. with comm. by W. D. Ross (1936; reprint, Oxford: Clarendon Press, 1960), 196b10–17, and *Metaphysics*, 1027a5–25. As Jaako Hintikka has shown, the definition of the possible (*to endechomenon*) in *Prior Analytics* 1.13 is synonymous with the definition of the contingent (*to sumbebekos*); see *Time and Necessity: Studies in Aristotle's Theory of Modality* (Oxford: Clarendon Press, 1973), pp. 29–38.

[32] *Prior Analytics*, ed. with comm. by W. D. Ross (1949; reprint, Oxford: Clarendon Press, 1965), 32b5–15.

When this trifold system is employed, necessary and usual events or attributes are grouped together and opposed to τὰ συμβεβηκότα, which in these contexts must be understood as random contingencies, or τὰ ἀπὸ τύχης, things that occur by chance and thus are incalculable, παράλογα.[33] One of the major purposes of joining the usual and the necessary in such passages is to establish the claim that there can be ἐπιστήμη, "scientific knowledge," only of attributes or events that occur in accordance with these principles, but not of those that are κατὰ συμβεβηκός. This position is a modification of the view found occasionally in the Aristotelian corpus and cited earlier, that knowledge is of the necessary and universal. "That there is no science of the accidental is clear; all scientific knowledge is of what is always or usually so—for how else could one learn it or teach it to another?"[34] And again, "There is no demonstrative knowledge of what happens by chance; for what happens by chance is neither necessarily nor for the most part, but something that comes about apart from them, whereas demonstration is of one or another of these."[35] In short, purely random contingencies are not amenable to systematic understanding; they stubbornly resist the pull of philosophical investigation because they are not definable by being always or usually so.

With the points drawn above in mind, we can return to *Poetics* 9 and inquire into the consequences of Aristotle's distinction between *poiesis* and *historie*. Assuming implicitly that human action, *praxis*, is in the realm of the contingent, [he is claiming for *poiesis* the ability to systematize relationships between character and event, so that the likelihood of a certain kind of person's performing a certain deed is perspicuous.] Poetry, in other words, takes indeterminate, random accidents in people's affairs, the radical contingencies of action, and makes them into calculable, intelligible possibilities, which are con-

---

[33] See *Metaphysics*, 6.2, *Physics*, 2.5, and *Posterior Analytics*, 1.30.
[34] *Metaphysics*, 1027a20–22.
[35] *Posterior Analytics*, 87b19–22.

formable to the precept of the usual (τὸ ὡς ἐπὶ τὸ πολύ), or the likely (τὸ εἰχός), to use the term that appears in the *Poetics*. As one commentator puts it, the poetic art "offers us a view of the *typology of human nature*, freed from the accidents that encumber our vision in real life."[36] But as much as *poiesis* may approach philosophy and scientific *episteme*, in the strict sense, through its presentation of the rational, explicable rules governing *praxis*, its necessity is in no way absolute or un-qualified and its universals not as binding as those of meta-physics, mathematics, or physics, the three speculative sci-ences. If we admit that necessity is an element of *poiesis*, it is so in the sense of being ἐξ ὑποθέσεως, as Aristotle says else-where, conditioned by the hypothesis that the end will come about. "There is absolute necessity [τὸ ἁπλῶς] in eternal things and hypothetical necessity in all things that come to be, as in the products of art, such as a house and anything else of this sort."[37] We can apply this point to drama as follows: assuming that the *muthos*, which is said in *Poetics* 6 to be the *telos* of tragedy, will be realized, certain other features become neces-sary, such as agents possessing distinct *ethe* that correspond to and motivate their actions. But the *muthos* itself is not ab-solutely necessary as, say, the axioms of mathematics are. So too poetic universals, which are drawn from the practical sphere, partake of the nature of the realm from which they come. They hold good for the most part, but not always and not in the same way. This can only be expected and one should not look for more, since, as Aristotle explains in the *Nicoma-chean Ethics*, an educated person "searches for that degree of precision in each field of study which the nature of the subject at hand allows; it is clearly just as foolish to accept arguments

[36] Else, *Aristotle's Poetics*, p. 305.

[37] Aristotle, *On the Parts of Animals*, 1.1, 639b24–26. For discussions of hypothetical and absolute necessity, see the useful translation with notes of *De Partibus Animalium*, vol. 1, by D. M. Balme (Oxford: Clarendon Press, 1972), pp. 76–84; and Richard Sorabji, *Necessity, Cause and Blame: Per-spectives on Aristotle's Theory* (Ithaca: Cornell University Press, 1980), pp. 21–23.

of probability from a mathematician as to demand strict demonstrations from a rhetorician."[38]

History, in the context of this view, cannot attain even to the limited universality of poetic art because it cannot eliminate indeterminate contingencies and random events from its account. It is bound neither to what is "always in the same way," by necessity, nor to what is "for the most part," according to likelihood. The particulars of which it treats, what Alcibiades did or had done to him, are not completely unreceptive of a likely account, but they cannot be assimilated as thoroughly to a causal teleology as the particulars of poetry can. Nor can they yield a systematic view of human nature and action, a view that tends toward the universal.

Aristotle's points about history, it should be observed, seem geared to a particular type of historical writing, the chronicle, whose temporal principle of organization typically omits explanatory hypotheses or interpretations that render a causality in explicit terms. Certainly the histories of Herodotus and Thucydides, which Aristotle probably read, take the ballast out of his claims, for they typologize characters and events virtually as much as tragedy does, at the same time as they establish clear directions in the tides of human fortune.[39] The oversimplified conception of *historie* in *Poetics* 9 is apparently employed for strategic reasons to draw a contrast important for the definition of *poiesis*. In any case, we should not regard Aristotle as chiding the historian and implying that the writer of history ought to be more like the poet, as a certain school of Hellenistic composers thought in their attempt to mix the principles of historiography and dramatic poetry, on the authority of the dictum in *Poetics* 9.[40] Rather, he is saying that much at the historian's disposal resists the control of poetic

---

[38] *NE*, 1094b23–27.

[39] See Ste. Croix, "Aristotle on History and Poetry," pp. 50–52.

[40] A discussion of this group of Hellenistic writers led by Duris of Samos is by Kurt von Fritz, "Aristotle's Contribution to the Practice and Theory of Historiography," *University of California Publications in Philosophy*, vol. 28, no. 3 (1958): 133.

likelihood or necessity and therefore cannot be totalized into the organic structure of a *muthos*.

Although tragedy, in this view, achieves a higher order of unity and causality than history, it nonetheless, according to Aristotle, can include surprises and unexpected actions. In fact, he thinks that pity and fear are best produced when events occur "παρὰ δόξαν δι' ἄλληλα"—that is, by surprise and yet on account of each other.[41] This is a key phrase in the *Poetics* and particularly important for the point that I am trying to make here. It confirms that the unexpected in tragedy is admissible only when recuperated by the poet within a larger pattern of coherence and order, to which the audience is supposed to be sensitive upon reflection. Unrelieved accidents and chance happenings, though integral to life as we live it and as history depicts it, are worthy of inclusion in tragedy only when they seem to have happened "of set purpose" (ὥσπερ ἐπίτηδες).[42] In short, the tragic *muthos* controls the randomness of surprises so that they appear designed—like the fall of the statue of Mitys at Argos on his murderer. Aristotle appeals to similar restrictions when discussing the irrational in chapter 25. Arguing that irrationalities (τὰ ἄλογα) and impossibilities (τὰ ἀδύνατα) are censurable when there is no inner necessity for introducing them, he says they may be justified (apparently either by poet or critic) according to the requirements of the poem, according to a higher end, or according to popular opinion.[43] But unameliorated by explanatory causes, they are unacceptable in tragedy.

The argument in chapter 9 is, in one way, Aristotle's response to Plato's charge that poetry is mere *paidia* and not *spoude*. By crediting literature—and tragedy is always foremost in both philosophers' minds—for its systematic and coherent presentation of action, Aristotle redeems it from the curse of being play, dangerous play that has no basis in *logos*,

[41] *Poetics*, 1452a4.
[42] *Poetics*, 1452a7.
[43] *Poetics*, 1461b9–10.

but rather originates in and caters to the baser part of man's soul. By bringing into view the necessary or probable connections that poetry draws in its subject matter, he manages to align it with the philosophical interest in universals. While this strategy undermines Plato's attack, it also imposes a serious limitation on the interpretation of dramatic art in the *Poetics*. If tragedy, as a privileged form of poetry, is distinguished from history by virtue of its elimination of the indeterminately contingent and by its teleological control of character and action, then what would Aristotle say about conflicts in plays arising from forces irrationally and unpredictably bearing in on humans from outside their intelligible universe? How would he account for the destructive powers of the cosmos that act in apparent defiance of moral, ethical, and causal laws, the powers that Plato said were so badly and so often misrepresented by the tragic poets?

He might account for them as anomalies or flaws in dramatic design and simply relegate them to an inferior sort of drama. But the important point is that he does not engage such questions at all. Aristotle's exclusion of these issues from his discussion in the *Poetics* is facilitated by a theory of action that is consistent with the contrast between *poiesis* and *historie* in chapter 9. We return to the model of *praxis* discussed earlier. The process and completion of a dramatic action, as already noted, are intelligible in terms of the moral disposition, the *ethos*, that an agent reveals through choice, *prohairesis*. Linking the act with the purpose of the agent are the rules of likelihood and necessity, which create a complete and logical circuit of causality between the origins and ends of *praxis*. Thus an action will be of the same quality as the character who conceives it: if the character is good, as Aristotle says he must be, his action will be good. A problem with this scheme is that it bypasses some salient features of Greek tragedy.

For one thing, Aristotle's view does not accommodate instances in which the tragic action, once set in motion by one or more agents, becomes so mired in ethical complexity that it eludes formulation in terms of "goodness." I will discuss this point in greater detail later. For the moment I simply note that choice or ethical predisposition and action are often not morally equivalent in tragedy. Even if we can characterize an agent as *spoudaios*—and sometimes it is impossible to do so—the chain of events that he or she initiates can become implicated in conflicts that disrupt a stable perspective on which the moral evaluation of a *praxis* as *spoudaia* depends. This difficulty of evaluation attaches to *praxis* both in the narrow sense of what an agent does and in the broader sense of what the tragedian "imitates," the *muthos*. Some might think that Aristotle's notion of hamartia embraces such ethical complexity; but, as we will see, his use of the idea does not appreciably qualify his sense of tragic *spoudaiotes*. Both terms are employed in the *Poetics* without acknowledgment of the moral dilemmas that may be entailed by a wrongdoing in which a good agent becomes involved.

There is a second difficulty in Aristotle's causally integrated view of character and action. He does not take into account what impinges on characters from without, the random contingencies that resist systematic explanation and that he elsewhere calls τὰ ἀπὸ τύχης. Gerald Else pinpoints the exclusion: "What happens to the tragic man, except so far as he himself is its cause, remains outside the grasp of Aristotle's theory, or can appear in it only as an inscrutable premise."[44] A consequence of this exclusion is that it bars from Aristotle's perspective tragic events revolving around a conflict between mortals and divine forces breaking in unpredictably upon their actions. *Heracles Mainomenos*, for example, would be a freak in Aristotle's system, not simply because it lacks organic structure, as critics have repeatedly observed, but because it shows man in the grip of a power that defies logical understanding and that operates without the determinacy that would render it amenable to the principles of likelihood or necessity.

[44] Else, *Aristotle's Poetics*, p. 306.

The dislocation in the action of the play arising from Hera's brute aggression against Heracles is calculated by Euripides to jar the expectations and sense of probability that he has elicited from an audience.[45] Structuring the first half of the tragedy as a suppliant drama, with the tyrant Lycus pitted against Amphitryon, Megara, and her children, he makes the movement of events build toward a theodicy. The conflict in this suppliant drama generates hope that the hero who has delivered the rest of the world from violent predators and monstrosities will appear before the savage Lycus can wreak disaster—and he does appear. With the arrival of Heracles, the prayers of the victims and the parallel anticipations of the audience are met. Thus the play satisfies moral outrage at gratuitous violence by short-circuiting Lycus's plans to kill Heracles' relatives. In this portion of the action, Euripides seems to validate a traditional religious view, initially questioned by the desperate Megara and Amphitryon, that divine justice may operate slowly but with ultimate predictability and efficacy. Moreover, the events depicted through line 814 can be characterized without much difficulty in Aristotelian terms. The action is well integrated and manages to prefigure its surprise in a way that renders it probable. Like the fall of Mitys's statue at Argos on the man who murdered him, Heracles' return to Thebes has an air of design.

Into this patterned *praxis* that has carefully manipulated our expectations, there is a sudden, violent eruption. Just as the chorus finishes its ode in celebration of the release from danger ("Disaster is reversed") and expresses faith in the jus-

---

[45] See William Arrowsmith's introduction to his translation of *Heracles*, in *Euripides II. The Complete Greek Tragedies*, ed. David Grene and Richmond Lattimore (Chicago: University of Chicago Press, 1969), pp. 44–58. Godfrey Bond in his edition and commentary of *Heracles* (Oxford: Clarendon Press, 1981), pp. xvii–xxvi, rehearses the various efforts of critics to find unity in this "broken-backed play" (Murray's phrase). Bond himself tries to outline a "unity of contrast," as he calls it, and in so doing reveals his essential complicity with Aristotelian norms of dramatic structure, which remain the norms of most scholars of the play.

tice of the blessed gods, there is a loud burst of thunder on stage, followed by a shocking epiphany of the goddesses Iris and Lyssa, Hera's henchwomen. They have been sent to taint Heracles with the curse of fresh blood. In the brief exchange between these two monstrous deities, Hera's wrath emerges as a terrifyingly irrational force of violence, which Lyssa renounces in a manner reminiscent of Hephaestus in *Prometheus Bound*.[46] The improbability that madness personified would utter words of reason to the bloodthirsty representative of her superior is only one of several shocks calculated to jolt the audience into confusion. Not even Heracles' bastardy is mentioned explicitly as the reason for Hera's hostility, though appeal to this mythologically well-known fact does not do much to bring her savagery into the area of substantial motivation. Theodicy is blatantly juxtaposed with unintelligible divine brutality and the spectators are left temporarily reeling.

Driven by a malignant goddess into the murder of his loved ones, Heracles becomes a vehicle of indeterminate violence (*bia*). Euripides strips away any possibility of construing his action by reference to purposive choice, for Heracles is bent on a completely different course than the one he is compelled in madness to take. Entering the palace after his arrival to greet the household gods and to purify himself ritually of the blood endangering his family with pollution, his aim is to protect his kin. But this deliberate and rational purpose is broken by the sudden onslaught of an aggressive force that turns him into the destroyer of the very ones he is attempting to rescue. This invasion of a deity into the orderly process of human action is disturbingly and undeniably *alogon*, "irrational," not only to Heracles, when he regains his senses, but to the characters and audience alike, who are refused a framework within which to rationalize the horrible wrath of Hera and so render its cause intelligible. The goddess' actions are not a rightful punishment for wrongs done, but as Lyssa says, recal-

---

[46] Aeschylus, *Prometheus Bound*, in *Septem quae supersunt tragoedias*, ed. Denys Page (Oxford: Clarendon Press, 1972), ll. 12–35.

citrant evils.[47] According to the explicit precept of the *Poetics*, the event on which *Heracles Mainomenos* pivots is inadmissible to tragedy, for it is neither necessary nor likely, but without determinate cause (αἴτιον ὡρισμένον); behind it stands a will fixed on senseless destruction. It is just this kind of divine violence that Plato censured the tragic poets for dramatizing and that Aristotle glosses over by focusing on the causal integration between a *spoudaios pratton* and a *spoudaia praxis* in tragedy.

Euripides is notorious for effects of dramatic dislocation, and *Heracles Mainomenos* is an especially famous example of his iconoclastic techniques and subversions of form. We can appreciate the extent to which he renders divine violence unintelligible by comparing his play with one by Sophocles that also features an act of divine aggression against man—*Ajax*.[48] In this drama, the goddess Athena intervenes in the human sphere to deflect the already fixed and self-determined violence of Ajax against the Greeks. Her strategy is to drive him mad so that he mistakes herds of cattle for his human enemies and wreaks havoc on livestock rather than on the Argive army. Like Heracles, Ajax's mental delusion is a product of divine control. But the whole portrayal of divinity in Sophocles' play is more amenable to Aristotelian terms. The motivation of the goddess is clarified at the outset of the tragedy, when Odysseus encounters her as he is tracking Ajax down and asks what cause (πρὸς τί, 40) prompted him to such bloodshed. Both Ajax's and Athena's motives are revealed when the goddess mentions the hero's grief over Achilles' armor as his inducement to violence and her own desire to protect the Greeks as the reason for her intrusion. The chain of causality is complicated in the action, because the preconceived anger of Ajax is derailed by a divinity who blinds him into thinking he is doing what he is not; but the deeds of god and man are rendered intelligible through an initial dialogue

---

[47] *Heracles*, l. 854. For a different view, see Bond's edition, pp. xxiv–xxvi.
[48] Sophocles, *Fabulae*, ed. A. C. Pearson (Oxford: Clarendon Press, 1971).

that responds to questions of motivation. We might look suspiciously at a deity who thinks there is nothing sweeter than laughing at one's enemies—the divine mockery stands out more starkly in tragedy than in epic—but that suspicion is very different from the disbelief we are made to feel at the queen of heaven destroying the hero who, "having tamed the pathless land and savage sea, / alone held up the honors of the gods / when they fell at the hands of unholy men" (851–53). Euripides presses hard on disjunctions that Sophocles mitigates.

The difference between plays such as *Ajax* and *Heracles Mainomenos* may be taken as a measure of the separation between Sophoclean and Euripidean dramatic techniques. The former's apparently greater adherence to standards of probability and causality is often taken as a hallmark of his art and the source of Aristotle's obvious admiration for his work. But we should be careful about generalizing these features to the whole corpus of Sophocles, for he too is preoccupied with the irrational, incomprehensible ways in which divinity obstructs human action and collides with the course set by personal choice. Even in Aristotle's most exemplary dramatist, we find representations of *praxis* that incorporate events unconformable to the expectations laid out in the *Poetics* about the sufficiency of *ethos* as a likely or necessary explanation of tragic action.

The *Trachiniae*, another Greek tragedy dealing with the figure of Heracles, portrays *bia* at several levels as an irrational force of violence operating in the human universe and defying capacities for understanding or efficacious planning.[49] The pivotal *praxis* around which the disaster in the play revolves is Deianeira's effort to secure the love of her husband by employing a drug given to her by Nessus the centaur, who assured her, when he died by Heracles' arrow, that she would

---

[49] On *bia* in the play, see Charles Segal, *Tragedy and Civilization: An Interpretation of Sophocles* (Cambridge, Mass.: Harvard University Press, 1981), pp. 60–108.

have in the substance "a magic charm / over Heracles, so he will never behold another woman / and love her more than you" (575–77). Claiming not to be a wife who knows evil daring, Deianeira believes that with this charm she can lay a spell on her husband and so eliminate her new rival, Iole. But the act designed to draw Heracles to her and guarantee their marital happiness sets loose a terrifying violence that brings on not only Heracles' death, but the suicide of Deianeira. In the last scenes of the play we learn how it has come about that the drug Deianeira thought had curative properties instead poisons her husband. Heracles' speech in lines 1159 and following reveals that Zeus's prophecy about his son's death has been fulfilled through the centaur's *pharmakon*:

> Long ago it was predicted by my father
> that I would die at the hands of nothing that breathes
> but by someone dead, an inhabitor of Hades.
> This, then, was the beast, the centaur, as was divinely
>   foretold,
> who, being dead, killed me as I lived.
>
> (1159-63)

Deianeira's action, which seems initially self-determined and personally conceived, the product of *prohairesis*, is also an instrument of divine will, with the disturbing twist that under Zeus's influence her intended remedy becomes a killing potion. The *peripeteia* hinges on the inherent doubleness of the *pharmakon*, its unstable magical properties, which is to say the properties that put it beyond the range of deliberative controls and in the realm of numinous powers. Indeed, the noxiousness of the *pharmakon* is unleashed at the precise moment it is wittingly administered as the cure it is supposed to be. We are dealing here with a matter that Aristotle's notion of hamartia, focused as it is on flaws in personal decision making, does not adequately address. For the thoroughgoing ambivalence of the *pharmakon* is not reducible to the strictures of rational thought processes, whose end in this case is to master

the substance by effectively limiting the conditions of its application.

Now it is typical of Sophocles' dramatic technique—once
again in contrast with Euripides' in *Heracles Mainomenos*—
that he lends an air of probability to the series of events issuing
in Deianeira's unwitting error. The likelihood that the drug
she supposed would cure in fact contaminates is strengthened
by her own late admission that the dying beast from whom
she received the substance could hardly have been motivated
by kindness. Nessus beguiled her to destroy the man who shot
him. But this string of likely events (εἰϰότα) at the human level
does not extend to the metaphysical powers operating pervasively, it seems, behind the action. What is brought into view,
with the revelation by Heracles that Deianeira is a vehicle of
divine force, is the savage unpredictability of the gods in the
play, who intervene in people's affairs to effect ends that are
not encompassed by human purpose. Divinity operates ran-
domly and with indeterminate violence; or, to put it differently, human understanding and foresight cannot plot its
movements with any regularity. This fact is borne out by the
poignant failure of Deianeira's search for information at the
beginning of the play to end with reliable facts. The character
who has gradually extricated herself from passivity and engaged in the pursuit of knowledge in order to act as an informed agent is destroyed through an ignorance manipulated
by divine will. Why Deianeira is the instrument of Zeus's
aggression against his own son is mysterious, which is to say
that the ultimate cause of her violence remains inscrutable.

Moreover, the destructive power of Kypris that moves
through her is also resistant to explanation. Sophocles presents *eros* repeatedly in the play as a destructive force that has
erupted not only into Deianeira's life but into Heracles' as
well. It precipitated the combat between the monster Achelous
and Heracles, in which Deianeira was the prize; it has driven
Heracles into fits of passion, in which he has killed to procure
his object of desire; and now, according to the chorus, it has
presided over Deianeira's recent disastrous effort to secure her

husband's love. "Kypris, the silent meddler," the choral members say, "is clearly the doer of all these things" (861–62). Like Hera in *Heracles Mainomenos*, she is an incalculable and irrational power who invades the course of human ends and actions with devastating effect.[50]

Though victorious even over the king of the gods in love, the *bia* of Aphrodite stands in close relation to the *bia* of Zeus, which is similarly enigmatic in the play. It is true that there is a symmetry between the ruthless use of force by Heracles, about which we have heard much before his appearance on stage, and the violence of Zeus in bringing about his fall. Moreover, the prominence of the Furies at the end of the play, especially the description of the robe of Nessus as a "woven net of the Erinyes," suggests that what Heracles suffers is intelligible in terms of his actions, for which he pays at the hands of the avenging spirits. The gods are savage just as Heracles is, and there is a kind of likely congruity in the parallel. But the end of the tragedy is designed to drive home the difficulties of comprehending Zeus's will not only in his son's death but in his life as well. The symmetry between culpability and punishment is broken in order to bring the indeterminate quality of divine action into view. Heracles, in his suffering, questions why Zeus repays him with such thanks for all his sacrifice to the god. The grotesque and extreme state of his pain lends a pathetic credence to this question, which expresses a doubt felt by others in the play, especially Hyllus.

When, in the last scene, Heracles imposes a set of constraints on his son that defies logic and understanding, we find affirmed an aspect of divinity that Heracles himself has experienced as the son of Zeus. Like Hyllus, to whom he issues the harsh and irrational orders of burning him on a pyre and marrying his concubine, Iole, Heracles, too, has been made to act under the force of commands whose reasons and ends he can-

[50] See the ode to Kypris in ll. 497–530. On the connections between Kypris, Zeus, the Erinyes, and violence, see R. P. Winnington-Ingram, *Sophocles: An Interpretation* (Cambridge: Cambridge University Press, 1980), pp. 212–15.

not fathom. The enigmas at the human level mirror those at the divine. Zeus, whose power Hyllus affirms in the "many and strange sufferings" he has witnessed, remains finally no less inscrutable than Kypris. The violence these gods release in human lives is *alogos*; it cannot be accounted for satisfactorily in terms of a larger divine scheme whose intelligibility is accessible to mortals, let alone in terms of dramatic *ethos*.

I have focused on two plays that feature the gods as incalculable forces of violence erupting in people's lives in order to suggest that an aspect of Greek tragedy excluded from Aristotle's conception of a unified *praxis* occurs with some frequency. Euripides is perhaps most often associated in our time with a view of the inscrutability of divine violence, but Sophocles and Aeschylus are also preoccupied with this issue. *Prometheus Bound*, for instance, comes readily to mind as a play interested in the compulsive, irrational power of Zeus in the universe and may be compared with *Heracles Mainomenos* and *Trachiniae* in this respect.

Else observes that Aristotle's move to bar the irrational in the form of indeterminate contingency from his dramatic theory poses a paradox: "Aristotle's theory of the practical world has no room for any systematic cause of action except man himself; yet the tragic 'action' involves not only man's own causality (which is amenable to the requirements of the *eikos e anankaion*) but something that breaks in upon him, 'happens' to him from outside."[51] He leaves it at that. But the inconsistency is more than a simple paradox. It reveals a blind spot in Aristotle's view. In his determination to invest tragic drama with *logos* and thus rescue it from the bind Plato put it in, he employs a contrast that makes poetic art serious and philosophical—precisely what it is not in the *Republic*. Although this strategy is not intended to debunk *historie*, it shifts the burden of irrationality and contingency away from *poiesis*. A result of the shift is to make Aristotle insensitive to or at least silent about the point at which the more philosoph-

51 Else, *Aristotle's Poetics*, p. 307.

ical tragedy can intersect history—in the contingent. His theory, consequently, blocks one of the ways in which a discussion of conflict could arise: in the random, accidental forces bearing in on humanity and precipitating struggle.

We are now in a better position to understand how Aristotle and Hegel can begin with the same interest in preserving reason in tragedy yet end with very different formulations not only of the tragic event, but of the relationship between history and tragedy. Only when human struggles in history have been brought under the control of a teleology and purified of the taint of contingency is the German philosopher able to define tragedy on the basis of collision, which is a rationalized version of turbulent change and dissolution. Because the Greek philosopher does not expunge history of accidents, he has to set it off from the structured teleology of dramatic poetry, and in so doing overlooks conflicts with sources in a contingency. For both thinkers the accidental is a bane.[52] But one has managed to bring everything attributable to chance under the "cunning of reason," thus making history into drama, while the other recognizes an irrational component in history, thereby eliminating it from drama. If Hegel falsifies the intelligibility of tragic rivalry with his rationalizing bent, Aristotle does so too, but less overtly by shelving a discussion of how tragedy unsettles the desire to see meaning in clashes with forces beyond one's control.

THE SPARE REMARKS on history in chapter 9 of the *Poetics* do not link accounts of the historical course of human affairs with disorderly conflict. Thus it would be misleading to say that the opposition of *poiesis* to *historie* is one of harmony to strife; this is not the gist of the passage. Rather, the contrast reveals a critical orientation that is never clearly articulated as a position: by removing the historically contingent from the dramatic universe, Aristotle also eliminates from his consid-

---

[52] Hannah Arendt speaks to this point in *The Life of the Mind* (New York: Harcourt Brace Jovanovich, 1978), vol. 2, *Willing*, pp. 14–15.

eration of tragedy conflictual events arising from what unex-
plainably and without determinate cause befalls a character.
Having said this, however, we have not gone far in understanding why Aristotle is predisposed to say nothing about
conflict in tragedy. The argument about contingency concerns
mainly the clashes beween mortals and gods. What about collisions among people or within an individual, which have less
to do with incalculable accident? Do these occurrences, so important a consideration in dramatic criticism from the time of
Hegel, have a place in the Greek philosopher's account of
tragedy, or do they too fall outside his purview? These questions can be approached through a study of Aristotle's theory
of the tragic *spoudaios*, to which we will now turn.

Chapter 6 of the *Poetics* offers a definition of tragedy as the
imitation of an action that is serious, complete, and of a certain magnitude (μίμησις πράξεως σπουδαίας καὶ τελείας
μέγεθος ἐχούσης). Action implies people who are acting and
who must be of a certain sort with respect to thought and
character. In this context, Aristotle introduces a connection
we have already had the occasion to examine briefly: character reveals moral qualities and moral qualities condition acts.
Thus a *spoudaia praxis* assumes a *spoudaios pratton*. Typical
of the style of the *Poetics*, which can be at once crabbed and
obvious, these comments are not elaborated in the context,
nor is anything more said by way of clarifying the term *spoudaios*, which is pivotal in Aristotle's dramatic theory. An understanding of the idea and particularly its nonagonistic bias
can be gleaned only from the fuller and more systematic treatments of it in the *Politics* and *Nicomachean Ethics*.

In turning to these texts, I am adopting a line of argument
that claims for the *spoudaios* in the *Poetics* moral associations
articulated with greater rigor in the ethical and political treatises. It should be noted, however, that Aristotle's use of the
term in his literary criticism has distinctly popular and non-
specialized overtones: the tragic agent, in accordance with the
ordinary Greek scale of aristocratically based values, is fa-

mous, royal, wealthy, and capable of significant action.[53] Thus, in contrast with comedy, which gives us figures of a lower type (*phauloi*) grotesquely rendered, tragedy deals with people of high status whose deeds are to be taken seriously. This distinction between *spoudaioi* and *phauloi* is conventional and may be traced to the archaic tradition of Homer, Simonides, and Theognis, among others, who predicate the worth of the two classes on social rank and public reputation.[54] But to restrict the definition of the *spoudaios* in the *Poetics* to these popular criteria is oversimplified. As various recent discussions have shown, Aristotle's literary terms, including *spoudaios*, are informed in often subtle but thoroughgoing ways by his ethical ideas and especially by his theory of the practical virtues (*aretai*), with its emphasis on the so-called cooperative excellences.[55] It is precisely the influence of the "quiet" values of justice, temperance, and peaceful coexistence that can be traced in Aristotle's nonconflictual treatment of character and action in the *Poetics*.

We might best approach an understanding of this influence by turning to some passages in the *Nicomachean Ethics*.[56] As Aristotle proposes in book 1, since man's proper function, or *ergon*, is the realization of happiness (*eudaimonia*), he who best conforms to this end becomes the standard, the *metron*

[53] See, for example, *Poetics*, ed. Lucas, pp. 63–64.

[54] See, for example, Simonides, Frag. 370, in *Lyrica Graeca Selecta*, ed. D. L. Page (1968; reprint, with corrections, Oxford: Clarendon Press, 1973), and Theognis, Frag. 305, in *The Elegies of Theognis and Other Elegies Included in the Theognidean Sylloge*, rev. text based on Mutinensis Ms. with comm. by T. Hudson-Williams (New York: Arno Press, 1979). Also see Werner Jaeger, *Paideia: The Ideals of Greek Culture*, tr. Gilbert Highet (New York: Oxford University Press, 1939), p. 10.

[55] See especially Arthur W. H. Adkins, *Merit and Responsibility: A Study in Greek Values* (Oxford: Clarendon Press, 1960), and "Aristotle and the Best Kind of Tragedy," *Classical Quarterly*, n.s., no. 16 (1966): 78–102.

[56] General studies of Aristotelian ethics that have been especially helpful to me are by Hardie, *Aristotle's Ethical Theory*, and Cooper, *Reason and Human Good in Aristotle's Ethics*. Alastair MacIntyre in *After Virtue: A Study in Moral Theory*, 2d ed. (Notre Dame: Notre Dame University Press, 1984), pp. 131–64, repeatedly stresses the nonagonistic bias in Aristotelian ethics.

and *kanon*, for determining the way things should be in human affairs.[57] Such a person is the *spoudaios*, defined as one whose activities are in harmony with the rational element (*logos*), that distinguishes human beings from plants and beasts and makes them what they are. "If the function of man is an activity in conformity with reason, or at least not without it, and if when we speak of the function of an individual we mean that it is the same as the function of an individual with high standards [τοῦ σπουδαίου] . . . then the good of man is an activity of the soul in accordance with excellence, and if there are several excellences, in accordance with the best and most complete."[58] More specifically, the excellence of the *spoudaios*, at least at the practical level, is said to reside in a settled disposition (*hexis*) toward the mean in emotions and actions. The controlling voice of reason has established itself so firmly in him that he does not feel conflict with unruly or extreme desires. Thus, his action is a natural, untroubled manifestation of his emotion, which is itself neither excessive nor deficient; he is without internal conflict. In this respect, he differs from the self-controlled man, whose actions are virtuous but contrary to his likes and dislikes, which are askew. Whereas the *spoudaios* conducts himself without struggle, the *egkrates* has to force himself to act well against his complaining *pathe*, or passions.[59] We will return to this psychological aspect of the good man shortly. But for now I want to examine the social implications of how he manages to live the good life and there-

[57] For a discussion of the complexities surrounding this point, see Kathleen V. Wilkes, "The Good Man and the Good for Man in Aristotle's Ethics," in *Essays on Aristotle's Ethics*, ed. Amelie O. Rorty (Berkeley: University of California Press, 1980), pp. 341–57. On the different accounts of *eudaimonia* in the *NE*—the "intellectualist" account in 10.7 and the "comprehensivist" account described as secondary at 1178a9—see Thomas Nagel, "Aristotle on *Eudaimonia*," and J. L. Ackrill, "Aristotle on *Eudaimonia*," both in Rorty's *Essays on Aristotle's Ethics*.

[58] *NE*, 1098a8–10.

[59] For Aristotle's discussion of these matters, see *NE*, 3.10–12 and 7.1; also see J. O. Urmson, "Aristotle's Doctrine of the Mean," *American Philosophical Quarterly* (July, 1973): 223–30.

fore live up to his name. Among other things, he does so by cultivating *homonoia*.

Found frequently in Aristotle's discussions of man in his social role as a communal being, the term has political overtones, meaning literally, "being of the same mind" or "thinking in harmony."[60] In the *Politics* and *Nicomachean Ethics*, books 7 and 9, it is considered the criterion of public living, the *metron* and *kanon*, for without it there could be no community.[61] *Homonoia* is what draws people together into a *koinonia*, a body living at one and striving for happiness by holding its own best interests in common. In other words, it bonds those who share the project of creating and sustaining the good life in the polis. As an expression of *philia*, it provides the basic social framework within which individuals work to fulfill their *erga*.

Since stability is the norm of man's life among other men, Aristotle, predictably, regards *stasis* as a disease marring the good health of the political organism. This attitude underlies his treatment of disorder in book 5 of the *Politics*, where an aversion to violence or disruptive behavior of any kind shows clearly.[62] Condemning the belligerence that attends radical changes in constitutions and rejecting rebellious struggle as an effective vehicle for political reform, Aristotle tries to suggest stabilizing strategies that can prevent the outbreak of war. Many of his recommendations concern the equalization of

---

[60] See Martin Ostwald's translation of the *Nicomachean Ethics*, with glossary (Indianapolis: Bobbs-Merrill, 1962), p. 309.

[61] *Politics*, ed. with comm. by W. D. Ross (1957; reprint, Oxford: Clarendon Press, 1962). The introductory comments in book 1 address the concept of *koinonia*, and the subsequent chapters discuss particular forms of *koinonia*. In the *NE*, see especially 8.9–12 and 9.6.

[62] The nature of *stasis* in Aristotle's *Politics* is treated in several essays collected in *Articles on Aristotle*, ed. Jonathan Barnes et al. (London: Duckworth, 1977), vol. 2, *Ethics and Politics*; see especially Kurt von Fritz and E. Kapp, "The Development of Aristotle's Political Philosophy and the Concept of Nature," pp. 113–34; Marcus Wheeler, "Aristotle's Analysis of the Nature of Political Struggle," pp. 159–69; Maurice Defourny, "The Aim of the State: Peace," pp. 195–201.

material disproportions in the state—of wealth, land, and power—on the assumption that different interpretations of justice and equality lead to conflicting claims of different parties.[63] But as much as economic imbalances contribute to the contest of opposing claims, ethical problems are the more fundamental causes of dissension. Often in the *Politics*, Aristotle overtly connects *stasis* with vice, by definition an excessiveness or deficiency in emotions and actions.[64] Thus, for example, he says repeatedly in book 5 that the desire for gain and honor sets men at odds. They fight for these things not so much because they want to have them, but because they see others, some justly and others unjustly, getting a larger share.[65] Even should pure equality exist, however, and people get a fair shake, there would be revolt: "The wickedness of men is insatiable. At first a two obol allotment to citizens for the theatre was sufficient, but whenever this becomes customary, they always ask for more, until they come to infinity."[66] No feasible solution for this moral dilemma of always wanting more is to be found in equalization of property. Rather, a method of training is needed, which teaches men to use property correctly, to have the right attitude about it. Only in this way, through moral education, is stability ensured.[67]

The association of social conflict with vice is a distinct feature of Aristotle's analysis of *stasis* in the *Politics*. Many of the most important ideas that inform this analysis are taken from Plato, who in the *Republic*, books 8 and 9, develops extensively the broad social implications of personal depravity. Describing how a degeneration from the highest to the lowest forms of government takes place, Socrates focuses on disorder within the soul as the prime cause instigating people to contend against each other for objects that the virtuous person shuns. As timocracy moves toward oligarchy and oligarchy

[63] *Politics*, 6.5–9.
[64] *NE*, 1106b24–35.
[65] *Politics*, 1302a38–b1.
[66] *Politics*, 1267b1–3.
[67] *Politics*, 1263b15–1264b26–31.

toward democracy and tyranny, conflict spreads, invading all aspects of life, until the entire polis is seething with strife. In a typically vivid passage, Plato characterizes the increasingly anarchical state of affairs as one in which "the father has grown accustomed to be like his child and is afraid of his sons, and the son to be like the father and neither respects nor fears his parents, in order that he may be free. And the resident alien is accustomed to equate himself with a citizen and a citizen to him, and likewise with the foreigner."[68] When the principle of differentiation on which hierarchy and order depend collapses, there is no way to go but down. Such chaotic dissolution is attributable to the fact that "reason blended with culture" (λόγος μουσικῇ κεκραμένος) has been usurped from its proper place of control within individuals and social groups.

In the *Sophist*, this view is affirmed: *poneria*, "foul conduct," is described as a result of discord and disease within the soul, of a violent disjunction between elements that are meant to be naturally related and subordinate to *logos*. "Perhaps you have not considered that disease and strife are the same? . . . Is that because you think that strife is anything else than a disagreement of what is naturally related brought about by some kind of corruption?"[69] Images of disease and contamination pervade Plato's analysis of the *stasis* produced by moral vice—a point we have already witnessed earlier in his discussion of the social effects of tragic drama. Aristotle agrees with this evaluation of conflict in the state. Like Plato, he believes that those whose desires war against and overcome the voice of reason are behind unrest in a community. There could hardly be a position more different from Hegel's in this respect. Whereas *Kollision* is for him a necessary experience driving the teleological direction of history and tied to a clash

---

[68] Plato, *Republic*, 562e–563a.

[69] *Sophist*, 228a. For a full treatment of *stasis* in the *Republic*, see White, *Companion to Plato's Republic*; on *stasis* and unity in the state, see pp. 13–20, 39–43, 107–108; on the parallel matter of *stasis* and unity in the individual soul, see pp. 87, 123–31, 223–24, 239–41.

of ethical values, for his Greek forbears it is an evil eliminable through proper moral education.

The connection of *stasis* with vice is the negative side of a positive precept in the *Nicomachean Ethics*, which is stated as a rule governing social relationships. Returning to the discussion of *philia* and *homonoia* in book 9, we find that the spirit of "being together on the same things" is found exclusively among good men and characterizes their partnership in action, in attaining common goals on which they all agree.[70] Only they are of one mind both with themselves and others, "ἐπὶ τῶν αὐτῶν ὄντες," as the Greek proverb goes. Wishing for what is just and profitable, they strive for it together. Thus the *spoudaioi* are the social backbone, making the group strong by agreeing among themselves and creating the unity of mind that heads off discord. They may be a minority in historical states, but they are still the standard for the way things should be.

If "the wishes of people like this remain constant and do not flow this way and that, as the Euripus does,"[71] the wishes of bad men, on the other hand, make it hard for them to live in concord and have friends. Because they try for more than their share when material advantages are to be had and leave the burdensome to others, because they spy on neighbors trying to get what they desire for themselves, the *phauloi* are always at each other's throats. They do not agree about what is best, nor do they pursue the common interest in a spirit of peaceful cooperation.[72] Echoing various passages from the *Politics*, these words in book 9 of the *Nicomachean Ethics* underscore Aristotle's ethical interpretation of social strife, for they valorize the dichotomy of *spoudaios-phaulos* by means of the antithesis *homonoia-stasis*. Unlike bad men, whose behavior is contentious, good men think the same things and do not fight.

This social and ethical interpretation of conflict, as I have

---

[70] *NE*, 1167b5.
[71] *NE*, 1167b7.
[72] *NE*, 1167b10–15.

already noted, is given a firm psychological basis in Aristotle's philosophy. In this respect, again, Aristotle follows Plato, who locates the roots of social disorder in the psyche. In book 9 of the *Ethics*, we discover that the socially harmonious nature of the *spoudaios* is grounded in the inner unity of his soul.[73] The good man has every one of those sentiments for himself that he has toward his friend: (1) he wishes for and does what is good for himself and does so for his own sake; (2) he wishes for his own life and preservation and he wishes them especially for that part of him with which he thinks (his divine part); (3) he wishes to spend time with himself, for he does so with pleasure—the memory of his achievements gives him delight; and above all, (4) he remains consistent in his judgment, desiring the same objects with every part of his soul. In him everything is in harmony with the leadership of reason.[74] These attitudes together comprise an axiom basic to Aristotle's ethical theory: stay at one with yourself and engage in nothing about which you will have regrets. Always be your own best friend.

The problem with bad men, the *phauloi*, is that they in no way fulfill the precepts of self-love.[75] Always at variance with themselves, they have appetite for one thing and wish for another. Their souls are wracked by contrary forces. Unlike the *spoudaioi*, they do not act in obedience to the rational faculty (*phronesis*), and as a consequence their pursuit of the noble end is perverted. Their goal is happiness, but not knowing how to define it properly they are mistaken about it.[76] Hence they veer from one tendency to another, reaching for whatever pleasurable is at hand, but then having regrets. "Such men do not share their pleasures and sorrows with themselves; for

---

[73] *NE*, 9.4.

[74] *NE*, 1102b25–28.

[75] For Aristotle's discussion of the bad man, see *NE*, 1166b2–29. Here, once again, we find Aristotle taking over a popular set of social terms, *spoudaios/phaulos*, and infusing it with moral and ethical distinctions of his own.

[76] See Amelie O. Rorty, "*Akrasia* and Pleasure," in *Articles on Aristotle*, ed. Rorty, pp. 271 ff.

their soul is at war and one part on account of its wickedness grieves when it refrains from certain things, but the other is pleased and one part pulls here and another there as if tearing them apart."[77] Bad men are their own worst enemies. Aristotle's vivid portrait of the *phaulos* as a man with two or more selves at constant war with each other shows how removed the experience of internal struggle is, in his estimation, from the *spoudaios*. To be at odds with oneself is the mark of a no-good, whose reason does not keep mastery over his psychic activity. It is for this reason that Aristotle can align the continent (*egkrates*) with the incontinent man (*akrates*) in the first chapter of book 7. Though the former acts well, he is like the acratic in that he struggles with himself; both, in this respect, differ from the *sophron*, "the good man," who, being at one in all parts of his soul, experiences no internal division when he acts.

These points, however, should not suggest that Aristotle is incapable of appreciating the fact that even good men can be confronted with competing claims on their conduct, that is, claims at least *prima facie* in conflict. In various passages, for example, he rejects a view of "reductive commensurability" such as the one argued by Socrates in the *Protagoras*.[78] He asserts in the *Politics* that the notion of universal commensurability is untenable. Similarly, in the *Eudemian Ethics* he says that knowledge and money do not have a common measure, nor, according to the *Nicomachean Ethics*, do the noble, the beneficial, and the pleasurable.[79] Nonetheless, Aristotle does maintain that the man who has the right idea about happiness (and the *spoudaios* or *phronimos* is such a one) can, whenever he must act, subsume the question of alternatives under *eu*-

---

[77] *NE*, 1166b18–23.

[78] Plato, *Protagoras*, in *Platonis Opera*, ed. John Burnet (Oxford: Clarendon Press, 1974), 354d–355d. See David Wiggins, "Weakness of Will, Commensurability and the Objects of Desire," in *Articles on Aristotle*, ed. Rorty, pp. 241–65, and Nussbaum, *Aristotle's De Motu Animalium*, pp. 210–20.

[79] *Politics*, 1283a3; *Eudemian Ethics*, 1243.22–23; and *NE*, 1104b50–1105a1.

daimonia and discern which course of action is best. Thus, when he discusses *phronesis*, "wisdom" or "moral intelligence," in *Nicomachean Ethics* 6.5, he indicates that "it is thought to be the mark of a man of practical wisdom to be able to deliberate well about what is good or beneficial to him, not in a partial sense, such as what contributes to health or to strength, but what sorts of things contribute to the good life generally." Implied by this view is the notion that there are a number of worthy actions or pursuits one aims at in life and they are capable of being coherently integrated with one another.[80] This suggestion is borne out earlier in book 6, where Aristotle notes: "There is a mark [σκοπός] toward which a man of reason looks and strives or relaxes [his activity], and there is a standard [ὅρος] of the means, which we say lie between excess and deficiency and which conform to right reason [κατὰ τὸν ὀρθὸν λόγον]."[81] Proper deliberation is supposed to yield this standard, though Aristotle is not quite clear about how the reasoning process will decide it.[82] The same commitment to a *horos*, or limiting term, in moral life is apparent in a passage from *De Anima*: "Whether one will do this or that is the work of reason to decide. And it is necessary to measure by a single standard, for one pursues the greater good. Consequently, it is possible to make one standard out of numerous sense perceptions [φαντασμάτων]."[83]

In short, Aristotle's unitary conception of *aretai* and belief in the efficacy of *phronesis* to fix the right standard generate a moral optimism that is not very different from the nonproblematic sense of morality in Plato's theory of commensurability. Both hold out for the ability of a good person to mediate between competing claims and decide on the better course of action. They would deny true or irresolvable moral dilemmas

---

[80] See Wilkes, "The Good Man and the Good for Man in Aristotle's Ethics," in *Articles on Aristotle*, ed. Rorty, pp. 341–42, and MacIntyre, *After Virtue*, pp. 156–58, 162–63.

[81] *NE*, 1138b22–25.

[82] See Hardie, *Aristotle's Ethical Theory*, pp. 214–17.

[83] *De Anima*, 434a5–10.

by attributing an impasse in "deciding the question" to a flaw
in practical intelligence or to inadequate possession or exercise of some virtue.[84] In each thinker, there is a marked tendency, when problems of ethical conflict arise, to fall back on
the idea that virtues complement rather than collide with each
other. This tendency is especially notable whenever the *spoudaios* is under discussion. As the exemplar of the ethical life,
he epitomizes the values of psychological, social, and moral
harmony.

While Aristotle's ethical works offer perhaps the greatest
insight into the nonagonistic bias of his tragic theory, signs of
this tendency are marked in another treatise that bears a close
relation to the *Poetics*. In the *Rhetoric*, Aristotle studies a science that he initially aligns with dialectic, insofar as it is not
concerned with any definite class of objects but instead given
to perceiving the available means of persuasion in any case.[85]
But like poetics and ethics, rhetoric deals with matters that lie
broadly within the realm of human action and are thus susceptible of probable, not absolute or definite knowledge. Of particular significance for my purposes is the fact that all the
branches of rhetoric discussed by Aristotle are implicated in
strife. Forensic and deliberative oratory particularly assume a
conflictual setting. To claim, therefore, that Aristotle avoids
treatment of conflict in his discussion of the *techne rhetorike*
would hardly seem tenable. But two different levels of activity
need to be distinguished, if my point is to be appreciated.

The practice of rhetoric in Greece is situated within the agonistic pressures of the law courts, the assembly, and the highly
diversified interests of the polis at large. In the fifth century,

[84] For a discussion of these issues in modern philosophy, with some consideration of Aristotle's position, see Philippa Foot, "Moral Realism and Moral
Dilemma," *The Journal of Philosophy*, vol. 80, no. 7 (1983): 379–98. Also
see MacIntyre, *After Virtue*, pp. 141–43, 157, 163.

[85] Aristotle, *Rhetoric*, ed. John Sandys with comm. by Edward Meredith
Cope, 3 vols. (Cambridge: Cambridge University Press, 1877), 1354a1–10.
Also see William Grimaldi, *Aristotle, Rhetoric I: A Commentary* (New York:
Fordham University Press, 1980), pp. 1–4.

theories of rhetoric are shaped in important ways by Sophistic ideas, which both take for granted and strategically exploit these pressures.[86] While a treatment of such ideas would take me too far afield of the *Poetics*, it may be said at the very least that Sophistic relativism is fundamentally tied to the rhetorical tool of *dissoi logoi*, the technique of effectively arguing both sides of an issue, and to the more general perception that language is the vehicle of shifting, nonabsolute, and contradictory "truths," the manipulation of which effects persuasion. Aristotle, needless to say, is not only keenly aware of this tradition, but he begins his own treatise with reference to it. He criticizes his predecessors in the rhetorical art for their preoccupation with "τὰ ἔξω τοῦ πράγματος"—things beside the point of a true *techne*. "The engendering of mutual dislike, pity, anger, and similar emotions has nothing to do with the proper subject, but is directed at the man who is judging the case."[87] While the remark is aimed immediately at teachers of rhetoric, its disapproval of speeches that embody such a theoretical orientation is also clear. In elaborating his reasons for regarding this approach as misguided and in presenting his own *techne* as the enlightened alternative, Aristotle reveals a profoundly critical sense of the contestatory field within which rhetorical truth is supposed to emerge and lays down guidelines for mediating or neutralizing the conflictual situation of speechmaking. Because these controls may be understood as expressions of the same philosophical temperament that produces the nonagonistic bias of the *Poetics*, they deserve brief scrutiny.

Aristotle specifies the chief problems of contemporary oratory and rhetorical theory from the point of view of the person

[86] G. B. Kerferd, *The Sophistic Movement* (Cambridge: Cambridge University Press, 1981); Michael Nill, *Morality and Self-Interest in Protagoras, Antiphon, and Democritus* (Leiden: E. J. Brill, 1985); A. T. Cole, "The Relativism of Protagoras," *Yale Classical Studies* 22 (1972): 19–45; Carroll Moulton, "Antiphon the Sophist, *On Truth*," *Transactions of the American Philological Association* 103 (1972): 329–66.

[87] Aristotle, *Rhetoric*, 1354a19–21.

judging a case. The emphasis in these passages is on forensic speaking, but the judge of the law court (*dikastes*) is actually a special example of the judge conceived more broadly, as one to whom language is addressed for approval or disapproval (*krites*)—a point that helps account for Aristotle's tendency to shift terms in his discussion. Claiming that appeals to emotion are irrelevant (οὐ περὶ τοῦ πράγματος) and directed at the judge (πρὸς τὸν δικαστήν), Aristotle establishes a contrast that informs his orientation in book 1. His attempt to ground rhetoric in the method of a *techne* involves first and most importantly a focus on subject matter rather than on audience. The aim of speechmaking is to represent the facts (τὰ πράγματα), not to sway the listener. In well-governed cities this aim is actually protected and guaranteed by the laws (οἱ νόμοι). The Areopagus, for example, forbids talk about nonessentials.[88] Here is an exemplary model, in Aristotle's opinion, of a forensic forum in which law forbids speaking "ἔξω τοῦ πράγματος" and where the judge is consequently insulated from the extraneous influence of emotions. Those who established laws to control discourse in this fashion, he says, legislated correctly. For, he continues, a litigant has only to show that the *pragma* "is or is not, has or has not happened." To warp the judge by moving him to anger or envy or pity is akin to warping a *kanon*, a rule or standard of measurement. As for the discriminations of the judge himself, whether something is great or small, just or unjust, he himself must know this and not learn it from those engaged in wrangling. Whatever the lawgiver (nomothetes) has not defined, the judge must define himself, without relying on the disputants.

But Aristotle does not stop with these admonitions about the securing of facts and trustworthy judgments. He goes so far as to say that well-established laws ought as much as possible to define and control everything and leave as little as possible to those who judge.[89] His reasons for investing such au-

[88] Aristotle, *Rhetoric*, 1354a24–27.
[89] Aristotle, *Rhetoric*, 1354a38.

thority in the laws are three: (1) to lay hold of one man or several who are sensible and capable of legislating and administering justice is easier than laying hold of many; (2) because laws come about from those engaged in examination a long time, whereas judgments (κρίσεις) are off-hand, it is difficult for those judging to render what is just and fitting; and (3) most important of all, the judgment of the lawgiver is not particular but prospective and general, whereas members of the assembly or law court make judgments about things that are present and specific.[90] Influenced in particular circumstances by loving and hating, they are not able to discern the truth adequately. "It is necessary," Aristotle sums up, "to make a judge preside as master over as few things as possible."

In this highly revealing introduction to his treatise, Aristotle adumbrates, within the field of rhetoric, a crisis of judgment, or perhaps better, "criticism," since that term preserves a telling ambiguity in the Greek κρίσις. The word means judgment, discrimination, decision making through separating out and dividing up, hence, critical thinking; but also dilemma, turning point, crisis. In the introductory paragraphs of his work on the art of rhetoric, Aristotle sketches a scenario that reveals the precariousness of grounding truth in the rhetorical sphere, that is, the realm of discourse in general, whenever language is submitted to the judgment of an audience. The discussion, characterized by a series of turning points from one site of truth to another, bespeaks an anxiety about where to locate authority.

A person engaged in debate ought simply to point out what the facts are. But the agonistic framework of disputation renders dubious the ascertainability of truth (τὸ ἀληθές) from the speakers themselves. Consequently, the listener, or *krites*, is substituted as a source of authoritative judgment, with the proviso added that he must not take his cues about what the case really is from the litigants. His decision making should be autonomous, dispassionate, and not embroiled in the interests

[90] Aristotle, *Rhetoric*, 1354b1–13.

of the contestants. But even this move to locate an authority for truth is vetoed by Aristotle, for there is no guaranteeing that the listener, the standard of judgment, will not be warped by appeals to emotions and the pressures of the agonistically charged issues. At this point in his discussion, Aristotle seeks to transfer the sanction for rhetorical truth to a province beyond the realm of rhetoric and beyond the judges presiding in rhetorical situations—to the law and the lawgiver. The gesture is telling. His effort to institutionalize rhetoric as a respectable *techne* that can aim at truth is performed by grounding it in an extrarhetorical, nonagonistic source of authority: the laws—product of the few rather than the many, conceived over time, with a view to the universal. To invest the authority of true judgments in *nomos*, as Aristotle does in this passage, is to imagine a standard that is ahistorical (not shaped by the pressures of the moment), oligarchical or autocratic (determined by one man or a small group), and philosophically respectable (since reflection on the universal rather than the particular is always the mark of a science). In short, Aristotle begins his treatise by putting in question the democratic, agonistic context of language as a locus for establishing truth. The social and political configuration of the Greek polis, which gave impetus to the study and practice of rhetoric, is treated as suspect, except in those rare instances where it has legislated the process of rhetorical debate and outlawed "things beside the point." The crisis of critical judgment is apparently truncated at the point where rhetoric defers to the rule of law.

As this discussion suggests, Aristotle relies in the *Rhetoric*, as he does in other treatises concerned with the productive and practical sciences, on principles of order and theoretical controls that subdue conflict and replace agonistically generated crisis with unequivocating, stabilizing criteria. The rule of *nomos* in the *Rhetoric* fulfills a function not unlike the rules governing the action of the *spoudaios* in the *Ethics* and *Politics*. Both defer indeterminacy and guarantee the security of normative standards of judgment. While the remaining bulk of the *Rhetoric*, especially on the topics of *ethos* and *pathos*, actually casts doubt on the viability of the law envisioned by Aristotle in the introduction, the point I wish to emphasize here is his methodological interest in establishing a nonagonistic basis for grounding a *techne*.[91] While conflict remains a fact of rhetorical practice, the Aristotelian science of rhetoric envisions institutions that can diffuse its threat to the attainment of truth.

My CLAIM in the preceding section, that the conception of the *spoudaios* shapes the nonconflictual view of character and action in the *Poetics*, holds even when one considers that the agent Aristotle has in mind as exemplarily tragic is a "middling" *spoudaios*, an individual between the two extremes of perfect virtue (*epieikeia*) and viciousness (*poneria*), one rather more good than bad and one who does not fall into misfortune through evildoing or turpitude but through some mistake. It could be argued that this adjustment allows for a wider range of characters and actions than unqualified *spoudaiotes* does: what Aristotle admits as proper to tragedy are boundary situations, forcing good and serious agents into untypical ways of acting, into deeds that, strictly speaking, would not count as virtuous, but that are necessitated by pressing circumstances. Such acts, one can insist, may well involve the protagonists in collision—a point to which Aristotle, arguably, was not insensitive.

Certainly the Greek plays offer abundant evidence of this view. Furthermore, Aristotle clearly admits that there are "mixed actions," ones classifiable neither as *agatha*, "good," nor as *kaka*, "bad," because they are complicated by the intrusion of misunderstanding, ignorance, emotion, or external constraint.[92] But there is an important distinction to draw at

[91] The question of Aristotle's success in fulfilling the program for rhetoric set out in the introduction of his treatise has been a longstanding source of controversy. For a recent discussion, see Grimaldi, *Studies in the Philosophy of Aristotle's Rhetoric*, Hermes Einzelschriften no. 25 (Wiesbaden: Franz Steiner, 1972).

[92] See T.C.W. Stinton, "*Hamartia* in Aristotle and Greek Tragedy," *Classi-*

this juncture. Notwithstanding Aristotle's reliance on the category of mixed actions in the *Poetics*, his formulations skirt around a discussion of internal or external conflict. The point is all the more apparent when we consider that a treatment of tragic struggle could very well emerge from an understanding of the dramatic agent as a good man who, for one reason or another, falls into error. That Aristotle does not exploit this view to articulate some thoughts about the nature of conflict is chiefly comprehensible, I think, in light of evidence from the ethical and political works presented earlier. A modern reader may think that the suggestion of conflict is rife in passages of the *Poetics* where the middling tragic agent is discussed. We must be cautious, however, of transforming into an element of Aristotelian theory a matter that remains, for specifiable reasons, vaguely implicit and unarticulated in the critical discourse.

Other passages lend support to this caveat and furthermore reveal how intent Aristotle is to conform his tragic agent to notions of harmony and uprightness set forth in the *Nicomachean Ethics*. Chapter 14 of the *Poetics*, on pity and fear, offers ample occasion for developing the topic of rivalry, but once again the critical discourse is carried along by premises that divert attention from the conflicts of the plays under consideration. The discussion in chapter 14 forms part of a larger section on the finest tragedy, which Aristotle introduces in the preceding chapter, saying that he will now consider "what things the makers of plots should aim at and whence the proper effect of tragedy will come."[93] The best play should have a complex plot, exciting pity and fear through the actions of a person who is good but who commits a great hamartia. Though this term, around which there is still a good deal of scholarly controversy, can have a variety of meanings, from deliberate wrongdoing to intellectual error, Aristotle appears

---

cal Quarterly, n.s., no. 25 (1975): 221–54. For Aristotle's discussion of *miktai praxeis*, "mixed actions," see *NE*, 3.1–5.

[93] *Poetics*, 1452b28–30.

to use it in this section as an act committed in ignorance of particular details and without evil intent.[94] In this narrower sense, hamartia is a characteristic only of the plays ranked highest in the *Poetics*—for example, *Oedipus Tyrannus*. This interpretation is borne out by the subsequent discussion.

Actions most likely to be pitiable and fearful are those involving violent deeds, but not between enemies, for we expect them to fight; they must be between persons dear to each other, relatives or close friends. The allusion to conflict is clear. However, Aristotle proceeds to talk not of the clash between characters, but of the various ranks of horrifying deeds, which are differentiated according to the degree of ignorance they contain.[95] Struggle between relatives is not what strikes Aristotle as tragic in this classification of pitiable and fearful deeds, a fact suggested by the Greek term τὰ ἀνήκεστα, which refers to hideous acts of wrongdoing without implying anything in particular about conflict. What produces the tragic effect is the ignorance (*agnoia*) that brings error; in the best drama the agent is not aware of the true identity of the persons involved. Thus he proceeds toward a wrongdoing of which he is morally innocent, since he is not consciously infringing a law; he knows what is right but acts mistakenly because he lacks specific knowledge of details—for instance, identity. Such an agent is conformable to the definition of the *spoudaios* in the *Ethics*, who is said never to act badly with full knowledge.[96]

When in chapter 14 of the *Poetics*, the issue of conflict breaks the surface of discussion, Aristotle confirms that his sight is on other elements of the tragic action: blindness and

[94] See *Poetics*, ed. Lucas, pp. 299–307, and Else, *Aristotle's Poetics*, pp. 378–85.

[95] *Poetics*, 1453b27–1454a15.

[96] *NE*, 3.1, 6.5, 8–13. It is important to note that although the *spoudaios* described in *Poetics* 13 is not a paragon of virtue and uprightness, he is most like the good and serious man of the *Ethics* in having correct knowledge of general principles and in acting badly only from ignorance of particulars, not intentionally.

discovery, error and enlightenment are his interests. Hence Sophocles' *Oedipus Tyrannus*, which does not focus on a central *agon* between agents but instead weaves a complex web around the dialectic of ignorance and knowledge, suits his theory well and becomes the model of the finely wrought play. Moreover, the wrongdoing in which the major character is implicated allows Aristotle to assert his status as a *spoudaios* without direct problems, for Oedipus's acts of parricide and incest are performed not in ignorance of general moral principles, which he surely grasps, but of particulars.

Still, the case of Oedipus, if pressed, strains Aristotle's theory not unlike the way it challenges Hegel's notion of ethical pathos. Though conflict, arguably, is not a prominent element in the play, contradiction is. We may easily grant the point that Oedipus's hamartia is unwitting, but the fact that he is unaware of his crimes during their commission does not relieve the disturbance that an audience experiences at the spectacle of a good man implicated in the most heinous of offenses against morality. Sophocles rivets our attention on an incongruity in the status of Oedipus that is so extreme it unsettles the notion of a stable, determinate goodness such as Aristotle would posit for his *ethos*. We could assimilate to the *spoudaios* a range of intellectual errors for which he is not morally responsible—and Aristotle himself in fact does so in chapter 14 of the *Poetics*. Nonetheless, the gap between who Oedipus and others in his world think he is and what he instead turns out to be is severe enough to put in question Aristotle's ascription to him of the laudable title *spoudaios*. A figure contaminated with *miasma* makes us question the adequacy of moral categories such as the ones Aristotle employs in his discussion of the play.

This is another way of saying that Sophocles' tragedy holds in balance irresolvable oppositions between goodness and criminal contamination that derive partly from an archaic notion of pollution, which Aristotle's ethical thinking had in various ways superseded or implicitly discounted as primitive. Plato, of course, laid much of the groundwork for this thinking, and yet he is close enough to the experiences dramatized in a play such as *Oedipus Tyrannus* to regard them as threatening to his own moral conceptions and consequently in need of censorship. Indeed, we are reminded of a passage in Plato quoted earlier, about anarchy in the state expressing itself through the perverse equality (τὸ ἐξιοῦσθαι) of fathers, sons, husbands, and slaves, when Oedipus describes his crimes at the end of the drama:

> O marriages, marriages,
> you begot me and having begotten me again
> bred the same seed and brought forth
> fathers, brothers, children, blood kin,
> brides, wives, and mothers
> and the most shameful deeds there are among mortals.
>
> (1403–1408)

With their jumbled lists and lack of logical connectives, these lines spell out the insidious crossing of established boundaries, exemplified in a man who is at once son and husband to his mother, brother and father to his children, and thus echo Teiresias's earlier attribution to Oedipus of a sordid equality between him and his progeny.[97] As a figure who finally recognizes that his identity lies in this grim sameness that transgresses social and moral limits, Oedipus eludes the more modern, homogeneous ethical terms according to which Aristotle would ask us to understand him.

If *Oedipus Tyrannus*, a play singled out in the *Poetics* for its masterful handling of character and action, challenges Aristotle's notion of tragic *spoudaiotes*, other plays do so even more overtly. Aeschylus's *Oresteia* and Sophocles' *Antigone*, for example, do not fit the Aristotelian bill. This is not only because they have "simple plots" (without reversal and recognition) of the type used by the older playwrights; unlike *Oedipus Tyrannus*, they center on deeds of violence per-

<hr>

[97] Sophocles, *Oedipus Tyrannus*, in *Fabulae*, ed. Pearson, ll. 424–25, 457–60.

formed by an agent fully aware of an opponent's identity—the
hamartia, in short, is conscious and voluntary. More important, these tragedies are engaged with problems that do not
fall under the scrutiny of a theory geared to showing the rational basis of action and the qualities of the *spoudaios*. As I
suggested in my earlier discussion of *Antigone*, one of the issues in this play is the stability of crucial cultural values, such
as *nomos* or *philia*, and the difficulty of maintaining a view of
ethical action as unified, integrated, and conformable to a universally valid principle. Conflict, in this drama, fragments
identity and moral coherence. Similar dilemmas inform the
Oresteian trilogy. Characters seem unable to conform their
conduct to a universal and consistent law, an *orthos logos*.
Choosing one way, they transgress in another. A collision between rival standards of justice, which Aristotle does not address in the *Poetics* but resolves in the *Nicomachean Ethics* by
appeal to the *spoudaios*, is precisely what does not get resolved in the *Oresteia* through the "good" agent's ability to
discern the *metron*. This point is underscored when Athena,
herself baffled by the competing claims of Apollo and the Furies, remarks in the *Eumenides* that "the matter is too great, if
any mortal man thinks he can judge [δικάζειν] it" (470–71).
In bringing his notion of ethical goodness to bear on the discussion of tragedy, Aristotle implicitly ameliorates what Aeschylus renders problematic: the idea of a moral universe governed by determinate values and criteria for judgment. In the
trilogy, as in other Greek tragedies, conflict is the expression
of a moral dilemma that puts in question a *horos*, or limiting
moral term, such as Aristotle holds out for in his ethical discussions. While the "resolution" in the *Eumenides* may seem
to provide such a term, it in fact postpones one, as we will see.

At the heart of the *Oresteia* is the dilemma of retributive
violence and the correlative problem of moral differentiation:
where does justice end and wrongdoing begin when an act of
righteous revenge is not only identical to the preceding crime
but itself the provocation for another act of revenge?[98] Orestes

[98] On the crisis provoked by the symmetry of crime and retribution, see

gives expression to the crisis in the *Choephori*, when he formulates it as a clash of war god with war god, of justice with
justice: Ἄρης Ἄρει ξυμβαλεῖ, Δίκαι Δίκα (461).[99] This is an
aspect of the tragedy into which Hegel's theory of drama, unlike Aristotle's, would seem to provide valuable insight. But
the notion of ethical claims, problematic when applied to the
Antigone, as we have seen, is no less problematic in the case
of the *Oresteia*, where the concept of justice cannot be accurately rendered in terms of subjective rights, whose moral legitimacy is predetermined and authorized by appeal to existing standards.[100] We will return to this point later.

In typically Aeschylean fashion, the crisis of retributive justice is first developed through an elaborate system of imagery
in the parados of *Agamemnon*. The simile of the eagles robbed
of their fledglings aligns Menelaus and Agamemnon with the
bereaved parents, who agonize over the loss of their young.[101]
And as the eagles were stricken, so will they strike in turn,
rendering like for like. The choral song advances, weaving a
complex response to the masters in the house of Atreus, who
have led the Argive army away to war on a mission of vengeance, and as it advances an ambivalence emerges more and
more forcefully: the eagle brothers of the simile become the

Anne Lebeck, *The Oresteia: A Study in Language and Structure* (Washington,
D.C.: Center for Hellenic Studies, 1971); Thomas G. Rosenmeyer, *The Art of
Aeschylus* (Berkeley: University of California Press, 1982), pp. 292–96; Eric
A. Havelock, *The Greek Concept of Justice: From Its Shadow in Homer to
Its Substance in Plato* (Cambridge, Mass.: Harvard University Press, 1978),
pp. 277–95. René Girard has interesting things to say about the crisis of retributive violence, though he does not directly address the *Oresteia*, in *Violence and the Sacred*, tr. Patrick Gregory (Baltimore: Johns Hopkins University Press, 1977), pp. 1–67.

[99] For a different reading, see Rosenmeyer, *The Art of Aeschylus*, p. 294.
On *dike* in Aeschylus, see V. A. Rodgers, "Some Thoughts on *Dike*," *Classical
Quarterly* 21 (1971): 289–301, and Havelock, *The Greek Concept of Justice*,
chap. 16.

[100] See Gernet, *Droit et société dans la Grèce ancienne* (Paris: Sirey, 1955),
pp. 61–81, and Rosenmeyer, *The Art of Aeschylus*, pp. 353–56. Also see my
discussion in chap. 2.

[101] *Agamemnon*, ed. Page, ll. 40–54. See Lebeck, *The Oresteia*, pp. 7–24.

wild birds of the portent, described in lines 104 and following, who tear to pieces a pregnant hare favored by Artemis. Calchas, the seer, interprets the omen as a sign that the Argives will destroy Troy but incur divine wrath in the process and thus suffer punishment at the hands of the city's protective goddess. In rapid succession at the beginning of the play, we are presented with two images that, when taken together, embody a pattern enacted throughout the trilogy: the transgressed is a transgressor. Acts of crime and punishment in the house of Atreus mirror one another. Thus, not only are Agamemnon and Menelaus implicated in the double bind of retributive justice, whereby a righteous act is simultaneously a crime, but the other agents of justice in the *Oresteia* are too—namely, Clytemnestra, Aegisthus, Orestes, and Electra.

Now, it could be argued that the dilemma encapsulated in the parodos and developed in *Agamemnon* and *Choephori* is not grounded in irresolvable moral strife. Rather, it is the result of an archaic system of values that is superseded in the establishment of the court of the Areopagus in the *Eumenides*.[102] In other words, the collision of justice with justice occurs only within a primitive moral framework that has not yet settled on a rational, conclusive standard for solving retributive violence. Presumably, this argument could validate Aristotle's view of an integrated hierarchy of values that resolves claims *prima facie* in conflict. For if we set the dramatic action in a developmental perspective invited by the trilogy, the vicious circle of the earlier struggles is finally broken—and could have been prevented altogether—by the institution of a legal tribunal that preempts individual revenge and mediates the question of rival claims through implementation of a standard higher than that encompassed in the ancient practice of retribution. This is a common view of the *Eumenides*, but an unsatisfactory one, for it bypasses the problematic ele-

---

[102] See, for example, Richmond Lattimore's introduction to the *Oresteia*, in *Aeschylus* I, *The Complete Greek Tragedies*, ed. Grene and Lattimore. Rosenmeyer has a good discussion of the inadequacies of this conventional view in *The Art of Aeschylus*, pp. 336–68.

ments of the trial scene between Apollo and the Furies, over which Athena presides.[103]

The *Eumenides* opens with a situation in which the retributive principle of like for like has reached a grave breaking point: Orestes' revenge for his father's death, which has been prompted by Apollo, is simultaneously a criminal matricide for which the Furies pursue him. Thus, the ambiguous moral status of the avenger is expressed in the final play of the trilogy through a full-blown struggle between rival deities, each with a different axe to grind. It has become commonplace in criticism to note the oppositions represented by the Furies and Apollo in the play and catalogue the conflicts that their feud embodies between the older and newer gods, the primeval and the Olympian world, archaic revenge and civilized rationalism, cruelty and enlightenment, and so on.[104] These contrasts are useful only up to a point; if taken too far or without qualification, they obscure significant parallels between the two rival deities, the most striking of which is that both stand by the justice of the principle of revenge. It is not the case, as is sometimes thought, that Apollo separates himself, as an enlightened Olympian, from an archaic system of bloody reprisals. He reminds us explicitly at the beginning of the *Eumenides* (84) that he made Orestes strike Clytemnestra down. Moreover, it should be observed that the highest Olympian, Zeus, is frequently aligned with, not opposed to, the Furies in the trilogy: he works with them in avenging the rape of Helen;[105] his purpose dovetails with their curse on the house of Atreus when Agamemnon is slaughtered;[106] and we have every rea-

---

[103] See Lebeck, *The Oresteia*, pp. 134–41, who reviews the major scholarship on the difficult elements in the resolution of the *Eumenides*. Among earlier critics to focus on these problems, Karl Reinhardt in *Aischylos als Regisseur und Theologe* (Bern: 1949), pp. 144–48, has an especially useful discussion. More recently, see Rosenmeyer, *The Art of Aeschylus*, pp. 355–68.

[104] See, for example, Lattimore's introduction to the *Oresteia*, pp. 29–31.

[105] *Agamemnon*, ll. 55–71.

[106] *Agamemnon*, ll. 1115–20; 1188–90; 1384–87; 1481–88.

son to believe, given the many prayers and appeals to him in the *Choephori*, that he approves of Orestes' murder of Clytemnestra, which is one that the chorus says the Furies also require.[107]

In short, complicity between the Olympians and the Erinyes in the trilogy is tighter than usually acknowledged. By the time we get to the *Eumenides*, they emerge as bitter opponents, but their opposition does not consist in the different views they have of retribution. I emphasize this point in order to assert that when Apollo and the Furies go to trial, they are not disputing the justice of revenge per se. Neither in the trial of Orestes nor in the establishment of the court of the Areopagus do arguments for or against the archaic law of retribution emerge and produce a criterion for judging the case at hand. We would expect such arguments to be quite to the point, since the principle of like for like has generated the crisis. The importance of this apparent deflection of attention away from the source of the problems in the *Oresteia* will be taken up in a moment.

If the issue in the trial scene is not the righteousness of revenge, what does the conflict revolve around? It revolves around two rather narrowly conceived claims, both of which lack a compelling core of thought and neither of which proves itself to be rationally or ethically superior. Having variously described their privilege (*geras*) in the play as punishment of those who (1) have shed human blood,[108] (2) have shed congenital blood,[109] and (3) are matricides,[110] the Furies focus their case on the third, most limited prerogative in the trial scene. They go so far as to deny the first when, in response to Orestes' question why they did not pursue Clytemnestra, they respond, "the man she killed was not of congenital blood." The partiality with which the Furies come down on matricides is itself unsatisfying, especially given the fact that the trilogy

[107] *Choephori*, ll. 244–63; 278–85.
[108] *Eumenides*, ll. 315–20; 334–40; 421.
[109] *Eumenides*, ll. 212; 356–59.
[110] *Eumenides*, ll. 210; 230–31; 261–65.

provides evidence for their having pursued a broader precept on other occasions. Moreover, their unwavering adherence to retribution seems to perpetuate blindly the dilemma that the trial has been called to settle.

It is true that by focusing their prosecution in the way they do, they establish a firmer basis for a purely legal victory. The case against matricide has an initial credibility and a claim to respect that are strengthened by the fact that the Furies track down a man who in no way denies he has killed his mother. But this legalistic expediency is one of the puzzling aspects of the trial scene, for the litigants seem bent at all costs on winning and less concerned with arguing for larger principles. Athena says to the Furies before the trial begins that "injustice should not win by oaths" (432), meaning that a well-reasoned defense should prevail over simple technicalities. In the course of the litigation, however, we suspect that right is winning by technicalities. If Aeschylus is said to be presenting the progress from an archaic system of reprisals to a more enlightened judicial system, how does one account for the unflattering and even parodic fashion in which he dramatizes the nit-picking arguments of the trial scene?

Apollo's case does not do much to relieve the impression of parody. He, too, has expressed various positions in the course of the *Eumenides*, first challenging the Furies' pursuit of matricides by showing how it undermines the sanctity of marriage.[111] Their hounding of Orestes, he says, and neglect of Clytemnestra demean the marital bond, and "ordained love between man and wife is greater than an oath, guarded by justice." At the trial, however, he changes his tack, launching an argument that implicitly contradicts his earlier expressed commitment to marriage. To overcome the case of the Furies against those who kill congenital kindred, Apollo uses a theory that seems both ad hoc and trivial, despite the fact that the audience may have recognized it as a familiar piece of reason-

---

[111] *Eumenides*, ll. 213–24.

ing from earlier philosophy.[112] He states that the male partner
in marriage is the real progenitor, while the woman is merely
the holder of his seed, not a parent at all.[113] The argument is
designed not only to get Orestes off the hook by disclaiming
congenital attachment to Clytemnestra, but also, indirectly, to
justify his revenge of his father, the male whose superiority
calls for special honor and retributive action when it is assaulted.

What is perhaps most notable about the positions of both
the Furies and Apollo is that neither is possessed of a cogency
that could invest it with the status of a mediating moral principle. They are marked by expediency, self-interest, and sophistic hair-splitting—points accentuated by their inconsistency with previously stated positions. Athena's espousal of
the Apollonian argument does nothing to help out the situation. She has self-aggrandizing recourse to the side that has
shown her personal favor (Athena is cited by Apollo as living
witness that mothers are not parents), and her preference for
the male is expressed with an arbitrariness that only underscores the speciousness of Apollo's claim:

> There is no mother anywhere who gave birth to me,
> and, excepting marriage, I praise the male in all things,
> with my whole spirit, and I am strongly for my father.
> Thus, when a women kills her husband, guardian of the
>   house,
> I will not honor her lot first.

> (736–40)

Thus the trial toward which the Oresteian trilogy moves
does not finally provide what we think it will—adequate and
satisfying criteria for judgment. Or, to put it differently, it fails
to offer the sorts of argument that rationally decide the case
of Orestes' revenge. Aeschylus's interest is not in forging an
abstract, general notion of justice to resolve the conflict. For
this reason, it is difficult to locate in the play what Aristotle

---

[112] See Rosenmeyer, *The Art of Aeschylus*, p. 361.
[113] *Eumenides*, ll. 657–66.

requires the *spoudaios* in times of trouble to rely on in getting himself out of a pinch—a *metron* and *kanon*. Such a standard is not only beyond the good person, but beyond the gods, too, it seems. Still, there is a resolution in the *Eumenides*, just as there is a transition from a retributive to a judicial system, and we would do well to look more carefully now at what it involves.

Although, as I have indicated, Apollo and the Furies, far from presenting a case against vengeance, in fact both assume its justice, we nonetheless come out the other side of the trilogy with a legal system that has halted a potentially endless chain of reprisals. Private violence has been replaced by a public tribunal that the community recognizes as sovereign and whose decisions no group can challenge (at least in principle). In Athena's words, "this council [βουλευτήριον] will be untouched by desires of profit, venerable, quick to anger, watchful over those sleeping, a protector of the land" (704–06). Moreover, through her powers of persuasion, she gradually assimilates the initially affronted and angry Furies to the function of this judiciary and explains their place to the court of the Areopagus:

> Such are the things I will do in good will toward
> these citizens: make these divinities,
> great and implacable, dwell here.
> They have as their portion the management
> of all affairs in men's lives.
> He who, never having met with these stern spirits,
> knows not from where the blows in his life come—
> for the wrong-doings of previous generations
> drag him before these powers and silent destruction
> utterly destroys with hateful anger
> even him who cries out loudly.
> ....
> Do you hear these things, guard of the city,
> what they bring to pass?
> Revered Fury has great power

both among the immortals and those who dwell under
the earth,
and concerning men, it is clear that
they accomplish their acts fully, bringing songs to some
and to others a life dimmed with tears.

(927–32, 948–55)

What is paradoxical and initially puzzling about this description of the Furies' new role in Athens is that it incorporates
features of their earlier office, including—and this is the significant point—violent revenge. The principle of retribution,
rather than being excluded or rejected in the establishment of
a new order, the court of the Areopagus, is instead internalized
into its machinery. But with a crucial difference. Now the judicial body, with the mollified but not tame Eumenides presiding alongside the judges, becomes the agency that strikes the
last blow. It claims, through its authority, which is universally
respected, a monopoly on vengeance and so stifles rather than
perpetuates retributive violence. Invested with a sanctified and
legitimate   revenge—"πότνι'   'Εοινύς"—the   legal   system
saves the community from a vicious circle of violence. Herein
lies its unique efficacy.

It is in this light, I think, that we can understand not only
why there are no arguments against revenge in the *Eumenides*
but also why the arguments that do emerge in the trial scene
are not possessed of a compelling rigor or an appeal to a
higher, absolute justice. Aeschylus saw clearly that the effectiveness of the judiciary lay in its special monopoly on retribution, not in its supersession of it, and dramatizes this insight
through the integration of the Furies into the workings of the
Areopagus. The pragmatic rather than morally cogent basis of
this effectiveness is driven home through the patently inadequate grounds on which the litigants rest their cases. They do
not resort to an undisputed, transcendent *dike* in making their
defense, but to particular, even idiosyncratic arguments that
nonetheless can be acted upon in a court of law. The relative
justice or, more accurately, persuasiveness of the arguments is

all the court needs to deliberate on in breaking the cycle of violence. Its ad hoc judgments, exemplified in Athena's arbitrary swing vote, are no less effective for being so; they terminate the bloody chain of reprisals, and that is the important thing. In short, a supreme, uncontendable good, around which an integrated hierarchy of values could be structured, is not Aeschylus's interest in the *Oresteia*. Implicitly rejecting the necessity of such a value or limiting term in ordering morality, he focuses instead on the practical and rationally unsatisfactory nature of the solution to retributive justice.[114]

It should be clear that the trilogy provides another insight into how tragic conflict can elude ethical closure, even while it achieves reconciliation, and can undermine the sufficiency of *logos* in fixing a moral standard capable of mediating between competing claims. Aristotle's approach to drama circumvents these aspects of conflict altogether. Had he tried to come to terms with them, however, he would have met with various dramatic facts that challenge the normative view of morality exemplified in the figure of the *spoudaios*. Because the trilogy is often read by modern critics as if it transcends archaic blood law in favor of a higher, rational principle such as Aristotle would want to see affirmed, it is important to recognize how Aeschylus disturbs this view.

A number of other plays from the extant corpus of Greek tragedy affirm, in different ways, the conclusions I have drawn from this interpretation of the *Oresteia*. I will single out for brief consideration another tragedy preoccupied, as the trilogy is, with violence and its containment—the *Bacchae*. Like Aeschylus, Euripides is concerned with the contagious properties of violence, its tendency to spread like wildfire and consume a community. But while the earlier playwright looks to legal sanctions for controls, Euripides probes religion for the ways in which it sets limits. Once again, in the case of the *Bacchae*,

---

[114] This discussion of resolution in the *Oresteia* is informed by several scholars, particularly Gernet, *Droit et société dans la Grèce ancienne*, pp. 61–81; Girard, *Violence and the Sacred*, pp. 1–38; and Rosenmeyer, *The Art of Aeschylus*, pp. 355–68.

we find that the source of the crisis is also the solution. As the court of the Areopagus puts a stop to retributive violence by assuming the position of institutionalized avenger, the religion of Dionysus appears to hedge in man's savage impulses by including as a central part of its worship acts of ritual violence. What is striking about both plays is their acknowledgment of the impossibility of superseding violence, as something irrational and immoral, through an ethical system that replaces it with a distinct alternative—something like Aristotle's cooperative excellences, for example. The "morality" toward which these dramas move—if it may be called that—incorporates the very experience that later Greek ethical thought excluded from the good and virtuous life. In their different appropriations of violence, the *Oresteia* and the *Bacchae* fly in the face of the Aristotelian conception of tragic *spoudaiotes*, with its implicit but pervasive anticonflictual understanding of "the good life."

It is the double status of Dionysus, as a divinity whose violence effectively meets and curbs violence, that engenders the ambiguity so troublesome to critics of the play, who go in search of unequivocal evidence whether Euripides is for or against the god and his religion.[115] In one sense, Dionysus is beyond morality, or at least beyond the questions of right or wrong action that a moral perspective encourages us to ask. This does not mean, however, that such perspectives are lacking in the play. To the contrary, there is no shortage of ethical ideas brought to bear on the god and his worshippers. In particular, discussions of *sophia*, "wisdom," and *sophrosyne*, "self-control" or "temperance," proliferate, as different aspects of Dionysiac religion are probed and set in a variety of perspectives. But this exploration, which reveals among other things an astonishing breadth and inconsistency in common fifth-century Greek moral terms, ultimately uncovers the in-

---

[115] For a recent treatment of the play and of this issue in particular, see Charles Segal, *Dionysiac Poetics and Euripides' Bacchae* (Princeton: Princeton University Press, 1982), pp. 7–26, and Girard, *Violence and the Sacred*, pp. 119–42.

adequacy of any moral system in comprehending Dionysus. In the figure of the god and his worshippers, ethical categories are continually mobilized only to be exploded. For example, while a conventional religious language of restraint, limitation, and quiet humility is used by the Bacchae in the first stasimon and elsewhere to describe their worship, the description not only fails as a definition but is hard to reconcile with a contradictory side of Dionysus: his violence, which breaks limits and rages across traditional boundaries.[116]

One way of understanding this sharp disjunction between the two most prominent sides of the god's religion is to explain the *sophrosyne*, the quiet moderation, which his followers respect and emulate, as a result of a savagery that has been allowed ritual channels for expression, that has not been repressed or denied, but given a legitimate place in the context of worship. We might say that Euripides gives us a view of violence brought within the pale of morality through its ritualization. Dionysiac turbulence, in its religious form, paradoxically humanizes violence and sets limits to its expression.[117] The alternative to this ritualized *bia* is embodied in the young, petulant king of Thebes, whose attempts to suppress the Dionysiac side of life has profoundly disruptive personal and social consequences. It produces within Pentheus a seething mass of conflicting emotions that is ready to erupt at the slightest provocation, and it also brings about a breakdown of effective leadership in the community. To refuse violence totally, as if it were a stranger to civilized, communal life, is to encourage its proliferation in the social group, its contagious dissemination. But this is to admit that both morality and social hierarchy are themselves possible only through the recognition and inclusion of violence. As a primordial, amoral force upon whose ritual control order can take shape and develop, violence is central to, not opposed to, morality and the life of

---

[116] On this doubleness of Dionysus, see Girard, *Violence and the Sacred*, pp. 126–42, and Segal, *Dionysiac Poetics and Euripides' Bacchae*.

[117] See Girard, *Violence and the Sacred*, p. 134.

the polis. If this is one of Euripides' insights into the god whose actions both command respect and elicit horror it is one that can hardly be encompassed in an Aristotelian framework. In a play that uncovers the profound complicity between morality and the amoral, between civilized existence and violence, Aristotle's notion of *spoudaiotes*, with its non-agonistic bias, pales.

Greek tragedy repeatedly brings to light insights into conflict, violence, and morality that challenge rather than affirm Aristotelian ideas. A similar point has been made by critics before. It is not news that the author of the *Poetics* operated within an ethical system whose contact with certain aspects of fifth-century morality was sometimes tenuous and whose understanding, consequently, of pivotal social and religious transitions explored by the tragedians was partial.[118] But what is not usually acknowledged is the extent to which the concept of the *spoudaios* and its affiliated assumptions act as powerful controlling terms in Aristotle's discussion of tragedy and generate an approach to dramatic character and action that bypasses such unsettling, unsystematic aspects of plays as those engaged earlier. Notwithstanding these limitations, Aristotle's views, in contrast to what Plato offers in his critique of tragic drama, have seemed to the later tradition both palatable and compelling. But the philosophical objections to tragedy raised in the *Republic* are paradoxically more in tune than the *Poetics* is with important features of classical drama. By singling out for criticism the ways in which tragedy questions the unity of values, the efficacy of reason in settling dilemmas, and the normative role of the *spoudaios* in deliberation and action, Plato draws our attention to the kinds of problems dramatized by the tragic poets that fourth-century philosophy tries to overcome, within a systematic ethical framework grounded in rationality. A more sympathetic reading of Plato, one that

---

[118] See especially Adkins, "Aristotle and the Best Kind of Tragedy," who explores some aspects of this disjunction between fourth- and fifth-century ethical ideas, without giving special attention to violence.

tries to come to terms with the reasons for his anxiety, suggests that he has as much to offer for an understanding of Greek tragedy as his now canonical follower.

ARISTOTLE'S THEORY OF TRAGEDY, as the foregoing discussion reveals, is limited by philosophical expectations of order and reason that are different in substance from Hegel's but that produce similar results for the reading of tragedy. If we look back to the *Oresteia* and the *Bacchae*, we could say that Hegel's view is able to take into account crucial elements of these plays that are omitted from consideration in the *Poetics*. For unlike the *spoudaios*, the identity of the tragic hero in the *Vorlesungen über die Ästhetik* is defined by a conflict between his or her own sense of right and an opponent's. The antagonistic side of dramatic character is the one that interests Hegel and leads him to call an action genuinely tragic only when it calls up "other opposing aims and passions in other individuals." What saves the conflict from becoming an expression of a serious, unmediated cleavage in the moral structure of the universe is the resolution at the end, which shows that truth resides in a reintegration of opposing claims, in recapturing the unity of the "ethical substance."

But his emphasis on reconcilable ethical claims allows Hegel to look past the problematic resolutions in Aeschylus's and Euripides' plays—past the unethical, parodic aspects of the concluding arguments in the *Oresteia* and past the elusive, ambiguous status of morality in the *Bacchae*. If Hegel provides a point of entry into the strife and conflict dramatized by the fifth-century tragedians, he also provides a way out of them by implementing his own philosophical version of Reason in history. In different ways, the rationalistic and ethically ameliorative orientations of both the Greek and the German philosopher tame the struggles represented in tragedy.

This point of similarity brings us to a final topic, which I would like to treat briefly in closing: the psychological disposition of dramatic protagonists, about which Hegel and Aristotle are also in agreement. Insofar as the inner life enters as a factor at all in tragedy, they believe it is simply as the firm and unswerving resolve to act without doubt and hesitation. Neither is interested in the "drama of the mind" or in pathological states of psychological dividedness or uncertainty. They do not consider internal conflict an attribute of tragic character, as many contemporary critics do, following in the footsteps of the Romantics. On the contrary, since they stress the fulfillment of an action, its "confident outward thrust," as one critic has called it, they correspondingly downplay the private, deliberative side of action, except as it issues in a choice, a committed purpose to carry on in a particular way.[119] The nonpsychological orientation of the Aristotelian model is apparent in the truncated scheme examined earlier that he adopts for describing a tragic *praxis*. By claiming that drama sets before us an action whose comprehensibility is rooted in *prohairesis*, the already fixed predisposition toward action, Aristotle indicates the importance of mental readiness in tragedy at the same time as he eliminates the deliberative process from the events depicted on stage.

Paradoxically, however, it is this same expectation of internal unity in the tragic agent that yields the different conceptions of action in Aristotelian and Hegelian dramatic theory. Hegel's characters enter into conflict because they are inextricably bound to realizing an ethical claim with a spirit of resolve that bends to nothing or no one. Insofar as that claim is particular and partial it is going to infringe on another, and if compromise or hesitation does not temper the drive of the antagonists, the battle is on. But Aristotle's *spoudaioi*, as we have seen, are in principle uninclined to bitter confrontations because they are at one within; their inner integrity and firmness of purpose condition the characteristic *homonoia* of their relations with others. What happens when good agents are obstructed from realizing their ends is not an issue that receives attention in the *Poetics*.

[119] Jones, *On Aristotle and Greek Tragedy*, p. 38.

BY SUPPLYING the Platonic background for Aristotle's distinctive reorganization of approach to Greek tragedy, I have tried to show in this chapter the extent to which central critical ideas in the *Poetics* can be fully appreciated only as responses to an earlier set of philosophical qualifications and attacks. Given Plato's disapproval of the socially and psychologically dangerous conflicts represented in tragic drama, the nonagonistic biases in Aristotle's formal definition of *praxis* and ethical conception of the *spoudaios pratton* become more intelligible. His systematic interests not only provide an alternative to his predecessor's views but implicitly exclude consideration of issues that troubled Plato and that cluster around the dramatization of conflict and crisis. Had Aristotle developed new attitudes toward *stasis*, ones that could have overcome its associations with irrationality, disorder, and a breakdown of values, his response to fifth-century tragedy might have been different. But, while departing from Plato's censure of dramatic art, he also preserves many of Plato's views of conflict. The result is that his rationalizing project in the *Poetics* excludes an experience that remained unamenable to the criterion of artistic *logos* and to the norms implied by tragic *spoudaiotes*.

We have seen that it is possible to interpret Greek tragedy against these Aristotelian principles, to locate in the plays explorations of ethical, religious, and social dilemmas that undermine rather than affirm what Aristotle sought to establish for drama. Through these interpretations, which uncover the gaps between the systematic preoccupations of the *Poetics* and the different concerns of the tragedians, I have wanted to bring into view the controlling, ameliorating function performed by the operations of critical theory. As I said earlier, we encounter for the first time in the *Poetics* the effort of philosophy to incorporate poetry, and tragedy in particular, into its orbit of the intelligible. The cultural advantages of this incorporation are strikingly apparent in the context of a Platonic attack. In one sense, then, Aristotle has performed a valuable service for tragedy; he has provided a way, against stringent opposition, to approach it with systematic rigor and to assign it a place of dignity among the arts. But his exclusions of the problematic, culture-questioning aspects of drama would produce an entire tradition of criticism that remained blind to an important side of tragic plays and that went beyond the *Poetics* in inventing ways of affirming tragedy as a salutary source for the indoctrination of virtue and order. It is to this later tradition of Renaissance and neoclassical theory that we now turn.

CHAPTER THREE

Renaissance and Neoclassical Dramatic Theory: Conflict and Didacticism

Take away order from all things, what should then remain? Certes nothing finally, except some man would
imagine eftsoons chaos. Also, where there is any lack of
order needs must be perpetual conflict.
—Sir Thomas Elyot, *The Governour*

The beautiful and great frame of the universall globe:
whereof the divinities, order, and equal firmenesse of all
the severall parts, together with the one perfect harmony
obeying the gracious and soveraigne government of their
Creator, by good right deserve to bee called pure, for
without so excellent a disposition, there would be nothing els but an uncleane, and polluted disorder and confusion.
—Pierre de la Primaudaye, *The French Academie*

THROUGH THE PROTECTIONISM of Aristotle's disciples
during the peak of Hellenistic bibliomania and the subsequent
vagaries of textual transmission, the *Poetics* seems to have
passed out of circulation shortly after the death of Theophras-
tus and was unknown in Roman antiquity.[1] The definitions of
tragedy familiar to Latin authors and handed down to the
Middle Ages by such grammarians as Donatus and Diomedes
were probably based not on the *Poetics*, but on an earlier,
more widely known dialogue of Aristotle's, since lost, entitled

---

[1] See A. P. McMahon, "Seven Questions on Aristotelian Definitions of
Tragedy and Comedy," *Harvard Studies in Classical Philology* 11 (1929):
99–108; J.W.H. Atkins, *Literary Criticism in Antiquity*, 2 vols. (Cambridge:
Cambridge University Press, 1943), vol. 1, p. 167.

On Poets. It was not until the turn of the fifteenth century that the *Poetics* was "rediscovered" and became the focal point for a spate of commentaries whose influence profoundly shaped the theoretical orientation of later views on drama. If Aristotle's ideas had a negligible impact on literary theory before 1500, they came to dominate the critical scene by 1550, and no discussion of poetry in general or tragedy in particular could respectfully proceed without reference to the Greek philosopher.[2] Considering the prominence and the authority of Aristotle in this period, one might predict that writings on tragedy would preserve not only the main lines of approach exemplified in the *Poetics* but its exclusion of conflict as well. The influence of Aristotle in the Renaissance, however, is substantially complicated by the form in which he was interpreted by major cinquecento critics, whose efforts at editing, elucidating, and translating the Greek text largely determined its reception in Europe. If we are to gain an understanding of the special factors operating in sixteenth- and seventeenth-century literary criticism that encourage a nonagonistic approach to tragedy, we must look to the distinctive ways in which Aristotle's poetic theory was assimilated in the first stages of its reemergence in the West.

For the early Italian pioneers in literary criticism, the *Poetics* posed formidable textual and exegetical difficulties, even though it had received some scholarly treatment in preceding centuries.[3] The work was known in the Middle Ages through the so-called middle commentary by the late-twelfth-century

[2] Joel Elias Spingarn, *A History of Literary Criticism in the Renaissance*, 2d ed., rev. and aug. (1924; reprint, New York: Columbia University Press, 1954), pp. 16–23; Baxter Hathaway, *Marvels and Commonplaces: Renaissance Literary Criticism* (Ithaca: Cornell University Press, 1968), pp. 9–19; Bernard Weinberg, *A History of Literary Criticism in the Italian Renaissance*, 2 vols. (Chicago: University of Chicago Press, 1961), pp. 349–423.

[3] On the manuscripts of the *Poetics* used in early Renaissance exegesis, see E. Lobel, *Greek Manuscripts of Aristotle's Poetics* (London: Oxford University Press, 1933), pp. 25–32; D. S. Margoliouth's edition of the *Poetics* (London: Hodder and Stoughton, 1911); Weinberg, *History of Literary Criticism*, pp. 361–71.

Arabic philosopher Averröes.[4] Based on an Arabic translation of a tenth-century Syriac manuscript translated from the Greek, Averröes' study proceeds by citing a brief passage or identifying phrase from Aristotle and then analyzing, explaining, and expanding the quotation, often through illustrative examples drawn from Arabic literature or through tag phrases from commonplace medieval notions about poetry. While Averröes was impressively knowledgeable about the Aristotelian corpus, having composed commentaries on all of Aristotle's major works, the philosophical understanding he brought to the *Poetics* was determined in important ways by his virtual ignorance of classical literature, his lack of familiarity with any form of drama, including Greek tragedy, and his pervasive importation of typically medieval views into the commentary. Indeed, this medievalization of Aristotle's text largely accounts for what little significance the *Poetics* had in the thirteenth and fourteenth centuries. Hermannus Alemannus, for example, first translated the Averröistic commentary in 1256, declaring in his introduction that he abandoned efforts to translate the original because of its very great difficulty.[5] This Latin version was preferred in the Middle Ages to

---

[4] See O. B. Hardison, "The Place of Averröes' Commentary on the *Poetics* in the History of Medieval Criticism," in *Medieval and Renaissance Studies: Proceedings of the Southeastern Institute of Medieval and Renaissance Studies, Summer, 1968*, ed. John L. Lievsay (Durham: Duke University Press, 1970), pp. 57–77; H. A. Kelly, "Aristotle-Averröes-Alemannus on Tragedy: The Influence of the *Poetics* on the Latin Middle Ages," *Viator: Medieval and Renaissance Studies* 10 (1979): 161–209; Judson Boyce Allen, *The Ethical Poetic of the Later Middle Ages: A Decorum of Convenient Distinction* (Toronto: University of Toronto Press, 1982), pp. 19–38; Weinberg, *History of Literary Criticism*, pp. 155–57.

On the slight influence of Aristotle's *Poetics* until the sixteenth century, see Hathaway, *Marvels and Commonplaces*, p. 9; William K. Wimsatt and Cleanth Brooks, *Literary Criticism: A Short History* (New York: Alfred A. Knopf, 1965), pp. 155–57; Marvin T. Herrick, *The Poetics of Aristotle in England* (New Haven: Yale University Press, 1930), pp. 8–13.

[5] Hermannus Alemannus's translation has been edited by William F. Boggess, *Averrois Cordubensis Commentarium Medium in Aristotelis Poetriam*,

a remarkably accurate but largely ignored translation of the Greek text made by William of Moerbecke in 1278. The conclusion seems ineluctable: Averröes' commentary on the *Poetics*, with its medievalizing sensibility, was more comprehensible and attractive to scholars of the period who turned their attention to Aristotle on poetry. While the circle of such scholars seems to have been quite narrow, the interest in the commentary nonetheless affirms the importance of Aristotle's assimilation to a complex of ideas influential for critics working in the cinquecento heyday of literary criticism.[6] We will turn to these ideas shortly. For now I note that the process of assimilation, which has been repeatedly singled out by modern scholars as the identifying trait of Renaissance appropriations of the *Poetics*, was under way already in the few medieval discussions of the text. Well before the great Latin commentaries by Francesco Robortello in 1548 and Vincenzo Maggi in 1550, the understanding of Aristotle was being mediated by an existing tradition of concepts about poetry whose orientation differed greatly from the formalism of the *Poetics*. Two beneficiaries of such medieval views, Robortello and Maggi, reveal their reliance on Averröes by quoting him and echoing his interpretations.[7]

It is well known that a major authority in this medieval tradition inherited by later centuries is Horace. His prominence is explainable in a couple of ways.[8] First, unlike the *Poetics*,

---

Dissertation at University of North Carolina at Chapel Hill, 1965. All references to the text of Averröes are to this edition of the Latin translation.

[6] See, for example, Kelly, "Aristotle-Averröes-Alemannus on Tragedy"; Hardison, *The Enduring Monument: A Study of the Idea of Praise in Renaissance Literary Theory and Practice* (Chapel Hill: University of North Carolina Press, 1962), pp. 12–18, 34–36.

[7] Francesco Robortello, *Francesci Robortelli Utinensis in librum Aristotelis De Arte Poetica Explicationes*; Vincenzo Maggi, *Vincentii Madii Brixiani et Bartholomaei Lombardi Veronensis in Aristotelis librum De Poetica Communes Explanationes*.

[8] On the prominence of Horace in Renaissance literary criticism, see Weinberg, *History of Literary Criticism*, pp. 71–110, and Marvin T. Herrick, *The*

the *Ars Poetica* was well known in the Middle Ages and came
down to Renaissance scholars accompanied by two commentaries from the late Roman period—those of the second-cen-
tury Acron and the third-century Porphyrion—as well as two
later commentaries by Landino and Badius. When cinquecento studies of Horace's text got under way, all four glosses
were regularly included in available editions, and critics took
their points of departure from them.[9] In short, sixteenth-century criticism inherited a tradition of well-developed Horatian
ideas and did not have to start from the ground up in their
scholarship on the *Ars Poetica*. Second, the rhetorical orientation of Horace's letter to the Pisos appealed to Renaissance
thinkers who often grouped poetics either among the sciences
of method, along with logic, dialectics, rhetoric, and gram-
mar, or with moral philosophy and ethics, whose aims are rhetorical in the sense of being directed toward the moral improvement of an audience. Both classifications were common
in the Middle Ages, as Averröes' commentary testifies; he vac-
illates between assigning poetics an ethical function and including it in the *Organon*.[10] While the affiliations of poetics
among the sciences were debated endlessly in the Renaissance,
its close associations with rhetoric remained strong and dictated what many critics had to say about it.

Since the ties between poetics and rhetoric were already secure when Aristotle's text on poetry resurfaced, the fate of the
Poetics in the sixteenth and seventeenth centuries was to be
absorbed into an existing tradition of interpretation centered
on the *Ars Poetica*. Facilitating this assimilation was the common Renaissance methodological strategy of systematically
comparing different texts from classical antiquity with a view

---

Fusion of Horatian and Aristotelian Literary Criticism, 1531–1555 (Urbana:
University of Illinois Press, 1946).

[9] See Weinberg, *History of Literary Criticism*, pp. 72–73.

[10] On the classification of rhetoric among the sciences, see Charles S. Baldwin, *Medieval Rhetoric and Poetic to 1400* (Gloucester, Mass.: Peter Smith,
1959); Weinberg, *History of Literary Criticism*, pp. 1–37; Hardison, *The Enduring Monument*, pp. 3–23.

to reconciling divergent opinions and rendering the great authorities from the past compatible with each other. This urge
to see consistency in the writings of Greek and Latin authors
produced a syncretism in Renaissance criticism, especially notable in the composite body of Aristotelian and Horatian ideas
that would come to form the basis of neoclassical literary doctrine.[11] Various modern works have traced the fusion of Aristotelian and Horatian criticism in the cinquecento, and it is
unnecessary to rehearse the stages of development in this context.[12] But the phenomenon is important for my purposes because it reveals a persistent bypassing of the formalistic approach of the Greek text as well as a tendency to impose a
more familiar audience-related orientation on Aristotle's theory.

The Horatian concern with language as a discursive instrument whose ends are to give pleasure and to teach carried over
to the *Poetics*, which was understood increasingly not only in
rhetorical but also in didactic terms. Unconcerned with the
subordination of ethical to structural matters in Aristotle's
thinking, Renaissance critics found in the *Poetics* affirmation
of their existing understanding of poetry as a vehicle of instruction in right action and an inducement to virtuous living.
They commonly took the Greek philosopher to be advancing
quite bluntly a view of tragedy as moral philosophy, pleasingly dressed up with literary embellishments in order to teach
more effectively. This interpretation yields a sense of Aristotle
distinctly different from the one for which I argued in the previous chapter. In supplying the ethical background for understanding the nonagonistic approach to tragedy in the *Poetics*,
I uncovered normative assumptions about choice and action
operating in Aristotle's definition of the tragic *spoudaios*. But
to see in the *Poetics* traces of values elaborated more fully in
the *Ethics* is not the same as making Aristotle a propounder

[11] See Weinberg, *History of Literary Criticism*, pp. 53–54.
[12] See especially Herrick, *The Fusion of Horatian and Aristotelian Literary Criticism.*

of a didactic theory of poetry. The *Poetics* may be said to remove the Platonic stigma from art and tragedy especially, by aligning them with philosophy and a system of ethics. But only through a detour such as Renaissance critics take via Horace does this alignment serve the end of morally indoctrinating an audience. To make a didactically minded rhetorician out of the author of the *Poetics* is to reinvent Aristotle on tragedy.

If the Renaissance assimilates Aristotle's poetic theory within a basically Horatian framework, then we must turn to this conflation of Greek and Roman influences in probing the reasons for the exclusion of conflict from critical discussions of tragic drama. At the outset we should take seriously the implications of the methodological bias toward harmonizing received ideas: the syncretistic tendencies in theory bespeak a fundamental suspicion of conflict and dissension, which is no less apparent in the orientation of individual branches of literary study. The mind-set determining this direction of thinking supposes the univocality and continuity of the great authorities: Horace and Aristotle ultimately agree. Within such a framework, it is not surprising that the rules governing institutions of Renaissance theorizing carry over to the understanding of a particular genre, tragedy, which is submitted to similar expectations of consistency, unity, and congruence. This is not to say that Renaissance literary discussion escapes disagreement and oppositional positioning, far from it. But an exegetical penchant of contemporary scholars was to reconcile critical views and align themselves with respected figureheads. This penchant influenced the ways in which they approached literary works.

The interpretive urge toward synthesis and reconciliation of apparent oppositions, so characteristic of sixteenth-century theory, was already well established in another, older tradition of hermeneutic activity—scholastic exegesis. Here, argumentation works through a series of *articuli*, or constituent parts and members, in which *similitudines* and *distinctiones* are drawn and contrary views are aired, with a view toward the final *concordantia* of the conclusion, in which all oppositions are resolved and all objections harmonized.[13] Thomas Aquinas's method in the *Summa* offers probably the most salient example of such a procedure. In this important respect, cinquecento critical practice seems indebted if not to the specific strategies than at least to the hermeneutic ideal of scholasticism.

Other cultural factors are also at work in reinforcing a nonagonistic bias toward tragedy. Objections to the art of poetry are concurrent with the rise of literary criticism in the sixteenth century, and in the last third of the cinquecento they occur with greater force and frequency.[14] It may be coincidence that the Council of Trent, whose sessions were held discontinuously between 1545 and 1563, was contemporaneous with the spurt of activity surrounding Aristotle's *Poetics* in midcentury. But there is little doubt that the critique of poetry, and of drama in particular, by tridentine Catholic reformers feeds a growing apologetic strain in the poetic treatises written during these years. In England, the Puritans often converge with their Catholic adversaries, notably those with a reformist bent, in expressing strident disapproval of dramatic literature and the stage, above all.[15] The barrage of condemnatory remarks in the British tradition reaches a culminating peak with the publication of William Prynne's *Histriomastix* in 1633, "a gargantuan encyclopedia of antitheatrical lore which scourges

[13] See the appendices for Thomas Aquinas's *Summa Theologiae*, 3 vols., vol. 3 tr. Michael C. Browne et al. (New York: McGraw-Hill, 1964), "The Structure of the *Summa*" and "The Method of the *Summa*." Also see the discussion of scholastic exegesis by Jesse M. Gellrich in *The Idea of the Book in the Middle Ages: Language Theory, Mythology, and Fiction* (Ithaca: Cornell University Press, 1985), pp. 65–69.

[14] See Weinberg, *History of Literary Criticism*, pp. 797–801; Basil Willey, *Tendencies in Renaissance Literary Theory* (Cambridge: Bowes and Bowes, 1922); Wimsatt and Brooks, *Literary Criticism*, pp. 167–72.

[15] See Jonas Barish, *The Antitheatrical Prejudice* (Berkeley: University of California Press, 1981), pp. 80–131; Russell Fraser, *The War Against Poetry* (Princeton: Princeton University Press, 1970); *Elizabethan Critical Essays*, ed. G. Gregory Smith, 2 vols. (Oxford: Oxford University Press, 1904), vol. 1, pp. xiv–xxxi.

every form of theater in the most ferocious terms, in a style of paralyzing repetitiousness from which anything resembling nuance has been rigidly excluded."[16] Not long after the appearance of *Histriomastix*, Parliament ordains the closing of all theaters in a way that suggests a deep complicity between the popularity of Renaissance plays and existing civil strife.[17] In seventeenth-century France, Jansenism fuels a controversy against drama that already reached major proportions elsewhere in preceding years.[18] While Christian arguments form an important part of this antipoetic and antidramatic wave of criticism, which at different times floods England and the Continent, Plato's censures are frequently wedded to them and adapted to Christian purposes.[19] Thus we find in these Renaissance attacks against poetry charges remarkably similar to those voiced in classical antiquity by the author of the *Republic*. Tragic drama, usually exemplifying the worst dangers inherent in all art, is rejected as morally degenerate, socially subversive, and generally threatening to the health, stability, and hierarchy of the cultural status quo. Once again, an entire system of values is mobilized in the critique, with unity, coherence, constancy, and order marshaled against forces of dissolution, fragmentation, and conflict.

Given an interpretive tradition with syncretistic leanings, an existing Horatian predisposition in favor of a didactically rhetorical approach to poetry, and an antidramatic tradition whose spokespersons could be rabid in the severity of their attacks on plays, it is no wonder that the Renaissance produces a body of literary criticism on tragedy notable, despite its heterogeneity, for its high valuation upon the normative, culturally affirmative aspects of drama. Tragedy, according to

[16] Barish, *The Antitheatrical Prejudice*, p. 83.
[17] Fraser, *The War Against Poetry*, pp. 13–14.
[18] On Jansenism and the drama of Racine, see Lucien Goldmann, *Le dieu caché: Étude sur la vision tragique dans les Pensées de Pascal et dans le théâtre de Racine* (Paris: Gallimard, 1955).
[19] See Weinberg, *History of Literary Criticism*, pp. 250–52, 293–96, 345–48, and Barish, *The Antitheatrical Prejudice*, pp. 5–37.

the dominant view, does not stand against society or question and threaten it, but instead encourages assimilation at a variety of levels, both ethical and artistic. Aristotle's *Poetics*, which was often regarded as a successful repudiation of Plato's complaints against literature, was a ready resource for critics who tried, in the face of new opposition, to shore up the ground of their defense, and it rapidly became indispensable to the often non-Aristotelian terms of their apologies. What is important for the present chapter is not so much the misappropriation of the *Poetics* in the sixteenth century, as the way in which the reception of this work girds the antiagonistic prejudice of theoretical approaches to drama. A poetics that renders moral coherence and instruction in virtue fundamental conditions of literary usefulness or profit (*utile*) will not be inclined to appreciate dramatizations of conflict in tragedy.

In Renaissance criticism, these obstacles often seem more repressive than the ones we encounter in Aristotle's *Poetics*. That is, the insistence on tragedy as a representation of moral order, as a clear delineation, if not a teleology, of vice and virtue is made in the face of so much contrary evidence in contemporary and classical drama that one is tempted to see a denial of tragedy in the interests of protecting the same dominant cultural ideology usually associated with the conservative, moralistic detractors of art. If the shrill voices of law and order try to stabilize traditional values through such radical tactics as banning plays and closing theaters, literary critics of the sixteenth and seventeenth centuries appear to perform a similar function but with a different strategy. They render tragedy amenable to an accepted system of beliefs by excluding its characteristically subversive aspects and treating it as an affirmation of conventional hierarchies and norms. The move to sanction drama puts Renaissance critics in a curiously double position. While often explicitly opposed to the censorious enemies of poetry, they are no less opposed, in their application of traditional values, to the culture-questioning, destabilizing spirit of tragedy, a form of literature they can extol only by transforming it into precisely what it is not—a purveyor of inherited truths. This paradoxical position is telling. It suggests the limitations of and pressures on critical theory, when it is beholden for its authority to an official culture whose validity is put to the test by the very literary works that are taken as examples of social and moral order.

The identity of this culture on which Renaissance dramatic theory rests its claim to authority is already, in certain respects, apparent from my remarks on the confluence of Aristotelian and Horatian ideas in the cinquecento. Generally, it may be described in terms of a medieval Christian heritage, reinforced in many ways, though also transmuted, through the influence of classical authorities. Because this Christian-humanist synthesis has been treated extensively by a variety of modern scholars, including Paul Oskar Kristeller, Ernst Cassirer, and Hiram Haydn, I do not analyze the conglomerate of ideas itself but study its manifestations in particular, representative critical treatises of the period.[20] At the outset, I note that the tradition carried forth by Renaissance and neoclassical criticism typically organizes its rhetorical and didactic interests around the terms discussed earlier in the case of Plato and Aristotle. Ethically, we find a similar emphasis on right reason as a guide for right action, on rationality and the correlative consistency of values as exemplary of the human state, and on social harmony as an extended consequence of the accord among those who adhere to the dictates of our highest faculty. Metaphysically, there is confidence in the existence of an order of creation, a hierarchy in which the articulation of differences is a condition of stability and in which human beings have a definably important place. The monarchies under which humanism thrived insert themselves into this

---

[20] Paul Oskar Kristeller, "The Place of Classical Humanism in Renaissance Thought," *Journal of the History of Ideas*, vol. 4, no. 1 (1943): 59-62; Ernst Cassirer, *The Individual and the Cosmos in Renaissance Philosophy*, tr. Mario Domandi (New York: Barnes and Noble, 1963); Hiram Haydn, *The Counter-Renaissance* (Gloucester, Mass.: Peter Smith, 1966), pp. 27–75. Also see Douglas Bush, *The Renaissance and English Humanism* (Toronto: University of Toronto Press, 1939).

cosmic order and sanction their own authority by appeal to parallels between, for example, the mortal ruler on earth and the divine primum mobile. We will examine these generalities in greater detail later.

For now, I simply want to stress that the complex of ideas in Platonic and Aristotelian philosophy, which connects reason with the desirable states of order and harmony, while linking irrationality to conflict and contagious disorder, is also operative in sixteenth-century thinking. As the epigraphs from Elyot and La Primaudaye suggest—they are echoed by Baldassare Castiglione, Erasmus, Thomas More, Richard Hooker, and any number of other representative figures in this tradition—strife retains contaminated associations with chaos, the collapse of values, and the distraction of human dignity. These connections have been amply documented in such classic books in the history of ideas as Arthur Lovejoy's *The Great Chain of Being*, Herschel Baker's *The Dignity of Man*, and Leo Spitzer's *Classical and Christian Ideas of World Harmony*.[21] The conclusion elicited by these studies and borne out in a reading of critical documents is that sixteenth- and seventeenth-century literary theory is informed by many of the same classical ideas that operated in the exclusion of conflict from Aristotle's discussion of tragedy.

While these ideas certainly form a heritage for Renaissance dramatists as well as critics, more often than not they are resisted or undermined in tragedy rather than affirmed. If criticism is a dominant voice of the official culture in the sixteenth and seventeenth centuries, tragic literature is a vehicle of dissent and opposition. Rather than sanctioning values identifiable with an inherited tradition, tragedy invokes these values in order to put them in question and explore the conflicts and

---

[21] Arthur Lovejoy, *The Great Chain of Being: A Study of the History of an Idea* (New York: Harper and Row, 1936); Herschel Baker, *The Dignity of Man: Studies in the Persistence of an Idea* (Cambridge, Mass.: Harvard University Press, 1947); Leo Spitzer, *Classical and Christian Ideas of World Harmony: Prolegomena to an Interpretation of the Word "Stimmung,"* ed. Anna G. Hatcher (Baltimore: Johns Hopkins University Press, 1963).

crises they repress. Thus, in the experiences dramatized by the great tragedians of the Renaissance, we find subversions, not consolidations of order. Their plays are instruments through which structures of authority are probed for their adequacy and destabilized in the process. Tragedy, in short, puts in doubt the validity of the ideas that criticism, following a more conservative path, deploys in its efforts at literary understanding.[22]

What emerges, once the claims to dissent dramatized in tragic plays are recognized, is a competition between discourses that seem in retrospect adversarial, although at the time the language of criticism is nonconfrontational and even acclamatory in its posture vis-à-vis drama. Renaissance literary theory, one could say, performs a kind of covert policing service, by bringing the works over which it assumes authority into line with established and generally acceptable norms. Within this perspective, we can understand why strife never assumes prominence in theoretical reflections on drama and is actually repressed by presuppositions of an order that tragedy represents and espouses.

Now it is true that standard definitions of tragedy by Scaliger, Minturno, Castelvetro, and Sidney mention wars, disturbances in the social order, and the falls of great people from prosperity to adversity. Partly inherited from the medieval tradition of *de casibus virorum illustrium*, this conception, which we will examine later, admittedly takes a superficial glance at the disruptive aspect of tragic action and the hero who is somehow out of step with the orderly functioning of cosmic

[22] For recent treatments of this relationship between tragedy and literary theory, see Stephen Booth, *King Lear, Macbeth, Indefinition, and Tragedy* (New Haven: Yale University Press, 1983), pp. 81–118, and Timothy Reiss, *Tragedy and Truth* (New Haven: Yale University Press, 1980). The disjunction between dramatic theory and practice in the Renaissance was addressed earlier in this century by Smith, in his edition of *Elizabethan Critical Essays*, vol. 1, p. xii. For a somewhat different view, focused more on rhetorical theory, see Joel Altman, *The Tudor Play of Mind: Rhetorical Inquiry and the Development of Elizabethan Drama* (Berkeley: University of California Press, 1978).

law. But the emphasis, as we will see, does not lead to deeper scrutiny, let alone appreciation, of conflict in tragedy. Critics, instead, remain concerned with the values of stability and constancy or with the ways in which upheavals produced by temporary imbalances are eventually set right. The more pressing and disturbing questions probed by the tragic dramatists recede behind a veneer of conservative values that are affirmed as the values of tragedy.

In studying the major developments in literary theory of the sixteenth and seventeenth centuries that shape the direction of inquiry on tragedy, my discussion will focus initially on Hermannus Alemannus's translation of Averröes' commentary on the *Poetics*, since it exemplifies the early transformation of Aristotle into a didactic theorist of poetry and continues to be cited with respect in the Renaissance by such people as Benvenuto da Imola, Coluccio Salutati, Alessandro Piccolomini, and Tasso. Next, I will turn to two Italian critics, whose influence on the later tradition is well known: Antonio Minturno and Julius Caesar Scaliger.[23] Their works on poetry reflect the characteristic conglomerate of Horatian and Aristotelian ideas, which had already been forged in the first great commentaries on the *Poetics* by Robortello and Maggi and which later passed to critics in England and France. Many of these ideas find their most polished and sophisticated formulation in Sir Philip Sidney's *Defense of Poesie*, an epitome of Renaissance critical attitudes, published in 1595 but probably written in 1583.[24] On the basis of these writings, it is possible to trace the emergence of the dramatic "rules" that become a hallmark of neoclassical criticism, especially as it is represented by Pierre Corneille in the *Trois Discours* and John Dry-

---

[23] I have used the partial translations in English of works by these critics: Julius Caesar Scaliger, *Select Translations from Scaliger's Poetics*, tr. and ed. F. M. Padelford, Yale Studies in English no. 26 (New York: Henry Holt, 1905); Antonio Minturno, *L'Arte Poetica*, in *Literary Criticism: Plato to Dryden*, ed. Allan H. Gilbert (Detroit: Wayne State University Press, 1962), pp. 289–93.

[24] Sir Philip Sidney, *Defense of Poesie*, in Gilbert's *Literary Criticism*.

den in *An Essay of Dramatic Poesy*.[25] Finally, we will take a brief look at intellectual developments in the eighteenth century that begin to undermine the neoclassical complex of ideas about tragedy and that make way for theories of the sublime, whose impact on critical attitudes toward tragic conflict is far-reaching.

BEGINNING HIS WORK by stating an intention to determine what is in Aristotle's *Poetics* "concerning the universal precepts of poetry common to all nations or the greater part," Averröes delivers his most inclusive judgment in the opening formulation of his commentary. "Aristotle said: Every poem and all poetic speech are either blame [*vituperatio*] or praise [*laudatio*]. This is clear through examination of poems and those things that are proper to them, which deal with matters of choice, both good and base [*honestis et turpibus*]."[26] Prompted by a characteristic medieval belief in poetry's ethical function, Averröes proffers a theory of poetry as praise or blame, which echoes earlier works, such as Tiberius Claudius Donatus's *Interpretationes Virgilianae* and Fulgentius's *Expositio Virgilianae Continentiae Secundum Philosophos Moralis*.[27] But whereas these authors are concerned specifically with an apology of Virgilian epic, Averröes aims at a broad definition of the ars poetica. In developing his thesis, he apparently transposes Aristotle's remark in chapter 4, that the original poetic forms were encomia and lampooning verses, to chapter 1, and in the process elevates it into a categorical assertion about poetry in general. The definition stuck, as did its attribution to Aristotle; Roger Bacon and Thomas Aquinas refer to it approvingly, and a popular *Parviflores* by Marsiglio

---

[25] Pierre Corneille, *Trois Discours*, in *Corneille: Oeuvre complètes*, ed. André Stegmann (Paris: Seuil, 1963), pp. 821–46; John Dryden, *An Essay of Dramatic Poesy*, in Gilbert's *Literary Criticism*. On French neoclassical theory, see René Bray, *La formation de la doctrine classique en France* (Paris: Nizet, 1966).

[26] Averröes, *Commentarium Medium in Aristotelis Poetriam*, p. 3.

[27] See Hardison, *The Enduring Monument*, pp. 33–35.

of Padua dating from the early fourteenth century quotes it.[28] In Averröes' text, the introductory generalization entails a related series of contrasts. Insofar as all poetry is praise or blame, it treats subjects that fall into the category of either virtue or vice: "All action and character [*omnis enim actio et omnis mos*] are concerned with one of these two."[29] It follows from this, says Averröes, that "good and virtuous men represent only virtues and virtuous men, while bad men represent evil and evil men."[30] He subsequently identifies tragedy and the composers of tragic plays with the former and comedy and comic writers with the latter, specifying that the first group aims at encouragement of what is proper (*assecutio decentis*), while the second aims at rejection of what is base (*refutatio turpis*).

In this unfolding set of divisions, Averröes relies simultaneously on a firm sense of the absolute differentiation between good and bad, on the identifiability of different genres with the portrayal of one or the other, and on the edifiability of audiences presented with such clear-cut alternatives. The poetics that emerges from this view is both ethical and ethically normative. Value judgments are as integral to the work of the poet as they are to the responses of the spectators. Moreover, the integrity and stability of these judgments are ensured by an a priori confidence in the ontological validity of moral distinctions. For Averröes, poems are parts of a cosmos in which all things are hierarchized and so rendered meaningful. Praise and blame, as the functions of poetry, are understandable only within such a context, which binds subject matter, representation, and audience (*res, representatio*, and *auditor*) in close interrelation and parallel. This is another way of saying that such a theory posits the poem's content as continuous, on the one hand, with unambiguous virtue and vice in the real world and, on the other hand, with the unambiguous rhetorical ef-

---

[28] See Kelly, "Aristotle-Averröes-Alemannus on Tragedy," pp. 172–86.
[29] Averröes, *Commentarium Medium in Aristotelis Poetriam*, p. 7.
[30] Averröes, *Commentarium Medium in Aristotelis Poetriam*, p. 7.

fects of praising and blaming. Poems achieve what they represent, without equivocation. The "assimilative" tendencies in this theoretical configuration are impressive.[31] Indeed, the word for Aristotelian mimesis regularly used by Averröes is not *imitatio*, as one might expect, but *assimilatio*. The term is resonant. It suggests not only the relationship of suitability or agreement (*convenientia*) between *res* and *representatio* that allows for "true speech" and "right description," but also, from a rhetorical angle, the absorption of the audience as a complementary party into the world of the poem. The situation of a work of art vis-à-vis the object of representation and the receiving subject is not oppositional, confrontational, or agonistic. Artistically and ethically, the circuit of poetic experience assumes continuities and compatibilities. This is why poetic works could provide a basis for conduct and act as a repository of normative values to be emulated by an audience.

It is probably clear from the foregoing discussion that Averröes substitutes *consuetudo* and *credulitas* (corresponding to *ethos* and *dianoia*) for Aristotle's *muthos* as the "soul of tragedy."[32] He can therefore state that tragic poetry does not describe people as perceivable individuals (*individua cadentia in sensum*) but is instead "concerned with their honest customs, praiseworthy actions, and beatifying beliefs."[33] According to this position, tragic *consuetudo* exhorts to the performance of the praised action, and tragic *credulitas* exhorts to the belief in what is praised. Significantly, by insisting that tragic personages are paragons of virtue, Averröes not only departs from Aristotle's notion of the "middling agent" but also from the patristic strain of criticism that focuses on the theme of the fall of great princes. The ideal tragedy, in Averröes' commentary, presents disasters occurring to great persons *praeter merita ipsorum*, "beyond their fault." Notwithstanding the refer-

---

[31] On this aspect of Averröes' theory, see Allen, *The Ethical Poetic of the Later Middle Ages*, pp. 19–39, 179–229.

[32] Averröes, *Commentarium Medium in Aristotelis Poetriam*, pp. 19–20. Also see Allen, *The Ethical Poetic of the Later Middle Ages*, p. 26.

[33] Averröes, *Commentarium Medium in Aristotelis Poetriam*, p. 20.

ence to disaster, conflict seems to be barred from this conception of tragedy—in particular, psychological struggle or collisions that render doubtful the existence of an undisputable criterion for conduct. "It is fitting that the impression of reciting and representing speech in tragedy be the impression and image of one certain, not doubtful [*certi, non dubii*], and saying serious, not playful things; such are the speeches of men of the best character, thoughts, and actions. It is fitting that a recitation speak the deeds and fortunes of such as these."[34] Moreover, in achieving this effect, the dramatist must strive to make the *sermo imaginativus* as unquestionable an image of reality as possible. The fictional presentation should not be "ambiguous" and "based on doubtful material," or else it does not produce the pity and fear conducive to moral improvement.[35]

As with most of Averröes' formulations, these bind poet and audience in an experience of moral certitude from which the indeterminacy generated by conflict in tragedy has been eliminated. The fact that Averröes had no contact with Greek plays only partly accounts for his nonagonistic bias. The ethical context guiding theoretical statements in the commentary determines from the outset an orientation toward normative value judgments and nonoppositional, assimilative relationships between world, poem, and audience. This context, as we will see, continues to influence Renaissance criticism, even as Greek literature becomes more available and as contemporary dramatic practice builds momentum.

We might detect signs of attention to conflict in other parts of Averröes' theory. Notably, he developed an unusual interpretation of the Aristotelian *peripeteia* and *anagnorisis* as *circulatio* and *directio*, to use Hermannus's Latin renditions of the Arabic. By *circulatio*, he says in chapter 10, he means "imitation of the opposite of what is to be praised, so that at first the soul rejects and abhors it, and then there is a change from

---

[34] Averröes, *Commentarium Medium in Aristotelis Poetriam*, p. 18–19.
[35] Averröes, *Commentarium Medium in Aristotelis Poetriam*, Chap. 9.

this to the imitation of the very thing that is to be praised. Just as when one wants to imitate or represent happiness and things pertinent to it, he would begin first by imitation of unhappiness and things pertinent to it and then change to imitation of happiness and things pertinent to it. And he will do this through the opposite of what was represented as pertinent to unhappiness."[36] *Directio*, on the other hand, "treats the thing itself," without modulation. Averröes caps this discussion by noting that Aristotle regarded *directio* as more excellent when combined with *circulatio*. "Reversal," in this interpretation, is conformable with Averröes' general dictum that all poetry is either *laudatio* or *vituperatio*: he treats *circulatio* not as a sudden shift in the action from fortune to misfortune, but as a shift in poetic technique from blame to praise or vice versa. Since he elsewhere rejects a change in tragedy from the representation of virtue to the representation of vice,[37] he must mean to identify tragedy in chapter 10 with the former reversal of direction, that is, from blame to praise. While this view is not easily compatible with the one discussed earlier, which focuses on disasters occurring to great persons who do not merit them, Averröes does not seek to reconcile the two possibilities. What is interesting about the second view, for our purposes, is that it suggests the possibility of a conflict in the subject who experiences first the failure that is blamed and then the success that is praised. But Averröes does not elaborate, and whatever hints at struggle there may be in such a conception are muted and implicit. The picture that surfaces is one in which the tragic encomium of virtue is justified by a figure who has adapted himself to a rightful and stable ethical system. Recuperation of goodness is the desired and reachable end of tragedy. This ultimate state of affairs confirms the harmony of the world and the edifying powers of assimilation in tragedy.

While Averröes' treatment of *peripeteia* and *anagnorisis* is

---

[36] Averröes, *Commentarium Medium in Aristotelis Poetriam*, pp. 34–35.
[37] Averröes, *Commentarium Medium in Aristotelis Poetriam*, pp. 38–39.

idiosyncratic, his representation of Aristotle's general theory
of poetry as *laudatio* or *vituperatio* appealed not only to medieval but to Renaissance critics as well. Moreover, in assigning a moral purpose to poetry and an encomiastic intention to
tragedy in particular, he rendered the Greek text compatible
with the Horatian *utile*. This compatibility was apparently appreciated by Hermannus, who notes in his introduction to the
translation that considerable aid in understanding the *Poetics*
is provided by the *Ars Poetica* of Horace.[38] Thus, as early as
the twelfth and thirteenth centuries, the Aristotelian theory of
poetry was being imbued with rhetorical functions. For these
reasons, the Averröistic *Poetics Commentary* was frequently
appealed to by later critics, who found in its approach vali-
dation of the continuing effort to synthesize the two great authorities on literature from Greek and Roman antiquity. Let
us now turn to sixteenth-century discussions of tragedy with
a view to examining other ideas influencing the nonagonistic
orientation of dramatic theory.

BECAUSE RENAISSANCE VIEWS on tragedy, like Averröes' in the
Poetics Commentary, often emerge within treatises on poetry
in general, it is important to understand how broader conceptions of the ars poetica determine what might be said about an
individual form. In this vein, we can distinguish a popular notion of the poet current in the sixteenth and seventeenth centuries that is formative in shaping ideas about the status and
function of the tragedian. Repeatedly, the poet is portrayed as
a learned man, whose wisdom is integral to his excellence as a
writer. For example, in Minturno's *De poeta*, which appeared
in 1559, the combination of wisdom (*sapientia*) and eloquence (*eloquentia*) is considered the key to a special duty enjoyed by the poet—his role as civilizer of men.[39] Skilled in

---

[38] Averröes, *Commentarium Medium in Aristotelis Poetriam*, pp. 1–2.

[39] In this discussion of Minturno, I have been helped by Weinberg, "The
Poetic Theories of Minturno," in *Studies in Honor of Frederick W. Shipley*,
Washington University Studies in Language and Literature no. 14 (Lancaster,

speaking and steeped in knowledge, the poet appears as the great founder and consolidator of communal life. He converts savages into polite beings by imparting values necessary for the stability of the social group. His poetry, possessed of a special power, or *vis*, is variously described as instituting, exhorting, preserving, and enlightening. Poetic language, according to Minturno, is both foundational and conservative. Once it has generated order, it maintains what it has created by validating the civilizing virtues at its origin. Essentially, poetry is united with state and government, which is why Minturno classifies it in the branch of civil philosophy, whose aim is to teach youth how to rule properly. This classification is followed by many later critics, who concur with the view succinctly stated by Jason DeNores, that the duty of poetry, as a part of moral and civil philosophy, is "to direct all the arts and all doctrines to their true and proper end, that is, public utility and benefit."[40]

Minturno's ideas about the poet may also be traced both in Scaliger's *Poetices libri septem*, published posthumously in 1561, and later in Sidney's *Defense*, which is probably indebted to the two Italian critics for many of its positions. Thus we find Scaliger beginning his treatise with a description of the early function of speech and poetry that also emphasizes its foundational role in culture.

> Since man's development depended upon learning, he could not do without that agency which was destined to make him the partaker of wisdom. Our speech is, as it were, the postman of the mind, through the services of whom civil gatherings are announced, the arts are cultivated, and the claims

Penn.: Lancaster Press, 1942), pp. 101–29. See *De Poeta* (Venice, 1559), pp. 8–9.

[40] For this popular classification, see Weinberg, *History of Literary Criticism*, pp. 16–31. The quotation is cited by Weinberg, p. 27, and is from DeNores' *Discorso intorno a que' principii, cause, et accrescimenti, che la comedia, la tragedia, et il poema heroico ricevono della philosophia morale, et civile, et da' governatori delle republiche*, pp. 43–43v. Also see Hathaway, *Marvels and Commonplaces*, pp. 133–66.

of wisdom intercede with men for man. It is of course necessary to secure from others those things which we need, to
give orders to have things done, to prohibit, to propose, to
dispose, to establish, and to abolish. Such were the functions of early speech.[41]

Later, Scaliger says, the usefulness and effectiveness of language were increased by rules, measure, and proportional
construction, that is, with the development of the formal and
decorative principles specific to poetry and oratory. Once
again, we find that the poet, as a skilled manipulator of language, is highly instrumental in the formation and preservation of civil society.

Sidney, appropriating these earlier views, cites mythological
exempla to confirm the point that the poet "hath been the first
light-giver to ignorance, and first nurse, whose milk by little
and little enabled them [the noblest nations] to feed after-
wards of tougher knowledges."[42] Amphion, whose poetry
moved the stones that built Thebes, and Orpheus, whose music attracted beasts and "indeed stony and beastly people," are
offered as prototypes of the poet as civilizer and educator. In
the *Defense*, we find, in particular, the notion of the poet as a
learned man whose skilled eloquence produces works that are
a propaedeutic to more advanced study. His special ability to
impart knowledge and to lead his audience to desire
"tougher" matter is a result not only of his embellished, pleas-
ing language, but of his creative power to bring forth "another
nature," to range "within the zodiac of his own wit" and, by
"making things either better than nature bringeth forth, or,
quite anew," to deliver a "golden" rather than a "brazen"
world.[43] The poet as *sapiens*, or wise man, is thus closely related, in Sidney's discussion, with the poet as divine maker
(*poietes*), a kind of second deity, who fashions in the manner
of the "heavenly Maker." Probably borrowed from Scaliger,

[41] Scaliger, *Select Translations*, p. 1.
[42] Sidney, *Defense*, p. 407.
[43] Sidney, *Defense*, p. 412–13.

who also speaks of the poet as a second deity (*Deus alterus*), this complex of ideas relates the ordering and civilizing function of poetry in society with the ordering process inherent in poetic creation, which itself mirrors a divine activity.[44] Metaphysical, cultural, and literary order is deeply interconnected according to such a view.

Before drawing out the implications of these notions for a theory of tragedy, we would be helped by looking briefly at some of the major sources on which Minturno, Scaliger, and Sidney draw in developing their positions. The classical background for the model of the poet found in their treatises provides a way of understanding some of the broad antiagonistic strains running in Renaissance literary theory. A conception of the poet as learned (*doctus*) imitator underlies much of what Horace has to say in the *Ars Poetica*.[45] In a passage that obviously appealed to many later critics and that became a *locus classicus* for the Renaissance commonplace of the poet as learned civilizer, Horace says that *sapientia* in the old days of Orpheus and Ampion meant "to separate public from private matters, things sacred and common, to forbid promiscuous union, to provide rules for married people, to build towns, and to engrave laws on tablets."[46] Because the poets were the agents of these fundamental social dispensations, they won honor and the name of divine. The ancient connection of poetry with the origins of civilized life and with wisdom is reaffirmed in Horace's enjoinders to writers elsewhere in his epistle, for example, when he asserts: "Wisdom is the origin and fountainhead of good writing. Socratic works will be able to set subject matter before you, and words will naturally follow

---

[44] Scaliger, *Select Translations*, p. 8.

[45] On Horace's literary criticism, see C. O. Brink, *Horace on Poetry: Prolegomena to the Literary Epistles* (Cambridge: Cambridge University Press, 1963), pp. 222–25 on the *doctus imitator*; Wimsatt and Brooks, *Literary Criticism*, pp. 77–94.

[46] Horace, *Ars Poetica*, in *Opera*, ed. Edward Wickham and H. W. Garrod (Oxford: Clarendon Press, 1975), ll. 396–98.

the prepared matter."[47] Apart from the passing reference to
Socratic philosophy in this piece of advice, Horace is not particular about the nature of the poet's knowledge or the types
of learning with which he must be acquainted in order to attain excellence. As with so many other dicta in the *Ars Poetica*, the wisdom of the poet seems to be conceived vaguely in
terms of the audience and the need to impress them: the poet
must have enough familiarity with his subject matter to appear informed and be persuasive. In any case, despite the
vagueness, Horace's coupling of the poet's wisdom with his
civilizing, educative role is formative of Renaissance views.

But important as the *Ars Poetica* is in popularizing this
commonplace, the Roman rhetorical tradition, especially as it
is embodied by Cicero and Quintilian, is no less influential.
Horace himself is probably implementing an idea already established in rhetorical writings when he refers to the poet as
doctus imitator. For Cicero, in the *De Oratore* and the *Orator*,
had propounded a theory of the orator as a broadly educated
moral man skilled in speaking.[48] Moreover, he had set forth in
some detail the requirements for "knowledge," when he elaborated an educational program in the liberal arts (*artes dignae
libero*) essential for the production of an orator.[49] Focusing on
the necessity of instruction in philosophy (particularly logic,
psychology, and ethics), history, and civil law, Cicero followed Aristotle's lead in the *Rhetoric* in articulating fields of
study, which became central to Renaissance pedagogy and
which were used by sixteenth-century critics to supplement
Horace's general admonition to the poets about learning. This

[47] Horace, *Ars Poetica*, ll. 309–11.

[48] Cicero, *De Oratore*, ed. with notes by A. S. Wilkins (Amsterdam: Adolf
M. Hakkert, 1962), 1.2–3; *Orator*, in *M. Tulli Ciceronis Rhetorica*, ed. A. S.
Wilkins (Oxford: Clarendon Press, 1978), 2.7–3.13. This view appears even
earlier in the first book of *De Inventione*.

[49] This program is laid out in detail in various portions of *De Oratore* and
Orator; see *De Oratore* 1.5–6 for a summary. Also see G.M.A. Grube, "Educational, Rhetorical, and Literary Theory in Cicero," *Phoenix*, vol. 15, no.
4 (1962): 234–57, who stresses the Platonic and Aristotelian overtones in
Cicero's notion of the orator.

plea for a broadly based education reflects Cicero's rejection of the overly specialized training associated with the "workshops of the orators" (*officinae rhetorum*). Wisdom and virtue, he contends, are fundamental conditions of eloquence; and it is precisely this combination that is apparent in Cato, the orator, general, statesman, and moralist who, according to Cicero, did much to advance civilized values in ancient Rome and bring the nation out of barbarity. "In my view, no one can be an orator fully equipped with every merit, unless he has attained knowledge of all things important and of the arts. For his language must be adorned and enriched from knowledge. Unless there is matter grasped and understood by the orator, his speech has something empty about it and almost childish."[50] Defining rhetoric as "wisdom in speaking well and acting uprightly" (*sapientia bene dicendi et recte faciendi*), Cicero links knowledge, ethics, and eloquence in a way that leads to Quintilian's seminal formulation of the orator as a "good man skilled in speaking" (*vir bonus dicendi peritus*).[51] Indeed, this definition of the orator is Cato's, to whom Quintilian implicitly refers.

If, then, in Horace's *Ars Poetica* we see a trend toward adapting Ciceronian ideals of the orator to the poet, we find this trend elaborately developed in Renaissance criticism. Following the cinquecento norm of assimilating rhetorical and poetic ideas, Minturno, Scaliger, and Sidney all transfer Cicero's qualifications for a good orator to the poet. In the process, the case for making the poet out to be a forger of civilized values and a preserver of cultural order is strengthened and invested with greater classical authority. Often, as in Sidney's *Defense*, the preceding assumptions may be girded by the addition of a neo-Platonic conception of the poet as a divine maker. In this example of syncretism, the creative power of the artist—his ability to draw order out of matter—is another

[50] Cicero, *De Oratore*, 1.6.
[51] Quintilian, *Institutio Oratoria*, ed. M. Winterbottom, 2 vols.(Oxford: Clarendon Press, 1970), book 10.

factor underlying his efficacy in the social sphere. For the per-
fected world he gives us elicits the urge for perfection from our
"erected wit": once again, poetic order and cultural order are
complementary and mutually reinforcing.

In this amalgamation of classical views that compose the
popular Renaissance notion of the poet as civilizer, we encounter factors not conducive to an exploration of the agonistic side of tragedy. While it is true that the epic writer, according to most sixteenth-century critics, epitomizes the culturally
stabilizing function of poetry—epic is the favored genre of the
period—the tragedian is incorporated into the complex of
ideas with no special consideration given to the orientation of
his drama.[52] Without testing inherited ideas against contemporary literary productions, or for that matter against extant
classical plays, theorists predispose themselves to a position
about the status of tragedy in culture that renders the genre
conformable to traditional values, but only at the cost of mis-
representing its role vis-à-vis the social system. To insist on the
foundational and consolidating function of the poet in society
is to block ways of approaching the culture-questioning and
destabilizing moves of tragedy. Commonly revolving around
dramatizations of conflict, these moves testify to the oppositional role tragedy typically adopts in relation to dominant
sixteenth-century beliefs about the continuity of order and hierarchy in the universe. In the Renaissance, then, we find that
a theoretical premise about the relationship between drama
and order takes precedence over literary evidence and transforms that evidence into an affirmation of the very structures
it is subverting.

In the case of Sidney's *Defense*, what makes the culturally
stabilizing and ameliorating role attributed to tragedy particularly interesting is that it emerges within an agonistic context. The struggle in which the contemporary status of poetry
is mired appears at almost every turn of the treatise. From Sid-

[52] Sidney's preference for epic in the *Defense*, p. 434, is typical of Renaissance critics.

ney's opening remark, that he has "just cause to make a pitiful defense of poor Poetry," since even philosophers have defaced it, "with great danger of civil war among the Muses," through the apologetic arguments mustered progressively on behalf of poetry, we are made keenly aware of the conflict that has generated the *Defense*.[53] Sidney's attitude toward this situation is characteristically complex, modulating from a rhetorically heightened outrage at the assaults of dull-witted detractors to a shrewd albeit implicit sense of indebtedness to the dissent that has generated his response. Nonetheless, his aim is to neutralize the conflict by demonstrating that poetry espouses and confirms normative values. Sidney's theoretical temper is not unlike Averröes' or his many cinquecento predecessors': he highlights the assimilating powers of poetry through argumentative strategies that diffuse opposition and overcome the conflicts of criticism. This temper is no less apparent in the posture he adopts toward the extended comparison between philosophy, history, and poetry, about which I will say more shortly. Often formulating their interrelationship in oppositional terms, Sidney also presents poetry as a mediating entity that couples the precepts of philosophy with the exempla of history and thus transcends both in the excellence with which it achieves its end—to teach and beyond that to move people to virtuous action.[54] Poetry, one could say, is constituted as a nonagonistic phenomenon in the context of a critical desire to head off "civil war among the Muses" and to unite the stability of civil society with the instructive power of the *doctus imitator*.

This point brings us to another salient position in Renaissance theory. The concept of the poet as *doctus imitator* goes hand in hand with the notion that the end of poetry is to teach and please (*prodesse et delectare*). Taken from Horace, and a long medieval Christian tradition that espoused the dictum from the *Ars Poetica*, these ends were commonly assimilated

[53] Sidney, *Defense*, p. 407.
[54] Sidney, *Defense*, p. 430.

in the cinquecento to the three rhetorical duties (*officia ora-toris*) propounded by Cicero, namely, that oratory strives to teach, to please, and to move (*docere, delectare,* et *movere*).[55] In particular, we find that poems are expected to persuade in the way that a well-conceived argument, fitted out with adequate proofs, enthymemes, and maxims, can persuade. Poems, like speeches, are taken to have a point, a lesson, or a moral to impart, which is best conveyed when the rules for *inventio, dispositio,* and *elocutio* are observed.[56] The emphasis on persuasion and on adequate mastery of rhetorical *praecepta* is especially notable in the writings of Minturno and Scaliger, where the lines between oratory and poetry become so blurred that distinctions are usually impossible to draw. Witness Scaliger:

> Now is there not one end, and one only, in philosophical exposition, in oratory, and in the drama? Assuredly such is the case. All have one and the same end—persuasion; for, you see, just as we were saying above, whenever language is used it either expresses a fact or the opinion of the speaker. . . . Its end is to convince, or to secure the doing of something.[57]

I note that Scaliger's emphasis on the "one end" of persuasion does not prevent him from linking this *finis* with the Horatian *prodesse et delectare*. All three are interconnected, since an audience is taught only by being convinced of what is presented to it. Pleasure, it seems, facilitates the process of persuasion; it is a sugarcoating that helps the medicine go down.

While Sidney avoids strict insistence on rules and rhetorical parts, he nonetheless, like many of his Italian predecessors, tends to conceive of poetry or the plot of a drama, for exam-

[55] On this conflation, see Weinberg, *History of Literary Criticism*, pp. 150–52, 805–6, and "Theories of Minturno," pp. 106–8; Charles S. Baldwin, *Renaissance Literary Theory and Practice*, ed. with intro. by Donald Leman Clark (New York: Columbia University Press, 1939), pp. 155–89.

[56] See Weinberg, *History of Literary Criticism*, pp. 66–68.

[57] Scaliger, *Select Translations*, p. 3.

ple, as an argument, in which a moral precept or truth is decorated in the "fittest raiment" and applied to a particular case, in order to move the spectator to right action. Once again, the rhetorical *officium* of persuasion is indirectly applied to poetry, where it supposedly catalyzes the audience's performance of virtuous deeds. Unlike the philosopher, says Sidney, who sets down "with thorny argument the bare rule," the poet takes "whatsoever the philosopher saith should be done" and "giveth a perfect picture of it in someone by whom he presupposeth it was done; so as he coupleth the general notion with the particular example."[58] At the heart of the poem is a moral exemplum, designed to be implemented in human life.

This point brings us to a central concept in Sidney's *Defense*, one that enjoyed substantial currency in the Renaissance—namely, that poetry is a speaking picture. By fusing a moral abstraction with the image of an actual character and setting, it supples a tangible, visualizable embodiment of a universal ethical rule.[59] If philosophy and history are identifiable with *gnosis* and *praxis*, respectively, poetry unites both and consequently better achieves the end of moving its audience to virtue. Knowledge, in short, is not the sufficient telos of the arts; ethically enlightened action is. "And that moving is of a higher degree than teaching, it may by this appear, that it is well-nigh the cause and the effect of teaching. For who will be taught, if he be not moved with desire to be taught, and what so much good doth that teaching bring (I speak still of moral doctrine) as that it moveth one to do that which it doth teach? For, as Aristotle saith, it is not *gnosis* but *praxis* must be the fruit."[60] Like Averröes' theory of *assimilatio*, Sid-

---

[58] Sidney, *Defense*, p. 420–21.

[59] Sidney, *Defense*, pp. 414, 420–22. On this aspect of Sidney's poetic theory, see Forrest G. Robinson, *The Shape of Things Known: Sidney's Apology in Its Philosophical Tradition* (Cambridge, Mass.: Harvard University Press, 1972), pp. 97–122; Andrew D. Weiner, *Sir Philip Sidney and the Poetics of Protestantism: A Study of Contexts* (Minneapolis: University of Minnesota Press, 1978), pp. 28–50.

[60] Sidney, *Defense*, pp. 426–27.

ney's rhetorical configuration of *docere, delectare,* and *movere* assumes continuities between the poetic object of imitation (moral exempla), the medium (decorous, well-balanced, proportionate language), and the receiving subject (man's "erected wit"). Within such a circuit of causality, poetry is conceived predominantly in images of assimilation and digestion: "The poet is the food for the tenderest stomachs, the poet is indeed the right popular philosopher";[61] he "ever setteth virtue so out in her best colors . . . that one must needs be enamoured of her";[62] he "doth not only show the way, but giveth so sweet a prospect into the way, as will entice any man to enter into it."[63] Whereas philosophy is "harsh and disputative" in its methods and history susceptible of misleading an audience in its overly particular orientation toward action, poetry is not only edifying but conciliatory as well.

The nonagonistic bias toward poetry is again unmistakable in Sidney's attitudes and language. But as I have noted in a different context, conflict is only barely suppressed in his discussion of the poet and the audience. While the poet, "ranging in the zodiac of his own wit," sets forth a golden world that appeals to our better self, our "infected will" keeps us from reaching what we know to be good.[64] In this passage and elsewhere, Sidney seems committed to a neo-Platonic sense that the final end of poetry "is to lead and draw us to as high a perfection as our degenerate souls, made worse by their clayey lodgings, can be capable of."[65] Mired in the prison house of the body, the soul is inevitably engaged in a struggle for excellence, since it resists the urges of passion only with difficulty and submits itself to moral instruction reluctantly. It is very telling, however, that Sidney does not showcase such moral battles in the *Defense.* Particularly when differentiating poetry from disputative philosophy, he centers on poetry's gentle

[61] Sidney, *Defense,* p. 423.
[62] Sidney, *Defense,* p.425.
[63] Sidney, *Defense,* p. 427.
[64] Sidney, *Defense,* pp. 413–14.
[65] Sidney, *Defense,* p. 417.

powers of amelioration, its tendency to assuage rather than exacerbate conflict. This point is crucial, for it indicates Sidney's typically Renaissance propensity to mobilize the relationship between philosophy, history, and poetry, not in the interests of foregrounding and investigating conflict, as Hegel did, for example, but with a view to suppressing it while emphasizing the virtues of poetic assimilation.

Because the Horatian ends of poetry and the *officia oratoris* are firmly established in the medieval tradition and the early cinquecento before the revival of Aristotle's *Poetics*, the challenge, once the Greek text resurfaces, is to reconcile it with the didactic function assumed for poetry. Notwithstanding the absence of a doctrine of moral instruction in the *Poetics*, Renaissance critics effectively draw one from it. Typically, the *katharsis* clause is adapted to the Horatian *prodesse* and interpreted morally. As early as the commentaries of Robortello and Maggi, we find both homeopathic and allopathic theories of *katharsis* propagated. Drawn by the rhetorical premise of utility in poetry, Robortello views *katharsis* as a purging of pity and fear by means of pity and fear, while Maggi thinks that pity and fear, themselves good emotions, remove other perturbations, such as wrath, avarice, and luxury, from the soul.[66] These two theories stand at the beginning of a long debate about a tantalizingly brief clause in the *Poetics*, which continues today. In either case, Aristotle is taken as advancing a theory of moral purgation, which supports the Horatian and Ciceronian notion of rhetorical *utile* as inducement to virtuous living. Despite the fundamental differences separating the *Poetics* from the Latin rhetorical tradition, Renaissance critics proceed in their interpretation as if the two complement and reinforce each other, especially on the didactic function of poetry.

[66] Robortello, *De Arte Poetica Explicationes*, pp. 53, 102, quoted and discussed by Weinberg, "Robortello on the *Poetics*," in *Critics and Criticism: Ancient and Modern*, ed. R. S. Crane et al. (Chicago: University of Chicago Press, 1952), pp. 322–23; Maggi, *De Poetica Communes Explanationes*, p. 98, quoted and discussed by Weinberg, *History of Literary Criticism*, p. 408.

The impact of these views about morality and teaching on Renaissance conceptions of tragedy is far-reaching. Generally, the orientation produces a sense of tragedy as a propositional and affirmative mode of discourse. Possessed of a moral precept that it sets forth charmingly and persuasively, a drama is typically regarded as declaring a universal truth, in language embellished with ornaments that ensure its acceptance by an audience. Central to this conception is an implicit belief in the unity and stability of ethical values supposedly advanced by the dramatic *argumentum*. Right action is understood unproblematically, as a standard discernible and practicable through the proper application of the rational faculty; "well knowing and well doing," to use Sidney's expression, are mutually dependent.[67] If characters within a play are not themselves good examples of reason aimed at virtue, then negative examples may exhort the spectator to right living by demonstrating the miserable consequences of inadequate deliberation, or overreaching, or whatever other personal flaw could be adduced in explaining disaster. The downfall of an important personage in tragedy, in other words, is attributable to a sin or a "tyrannical humor," which sets the hero at odds with an objective order. Those who, in achieving worldly prosperity, become complacent and unguarded about their exercise of power ride for a fall. In a formulation that is strikingly medieval in its spirit of *contemptus mundi*, Sidney notes that tragedy "teacheth the uncertainty of this world, and upon how weake foundations guilden roofs are builded."[68] The lesson for an audience lies in perceiving the punishment of exemplary figures in high places, whose lapse from success is a consequence of being out of tune with a more inclusive system, a chain of being that both fixes and sustains moral norms. Thus the tradition of tragedy summed up in *de casibus virorum illustrium* as well as the tradition exemplified in Averröes' concept of good men who suffer disaster *praeter merita ipsorum*

[67] Sidney, *Defense*, p. 418.
[68] Sidney, *Defense*, p. 432.

both assume the unequivocality of virtue. Whether tragedy is the art of blame or praise, it fits into an ontologically secure scheme of value. While conflict may be indirectly or briefly acknowledged in these conceptions, neither features it as a defining element of the genre.

Christian influence on these views of tragedy is probably apparent, but we should also note the impact of Stoic philosophy on the idea that one is equipped to know and act upon what is virtuous. Renaissance ethical theory commonly adapts to Christian theology the Stoic maxim "virtue is nothing other than right reason" (*virtus non aliud quam ratio recta est*).[69] While Seneca is an important figure in this synthesis, so too are the highly eclectic Plutarch and Cicero, the latter of whom devoted the fifth book of *De Finibus* to a demonstration of the similarities between Academic, Peripatetic, and Stoic ethics. This "Platonizing stoicism," as it has been called, is taken over by some of the most representative early Renaissance humanists, including Erasmus and Sir Thomas More.[70] In their works and others, we find a broad and unspecialized notion of *ratio recta* as "that which bindeth creatures reasonable in this world and with which by reason they most plainly perceive themselves to be bound."[71] Both epistemological and practical, right reason not only grasps the hierarchy of values established by divine plan in the universe, but also conforms a person's behavior to the perception of this structure; it enables the individual to gain access to moral truth and to implement it in his life. Within such a conceptual framework, lapses from

[69] Seneca, *Ad Lucilium Epistulae Morales*, ed. L. D. Reynolds (Oxford: Clarendon Press, 1965), 61.33 and 76.22. For a discussion of the Stoic conception of *ratio recta* and its influence on Renaissance ethics, see Robert Hoopes, *Right Reason in the English Renaissance* (Cambridge, Mass.: Harvard University Press, 1962), pp. 33–45, 123–45, and Haydn, *The Counter-Renaissance*, pp. 27–67. For the influence of Stoicism on Renaissance theories of tragedy, see von Fritz, "Tragische Schuld und poetische Gerechtigkeit in der griechischen Tragödie," in *Antike und Moderne Tragödie*, pp. 32–52.

[70] Haydn, *The Counter-Renaissance*, p. 55.

[71] Richard Hooker, *Of the Laws of Ecclesiastical Polity*, ed. Ronald Bayne (Everyman ed.), 1.2.3, quoted by Haydn, *The Counter-Renaissance*, p. 39.

virtuous behavior suggest a bluntness or failure of reason for which the agent is responsible. The good person knows and acts unambiguously. This Stoic ability of shaping one's life to moral truth does not necessarily exclude conflict. But when Marcus Aurelius, for example, states that the end of human life is a tranquillity, or *ataraxia*, to be achieved within a tension of moral opposites, he is speaking of a peace experienced when one does what one knows is just.[72] Conflict is neutralized because *ratio recta*—or *to hegemonikon*, that which leads—can and does impose a standard. And on this standard the value of human conduct stands or falls. Virtue, accordingly, is often defined in Stoic terms as "consistency in life, an even steady course of action, self-consistency, a principle in agreement with its applications. The opposite of virtue is the unending restlessness and indecision of the man in the crowd."[73]

The Stoic doctrine of right reason and its Renaissance adaptations share some essential points with Aristotle's definition of *to spoudaion*, discussed in the last chapter, and its foundations in the principle of right reason (*orthos logos*). In particular, both positions treat virtue and goodness as synonymous with a condition of peace and propriety of conduct, attainable through the exercise of the rational faculty and the implementation of its dictates. But the bias of Aristotle's ethics against conflict does not affect his dramatic theory in the same way as Stoic or sixteenth-century Christian ideas influence formulations of tragedy. Admittedly, the notion of *spoudaiotes* militates against an agonistic view of tragic action. This notion, however, is introduced into the *Poetics* to serve

[72] Marcus Aurelius Antoninus, *The Communings with Himself, Together with his Speeches and Sayings*, Greek text with tr. by C. R. Haines (1916; reprint, Cambridge, Mass.: Harvard University Press, 1961), 6.1–12, 7.48, and 12.1–22.

[73] E. Vernon Arnold, *Roman Stoicism: Being Lectures on the History of the Stoic Philosophy with Special Reference to Its Development within the Roman Empire* (1911; reprint, London: Routledge and Kegan Paul, 1958), p. 282.

the aesthetic requirement that only characters of the better
sort, the *spoudaioi*, can arouse the emotions of pity and fear,
and characters of the better sort are not, in Aristotelian ethical
terms, mired ineluctably in struggle. The ethical side of the
Poetics does not buttress a didactic argument about the ends
of tragedy. On the other hand, the ethical component in Renaissance attitudes reinforces an overtly moral purpose—to differentiate virtue from vice, for an audience expecting a lesson
in proper conduct.

Foreclosed in theories of tragedy centered on the doctrine of
instruction is an approach to plays as open-ended explorations of crises and struggles, as interrogative forms that test
traditional values, along with assumptions about normative
order on which they are based, without offering rational solutions or adhering to conventions of poetic justice. The didactic *officium* attributed to tragedy is conservative to the
core. Even among later English neoclassical critics as diverse
as Ben Jonson, Thomas Rymer, and John Dryden, who write
during or after the great heyday of dramatic activity in the late
sixteenth and early seventeenth centuries, we find efforts to
consolidate a complex of ideas about order and moral determinacy that is disturbingly fractured in the plays of Marlowe,
Shakespeare, and the Jacobeans.

If the poet as *doctus imitator* is invested with the function
of pleasurably teaching an audience, there are different means,
according to Renaissance critics, through which he accom-
plishes this end. Despite the variety of instruments at the
poet's disposal, it would be fair to say that they are without
exception related within a more general controlling framework—the doctrine of decorum. Organizing all elements of
poetry around the concepts of appropriateness and congruity,
decorum assumes normative and fixed relationships between
human status, experience, and expression that become the
ground for propriety in art. According to the doctrine, a fundamental concern of the writer is to adapt character traits to
character, values to types, diction to subject matter, and style
to genre. There is not only a proper, but an ideal form for

every kind of content. That this is so follows from a premise about the natural world and the order of creation: everything has its place as well as its function within an all-embracing, well-articulated system. A passage from George Puttenham's *The Arte of English Poesie* (1589) affirms the connection between literary decorum and the *ordo mundi*:

> This lovely conformitie or proportion, or conveniencie, between the sence and the sensible hath nature her selfe most carefully observed in all her owne workes, then also by kinde graft it in the appetites of every creature working by intelligence to covet and desire, and in their actions to imitate and performe; and of man chiefly before any other creature aswell in his speaches as in every other part of his behavior. And this in generalitie and by an usuall terme is that which the Latines call *decorum*.[74]

Once again, as in the case of other Renaissance critical doctrines, this one is consolidated through appropriations of not only Latin authors, as Puttenham suggests, but of Greek authors, too, namely, Aristotle and Plato.

Decorum, of course, is a pivotal idea in Horace's *Ars Poetica* and informs virtually every criterion for excellence that he sets forth.[75] Though the concept is perhaps more affectively and socially oriented in his discussion than in typical Renaissance treatments, where rhetorical considerations are often explicitly made to rest on natural order, it nonetheless typologizes form and content in a fairly rigorous system of congruences. Adherence to convention and to the familiar is basic in Horace's view of decorum. Only by conforming style, character, and subject matter to popular expectations will the writer meet with success. Thus, in the case of tragedy, the

---

[74] *Elizabethan Critical Essays*, ed. Smith, vol. 2, p. 174. Chaps. 23 and 24 in Puttenham's treatise are worth reading in full. For a discussion of the Renaissance doctrine of decorum, see Herrick, *The Fusion of Horatian and Aristotelian Literary Criticism*, pp. 48–57, and Weinberg, *History of Literary Criticism*, pp. 71–72, 804–8.

[75] See Wimsatt and Brooks, *Literary Criticism*, pp. 80–91.

playwright must note the manners of each age and match temperament with years; not bring on stage revolting sights best transacted behind the scenes; structure his play in five acts, a length perspicuous and engaging; not allow a *deus ex machina*, unless a complication develops necessitating its appearance; present the chorus as a group of friendly counselors, seasoned in traditional wisdom; and so forth.[76] Such admonitions to the dramatist come to form the core of "the rules" for tragedy, refined in the Renaissance and codified in the seventeenth century, particularly by the French.[77] According to this way of thinking, the aim of poetry is to satisfy, settle, and appease spectatorly expectations. The position of the poet vis-à-vis the audience and its standards is affirmative and nonoppositional.

Central to Horace's understanding of poetry, decorum is no less important a notion in early Latin rhetorical theory, where it is given exemplary formulation by Cicero in the *Orator*. Supplying a Greek philosophical background for the doctrine, Cicero demonstrates how the concept of form, or *eidos*, which is basically hostile to art in the Platonic system, had by his own time developed a popular literary application.

> Truly, when that great artist [Phidias] was making a statue of Jove or Minerva, he was not looking at a person from whom he derived his likeness, but in his mind there resided a certain surpassing image of beauty, gazing intently upon which he directed his skill and his hand in producing a likeness of it. Therefore, just as there is something perfect and excellent in statues and figures, an intelligible form by imitation of which things not visible are represented, so too do we see in our mind the form of perfect eloquence. These forms of things Plato, that most eminent writer and teacher

---

[76] Horace, *Ars Poetica*, ll. 153–201.

[77] Bray, in *Formation de la doctrine classique en France*, pp. 59–61, underestimates this influence by focusing too exclusively on the cult of Aristotle, which is undoubtedly strong but conditioned pervasively by earlier assimilations of Horace.

of thinking and speaking, calls ἰδέας, and these he says do not come into being but they always exist and are contained in our reason and intellect; other things come into existence, die, are in flux, pass away, and do not stay long in the same state. Therefore, whatever is to be discussed rationally and methodically must be reduced to the ultimate form and type of its class.[78]

In the minds of most Renaissance critics, what holds good for the rational and methodical discussion of oratory is no less applicable to art. This passage from Cicero underscores an important complicity between the doctrine of decorum and a notion of poetry as ideal representation, based on exemplary models and experiences from which the vagaries of quotidian life have been eliminated. The influence of his thinking is apparent in Sidney's golden world and its many contemporary parallels, where nature is "wrought up to a higher pitch" at the same time that morality is heightened and universalized.[79] In a formulation remarkably similar to Cicero's, Sidney tells us that "the skill of the artificer standeth in that idea or foreconceit of the work, and not in the work itself. And that the poet hath that idea is manifest by delivering them forth in such excellency as he hath imagined them."[80] It is quite likely that a vaguely neo-Platonist view such as this, linked with Horace's more pragmatic, socially oriented dicta, shaped the specific Renaissance literary canons of decorum, which were frequently bound up, as the preceding quotation from Puttenham implies, with an objective and ideal *ordo naturalis*. Pagan and Christian philosophical ideas converge to generate a lit-

[78] Cicero, *Orator*, 2.8–3.10.

[79] Baxter Hathaway, *The Age of Criticism: The Late Renaissance in Italy* (Ithaca: Cornell University Press, 1962), pp. 144 ff. Other useful discussions of poetic ideality are by R. D. Stock, *Samuel Johnson and Neoclassical Dramatic Theory* (Lincoln: University of Nebraska Press, 1973), pp. 29–56; Walter Jackson Bate, *From Classic to Romantic: Premises of Taste in Eighteenth-Century England* (1945; reprint, New York: Harper and Row, 1961), chapter 1.

[80] Sidney, *Defense*, p. 413.

erary concept that again affirms a symmetry between the order of art and an objective, divinely instituted order.

For sixteenth-century critics, Aristotle's *Poetics* was a text that refined and further developed standards of artistic propriety, already more or less established in critical discussions of poetry. For example, ideas about the perfectability of form in poetry, and about the particular rules for realizing this perfectability, are girded by Aristotle's dictum in the *Physics* that "in general art completes the things which nature is unable to finish and imitates them."[81] This conception takes form to be an indwelling dynamic purpose or entelechy in the poetic object, a principle directing the whole to an end. If, according to Aristotle, a thing is properly said to be what it is when it has attained to fulfillment rather than when it exists potentially, then poetic art may be said to realize the potency contained in its raw material, by bringing human actions to their *telos* within the guiding structure of a *muthos*.[82] One of the most crucial principles articulated in the *Poetics* for securing this entelic unity is likelihood or necessity.

In the Renaissance, the principle is frequently taken to be an admonition about conformity to rules of decorum, with the end of convincing and moving an audience. If, for example, characters in a play are like their counterparts in nature and society, they will be more persuasive and hence consequential in teaching. As Bernard Weinberg points out, "Aristotle's requirements of 'necessity' and 'probability' were thought to pertain, not to conditions of the action as represented, but to conditions of real actions chosen as the objects of imitation. That is, the action as an object in life must be verisimilar, probable, convincing, natural. Insofar as the poem reflected the 'verisimilitude' and the 'probability' and the natural necessities of actions known to the audience, it would produce the impression of reality."[83] Thus, Aristotle is made into an ex-

---

[81] Aristotle, *Physics*, 199a15–17.
[82] Aristotle, *Physics*, 2.1.
[83] Weinberg, *History of Literary Criticism*, p. 800.

plicit proponent of the view that decorum in art assumes a preexisting decorum in the structure of reality. As in the case of many other Aristotelian ideas, so too with likelihood and necessity: formal criteria are treated as rhetorical rules, which predicate a congruity between the natural and the poetic as a condition for persuading and instructing an audience. While a parallel between the natural and the poetic certainly informs Aristotle's thinking in the *Poetics*, it is a parallel, as I have suggested, based on the notion of two kinds of processes, whose direction is structured by an indwelling form particular to the object. Because poetry can bring this process to completion in an efficient and perspicuous manner, through the implementation of likelihood or necessity, it may be said to improve on nature. But Aristotle does not have a static conception of "verisimilar" objects as types or preconceived ideas that the poet seizes upon; nor is believability (*to pithanon*) secured in his mind through such simple appropriations. To interpret Aristotle in this fashion is to superimpose on the "probability or likelihood" of the *Poetics* a kind of watered down version of the Platonic ideas, as a system of classifiable, immutable things—a wise king, a pious prophet, a courageous general—to which the characters and actions of poetry correspond.

The tendency to appropriate Aristotle in this vein is also discernible in the way Renaissance critics frequently take over the requirements for ethos listed in *Poetics* 15: that it be *chreston, harmotton, homoion*, and *homalon*. Trying to bring these criteria in line with Horace's *Ars Poetica*, sixteenth-century interpreters reinforce their predisposition toward a normative, conventional approach to poetry and to tragedy, in particular, the genre in connection with which Aristotle developed his theoretical views. Thus, we find Robortello translating *to chreston* as *probitas* and arguing, in a didactic spirit, for the elimination of wicked characters from tragedy.[84] We have al-

---

[84] Robortello, *De Arte Poetica Explicationes*, pp. 167–69, quoted and discussed by Weinberg, "Robortello on the *Poetics*," pp. 332–33.

ready seen that Renaissance critics had available in Aristotle's *katharsis* clause a way of moralizing bad characters; but Robortello's emphasis embodies a strain of thinking that tries to debar turpitude and vice of any sort from drama. Moreover, he believes the requirement of *probitas* involves the establishment of a set of typical characteristics appropriate to persons of different social stations, genders, ages, and so forth: goodness has a basis in cultural norms. *Convenientia*, or *to harmotton*, refers even more specifically to status. Robortello understands the term according to the Latin rhetorical tradition, which derives from the particular circumstances surrounding a person a complex of traits that necessarily and suitably characterizes him. If *convenientia* is tied to social considerations, *similitudo* or *to homoion* refers to consistency of character in relation to a traditional conception inherited from past writers—in short, literary convention. Finally, *aequabilitas*, Robortello's translation of *to homalon*, refers to constancy of character especially in the case of a newly invented figure, for which the poet does not have recourse to tradition; consistency is crucial in the case of innovation, when the audience's scrutiny will be especially keen and prone to criticism of anomalies. In every instance, parallels for Aristotle's four requirements of ethos are adduced from Horace's *Ars Poetica*. This procedure of cross-reference is typical of Robortello and of the many cinquecento critics after him, who may have come up with different interpretations of ethos, but who nonetheless syncretized Aristotelian and Horatian views to produce their peculiarly rhetorical and didactic versions of dramatic character and action.

In general, then, the doctrine of decorum establishes a set of laws for tragedy, whose authority resides in the supposed fact that they mirror a precedent order, either social or universal in scope, but in both cases sanctioned, if only implicitly, by an official culture. Imitation of ideal nature converges with imitation of classical *auctoritates*. Stipulations about generic integrity, dramatic unities of time, place, and action, the five-act structure, conventionalized characters all proceed from the assumption of an *ordo naturalis*, to which one is enabled to accommodate oneself through the observation of decorum in dramatic works. There is a purposeful circularity at work in this conception. Poetic laws drawn from a larger order in turn validate that order, by leading spectators to greater appreciation of and conformity to it.

To sum up, decorum, being firmly rooted in a sense of the universe as a well-balanced, harmonious system, is antithetical to what I have been calling the culture-questioning, explorative orientation of Renaissance drama. Plays by the English tragedians, in particular, repeatedly undermine assumptions about proprieties of rank, congruences between status and function, and equations of human experience with conventional styles or linguistic form. In the Renaissance concept of appropriateness, we have yet another example of a critical doctrine, whose authority both Christian and classical sources affirm, promulgated in the face of abundant challenges from the dramatic evidence. Tragic conflict puts in doubt precisely that hierarchical stability which rules of decorum take as normative.

As we pass from the general principles of Renaissance dramatic theory to the nature and ramifications of conflict in contemporary tragedies, I emphasize that sixteenth-century critics tend to think of form, content, and affect in reciprocal, mutually reinforcing ways. This integral relationship is epitomized, of course, in the doctrine supported almost unanimously by critics from Robortello to Pope: poetry's end is to teach pleasingly. Though emphasis is variously laid on one or the other element of this precept, the result is still by and large to affirm that formal organization elicits a particular effect.[85] Orderly arrangement of parts mirrors objective order, and both in turn are conditions for an audience's education in moral rectitude. Thus, as the didactic imperative imposed on

[85] On the complicity of formal order and moral utility, see Hathaway, *Age of Criticism*, pp. 129–70.

tragedy requires a coherent, clearly delineated ethical system in terms of which vice and virtue may be gauged, so too does the Renaissance aesthetic of form require a unified, closed structure whose integrated parts strengthen the feeling of finality, completion, and composure.[86] Instruction in the stability of moral values and the formal sense of an ending are intimately related as aesthetic ideals. This understanding of form and content as complementary raises yet another way in which theory collides with dramatic practice in the period we are discussing. The subversion of values in tragic plays is often attended by fragmentations of structure or unsettling manipulations of strategies for closure. In Renaissance dramas by Marlowe and Shakespeare and in Jacobean plays by Webster, Tourneur, and Chapman, the testing of traditional values is carried out through various techniques of structural dislocation. If, as I have claimed, the orientation of sixteenth-century criticism excludes tragic conflict, it also obstructs an appreciation of iconoclastic and agonistic formal devices. In both cases, the principles of theory advance a set of dramatic conventions that are typically points of departure for the more radical moves of tragedy.

Marlowe's *Doctor Faustus* is a useful testing ground for some of these points, because it consistently engages both standard Christian doctrine and conventional dramatic form, only to subvert them or implicate them in a dense web of ambiguities.[87] At the outset, it seems that the story of the destruc-

---

[86] See Barbara Herrnstein Smith, *Poetic Closure: A Study of How Poems End* (Chicago: University of Chicago Press, 1968).

[87] This discussion of *Doctor Faustus* relies on a number of recent scholarly works, notably Max Bluestone, *"Libido Speculandi*: Doctrine and Dramaturgy in Contemporary Interpretations of Marlowe's *Doctor Faustus*," in *Reinterpretations of Elizabethan Drama*, ed. Norman Rabkin (New York: Columbia University Press, 1969), pp. 33–88; Wilbur Sanders, "Marlowe's *Doctor Faustus*," *MCR* 7 (1964): 78–91; Marjorie Garber, " 'Infinite Riches in a Small Room': Closure and Enclosure in Marlowe," in *Two Renaissance Mythmakers: Christopher Marlowe and Ben Jonson*, ed. Alvin Kernan, Selected Papers from the English Institute, 1975– 1976, n.s., no. 1 (Baltimore: Johns Hopkins University Press, 1977), pp. 3–21; Stephen Greenblatt, "Mar-

tion of a man, who willingly contracts with the devil in an effort to gain "a world of profit and delight, / of power, of honor, and omnipotence" (1.1.54–55) and who is damned in the end for doing so, is apt material for a morality drama.[88] Faustus's demise is a suitable punishment for one who transgresses human limits and spurns the efficacy of Christian redemption. Renaissance critics would have found confirmation of this didactic reading in the homiletic choral frame of the play: while the prologue speaks of a man whom "the heavens conspired to overthrow" for mounting "above his reach" (21–22), the epilogue makes summarizing reference to the "hellish fall" of Faustus, "whose fiendful fortune may exhort the wise, / Only to wonder at unlawful things / Whose deepness doth entice such forward wits / To practice more than heavenly power permits". Such a view of Faustus's decline can find support in various elements of the play as well, but at the same time it adapts the dramatic action to a thesis, a moral assertion that ignores the disturbing questions about doctrinal beliefs raised in the course of the protagonist's career and that bypasses the haunting ambiguities suspended rather than resolved at the end of the play.

Marlowe's strategy in employing a choral framework whose perspective forces the *praxis* into a preconceived traditional formula is not unlike Thomas Kyd's in *The Spanish Tragedy*.[89] The inadequacy of a moralistic reading is anticipated within the drama itself, where the platitudinous certainties on which it resides are made to clash with the far more unsettling, problematic termination of the action. In this juxtaposition of the didactically assertive and subversively interrogative modes, Marlowe provides an insight into a broader dynamic operative in the Renaissance: the voice of the official

---

lowe and Renaissance Self-Fashioning," also in *Two Renaissance Mythmakers*, pp. 41–69.

[88] Citations are from the edition of the play by Russell A. Fraser and Norman Rabkin in *Drama of the English Renaissance*, 2 vols. (New York: Macmillan, 1976), vol. 1.

[89] For a different view, see Altman, *The Tudor Play of Mind*, pp. 372, 384.

culture, in this case the chorus, with its emphasis on normative categories for evaluating human experience, tries to bring tragedy into the orbit of the conventional, by appropriating its unorthodoxies within a neutralizing context, namely the doctrine of sin and repentance. But we are enabled to grasp the ideological nature of such an appropriation by its very insufficiency as an account of the tragic action.

The pervasive enigmas in *Doctor Faustus* begin in the prologue, whose apparently homiletic edge is blunted in a variety of ways, most notably perhaps by a phrase that suggests from the outset an inherent ambivalence in the spectacle about to be staged.[90] In referring to Faustus's fortunes "good or bad," the chorus not only implicitly puts in question the determinacy of moral judgment, but also anticipates a disjunction between Christian and secular appreciations of the play. The obsessive restlessness and the impatient urge to break through boundaries that characterize Faustus's conduct throughout Marlowe's drama are simultaneously the conditions for a Christian abjuration of his actions and a secular or aesthetic capacity to admire, if only at a distance, the hero's remarkably voracious will to power. The incompatibility and yet viability of both frames of reference are pressed on an audience in the first scenes of the drama, where Faustus's skeptical rejection of the traditional disciplines of logic, medicine, law, and divinity appears to be a positive liberation from stifling orthodoxies that repress humanity at the same time that it elicits fear about the dangers of denying such institutional instruments of salvation as theology. Marlowe's tragedy, however, does not allow us to fix on a perspective in which these divergent judgments could merge to form a unitary interpretation. Neither the heroic nor the Christian framework is negated in *Doctor Faustus*, and neither, on the other hand, assumes unequivocal privilege; they are both suspended in irresolvable counterpoint. Moreover, what constitutes Christian and heroic value is itself rendered ambiguous in the dramatic action, and con-

[90] See Bluestone, "*Libido Speculandi*," pp. 33–36.

sequently the criteria for evaluating Faustus within each perspective are also destabilized.

Uncertainties surrounding various aspects of Christian doctrine proliferate in the play and render conventional moral interpretations difficult. For our purposes, we can focus briefly on an issue that has particularly unsettled audiences and critics: whether the opportunity for repentance is excluded from the time of Faustus's pact with Mephistophilis.[91] Mephistophilis claims that it is, and Faustus often acquiesces in this view:

> FAUSTUS: Why, dost thou think that Faustus shall be
>   damned?
> MEPHISTOPHILIS: Ay, of necessity, for here's the scroll
> In which thou hast given thy soul to Lucifer.
> FAUSTUS: Ay, and body too.
>
> (2.1.129–32)

On the other hand, standard Christian doctrine holds out for the possibility of efficacious repentance until man's death. As the good angel continually reminds Faustus, and as the old man says in act 5, when time is running out:

> Though thou hast now offended like a man,
> Do not persever in it like a devil;
> Yet, yet, thou hast an amiable soul,
> If sin by custom grow not into nature.
>
> (5.1.42–45)

The problem of whose authority prevails cannot be determined by assuming the unreliability of the devil's views about Christian salvation or of Faustus's testimony, as a man who has sold his soul, about such matters. Those who reject demonic information out of hand as deceptive have to deal not only with the fact that Mephistophilis often accurately represents traditional Christian belief, but that Heaven itself appears to act as if Faustus is damned well before the end. A notorious example occurs in act 2, scene 2, when, in a moment

---

[91] See Bluestone, "*Libido Speculandi*," pp. 65–69.

of repentant prayer, Faustus cries out to Christ for help and is answered by the arrival of Lucifer. Mephistophilis has just exhorted him to "think of hell," since he is damned, and he instead prompts himself to "think upon God that made the world" (2.2.80). Though a conflict ensues, with the voices of the good and bad angels acting out the ambivalences within Faustus himself, the result for the moment is a change of heart and a plea for mercy. In turning his soul heavenward, he fulfills a prerequisite for salvation and, moreover, proves that sin has not yet by custom grown into nature. Standard Christian belief, echoed in the play, would lead us to expect divine intervention at this point or some indication of a responsive God. When Lucifer appears, instead, answering, "Christ cannot save thy soul, for he is just" (2.2.93), we are presented with a disturbing spectacle that undermines orthodoxy: the devil refuses Christ's efficacy at the same time Faustus is probably crossing himself in a gesture for help.

We may conclude that the infernal judgment about Faustus's soul is confirmed in such an action, but Marlowe does not allow even this opinion to stand firm: Lucifer and his cohorts have appeared, but Faustus has not been razed to pieces as the devil has promised he would be if he repents. Prediction and fact do not concur, and consequently we are not sure how to evaluate the demonic assertions. Nor can an audience find grounds in this scene for validating traditional religious belief about salvation. Redemption appears beyond reach not because Faustus's hardened heart refuses to repent, but because hell closes in rapidly and irresistibly around him, while heaven becomes a remote abstraction. Add to these doctrinal disjunctions the problems of evaluating the heroic quality of Faustus's temporary appeal to God: the vulnerability that looks like courage from a religious vantage point is weakness and cowardly wavering in the context of heroic norms for character, which sanction the protagonist's iconoclastic departure from safe human boundaries. In the configuration of action set up in *Doctor Faustus*, ambiguities proliferate both within the Christian moral perspective of the play and between the moral and heroic as well.

The conflicting views raised in this scene about salvation and its requirements are dramatized with increasing intensity at the end of the play, where they are accompanied by some striking subversions of conventional form.[92] As Faustus nears the termination of his twenty-four-year contractual period in act 5, the audience is presented with several devices signaling the movement toward conclusion. Not only are these devices unsettling, as we will see, but they help throw into relief a fact about dramatic time that has never been far from view: the action blatantly exceeds the traditional expectation of Renaissance and neoclassical critics for a limit of one day in the events represented.[93] This manipulation of convention anticipates others. After Wagner's announcement that his master "means to die shortly, / He has made his will" (5.1.1–2), there is a rapid contraction of time, during which the last hours of Faustus's life are radically foreshortened and the gaping hell-mouth is revealed to him as "that vast perpetual torture-house" (5.1.258) awaiting him. Such strategies bode dramatic closure as well as metaphysical enclosure, the unequivocal containment of Faustus's soul in the infernal beyond. But Marlowe deploys these strategies in such a way as to defer a sense of a resolved ending, to jar rather than placate spectatorly expectations for answers to troubled doctrinal issues in the play.

At the level of moral action, the drama leaves suspended a number of ambiguities about Faustus's spiritual status. For one thing, the internal struggle in his soul between repentance and the refusal to believe in salvation is carried on until the

[92] See Bluestone, "*Libido Speculandi*," pp. 73–83, and Garber, " 'Infinite Riches in a Small Room,' " p. 11.

[93] See, for example, Lodovico Castelvetro, *The Poetics of Aristotle Translated and Explained*, tr. Robert Montgomery, in *Critical Theory Since Plato*, ed. Hazard Adams (New York: Harcourt Brace Jovanovich, 1971), pp. 152–53. Castelvetro is known for having formulated the three unities time, place, and action, later endorsed by many neoclassical critics.

very end, as is the debate between the good and bad angels, which is both a reflection of the protagonist's personal struggle and a dramatization of the metaphysical battle for his soul. Then there is the problem raised once again by Faustus's increasing gestures to God for deliverance, which are met as before with the convergence of demons around him.

> My God, my God, look not so fierce on me!
> Adders and serpents, let me breathe a while!
> Ugly hell, gape not! Come not, Lucifer!
>   (5.1.228–30)

These words have the effect of intensifying the image of a wrathful Almighty, whose "ireful brows" Faustus thinks he sees earlier, but they also hold in suspense questions the tragedy never conclusively answers: at what point is it too late for Faustus to repent, and how are we to construe the fact that his pleas for mercy are met by an unresponsive God?

The interrogative frame of mind engendered by the play extends beyond the unresolved moral conflicts and includes, as Max Bluestone has observed, the impressive ambiguities in the theatrical spectacle. Heaven and hell are blurred or confounded in the last scene. When Lucifer and company ascend from Dis to assume their place in "state," that part of the stage traditionally reserved for divine and earthly kings, we witness a visual inversion of the Renaissance hierarchical conception of the universe. Moreover, the throne let down from the "heavens" above stage, to let Faustus know in "what resplendent glory" he could have sat (5.1.252), is conspicuously and disturbingly without its figurehead. The absence of God, which the audience felt earlier when Faustus's prayers for mercy were not met by a celestial power, is now given vivid theatrical form. As the empty throne of Elysium ascends and hell is discovered on stage, the confusion attendant on the confounding of traditional stage space gives way to a sense of an all-encompassing inferno that has literally crowded heaven out: Faustus is surrounded by demons in state as he gapes into the yawning hellmouth. At the moment the clock strikes twelve, stage directions indicate that devils enter and take away his body, but what happens to Faustus's soul remains enigmatic. His last words in the play, "I'll burn my books!— Oh Mephistophilis!" (5.1.331), are thoroughly ambiguous and do nothing to settle the question of repentance and the doubt about whether hell has claimed more than his limbs, later found "all torn asunder by the hand of death" (5.1.338). Why the scholars find anything at all left of Faustus, who was supposed to have been issued away earlier, is questionable. But the more important point is that nothing precludes the devils' having torn Faustus without acquiring his soul. As one critic reminds us, "Among Faustus's fifteen wishes, prayers, and commands in the final soliloquy is his wish to be drawn into a cloud's entrails so that when they 'vomit forth into the air,' as he says, his 'limbs may issue from' their 'smoky mouths / So that [his] soul may but ascend to heaven.' "[94] The words of the first scholar only prolong the audience's doubt in exhorting all to "pray heaven that the Doctor have escaped the danger" (5.1.336).

If the uncertainties sustained at the end of *Doctor Faustus* are themselves challenges to the dogmatic truths of Christian orthodoxy, it is tempting to regard Marlowe, as many have, in iconoclastic terms. The interpretation is strengthened when the critique of conventional moral beliefs is linked with the eliciting of admiration for a heroic figure, who seems to achieve a kind of transcendence by resisting expectations of social and religious order and its prescriptions for success. But Marlowe, as I have already suggested, undermines even a secular valorization of Faustus's breaches of traditional systems. While dismantling the conditions for a cautionary tale in his dramatic material, he distances us from the protagonist's displays of power and ingenuity, so that even within a nonreligious heroic framework our responses are unsettled. This point has been well appreciated by Stephen Greenblatt, who remarks, "If the heart of Renaissance orthodoxy is a vast sys-

[94] Bluestone, "*Libido Speculandi*," p. 81.

tem of repetitions in which paradigms are established and men gradually learn what to desire and what to fear, the skeptics, [such as] Faustus, remain embedded within this orthodoxy; they simply reverse the paradigms and embrace what the society brands as evil. In so doing they imagine themselves set in diametrical opposition to their society where in fact they have already unwittingly accepted its crucial structural elements."[95] Specifically, Faustus's conduct is structured as a set of repeated expressions of will, whose illicit objects of desire are inevitably parodic versions of Holy Communion or of the Christian conception of divinity. If his incessant assertions of desire actually confirm him in the very doctrine of repetition, which he thinks he is rejecting when he spurns conventional knowledge at the beginning, his subversive moves become far less radical. Faustus's irreverent critique of the official culture adopts its patterns of order. Herein lies another source for the dislocation of perspective that characterizes Marlowe's play. Not only are the moral and heroic interpretive contexts held in irresolvable suspension, but a pervasive ambivalence informs each perspective taken by itself.

It is for this reason that the strategies Marlowe employs in unmasking the shallowness of his protagonist's iconoclasm do not bring us back to a comfortably Christian view of Faustus's fall. So persistent is the impulse in this play to test both authority and the more spectacular forms of opposition to it that we are prevented from easy assessments of the drama either as an orthodox work, whose characters exemplify moral lessons, or as a rebellious one to be identified with the hero's obsessive urges to transgress. In short, Marlowe's drama not only resists traditional Renaissance critical principles of tragic didacticism and the theory of decorum they spawn, but he eludes being pegged as a simple detractor of convention. His dramatic explorations of order and subversion sustain a profoundly questioning view of human experience and the literary models that

[95] Greenblatt, "Marlowe and Renaissance Self-Fashioning," p. 54.

contain it, even when they may seem to opt for the values of iconoclasm.

Readings of Marlowe's other plays, such as *Tamburlaine*, parts 1 and 2, and *Edward II*, would confirm the pervasiveness in his work of this uncompromising spirit of interrogation and antididacticism.[96] The constant breaking of boundaries, transgressions of norms, and collisions with authority that distinguish Marlovian protagonists are at once ways of testing established values and the forms of opposition they generate. Such a questioning or adversarial sense of the official culture inhabits many Renaissance plays. While the diversity of Shakespeare's mature tragedies make generalizations difficult, we often find in them dramatizations of conflict that subvert rather than consolidate the hierarchical conception of the universe in which metaphysical, social, ethical, and literary order is implicated. Because a good deal of contemporary scholarship has in various ways illuminated this side of the plays, I will mention briefly in the present context some aspects of Shakespearean tragedy with which neoclassical critics take special exception.[97] In their attitudes toward Shakespeare, we find ample proof that the precepts of criticism in the age fly in the face of contemporary drama and are increasingly perceived as incompatible with one of the greatest tragedians of the time. It was a long while, however, before critics saw in this discrepancy between theory and practice the repressive role that Renaissance and neoclassical literary precepts play vis-à-vis tragedy. Typically, the divergence of drama from "the rules" and traditional values was construed as the fault of the dramatist, an example of his waywardness or ignorance

[96] See, for example, Greenblatt's readings of these plays in "Marlowe and Renaissance Self-Fashioning."

[97] Some recent scholarly works that move in this direction include Booth, *King Lear, Macbeth, Indefinition, and Tragedy*; Bernard McElroy, *Shakespeare's Mature Tragedies* (Princeton: Princeton University Press, 1973); Norman Rabkin, *Shakespeare and the Common Understanding* (New York: Free Press, 1967).

about the social function of civilizer with which he is supposedly invested.

In light of our earlier study of *Hamlet*, it is possible to note just briefly the difficulties encountered by a didactic reading of the play and by Renaissance expectations of formal unity and causality in the development of action.[98] The misdirection of these expectations never occurs to Thomas Rymer, the rather ill-tempered author of *A Short View of Tragedy*, who is nonetheless a representative critic, deriving his principles largely from the French neoclassicists and winning the respect of Dryden among others.[99] He repeatedly censures Shakespeare's plays for their "irregularities" of plot, on the one hand, and their departures from standards of decorum and morality, on the other. The criticism is easily intelligible in view of the various strategies put in motion by Shakespeare to destabilize a sense of logical dramatic progression and of probable outcome in the action.[100] From the initial discontinuities in the routine of sentry change to the false leads about the threat to Denmark necessitating a midnight watch, the play draws us into a world marked, as Horatio says in the end, by "accidental judgments, casual slaughters . . . and purposes mistook" (5.2.383–85). *Hamlet* resists the kinds of assumptions about propriety of form and causality of action made by Rymer. The resistance is not gratuitous. Formal subversions of conventional dramatic structure are complementary with a more general tendency in the tragedy to test epistemological certainties and moral truths. Disjunctions in the unfolding of dramatic events are an immediate assault on spectatorly expectations

[98] See chap. 3.

[99] Thomas Rymer's criticism of Shakespeare appears chiefly in *A Short View of Tragedy*, ed. Arthur Freeman in the series *The English Stage: Attack and Defense, 1577–1730* (New York: Garland, 1974). On Rymer's criticism of Shakespeare, see Joan C. Grace, *Tragic Theory in the Critical Works of Thomas Rymer, John Dennis, and John Dryden* (Rutherford, N.J.: Fairleigh Dickinson University Press, 1975), pp. 33–60.

[100] See, for example, Stephen Booth, "On the Value of *Hamlet*," in *Reinterpretations of Elizabethan Drama*, pp. 137–76.

that correspond to the disjunctions encountered by Hamlet in his attempts to anticipate the right responses in his own environment within the play.

Thus, as formal conventions are disrupted so too are the moral bases for deciding ethical action. We have already given some attention to this matter in chapter 1. At this point, I simply want to reconfirm that a play distinguished by foiled efforts to decide the question of a right standard for human conduct operates in the interrogative not the didactic or ethically assertive mode.[101] If Shakespeare's tragedy undermines the Renaissance critical ideal of moral teaching by unhinging the hierarchies on which it depends, it also disregards the principle of poetic justice, which is commonly an adjunct to the doctrine of instruction. As John Dennis writes in his essay "On the Genius and Writing of Shakespeare," which appeared in 1712, "the good and the bad perishing promiscuously in the best of Shakespeare's tragedies, there can be none or very weak instruction in them: for such promiscuous events call the government of providence into question, and by skeptics and libertines are resolved into chance."[102] We might add that Dennis's difficulties multiply, once it is admitted that categories such as good and bad are repeatedly broken down through the conflicts in Shakespeare's plays or so thoroughly confounded that questions of moral difference and identity become very hard to answer. In Jacobean tragedy, to which we will turn shortly, the questions become even more pressing. These aspects of Shakespearean tragedy, especially notable in *Hamlet*, make the playwright an extremely problematic writer for neoclassical critics, who are frequently obliged to qualify his genius by condemning his amorality. Samuel Johnson articulates a longstanding opinion, one shared, for example, by

[101] See Maynard Mack, "The World of *Hamlet*," in *Tragic Themes in Western Literature*, ed. Cleanth Brooks (New Haven: Yale University Press, 1955), pp. 33–34. Also see Harry Levin, *The Question of Hamlet* (New York: Oxford University Press, 1959), pp. 20–21.

[102] *The Critical Works of John Dennis*, ed. Edward N. Hooker (Baltimore: Johns Hopkins University Press, 1943), vol. 2, p. 7.

Shakespeare's younger contemporary Ben Jonson, when he observes that the bard's "first defect is that to which may be imputed most of the evil in books or men. He sacrifices virtue to convenience, and is so much more careful to please than to instruct, that he seems to write without any moral purpose."[103] Attuned to a system of values that stigmatizes Shakespeare's manipulations of ethics and moral standards, these critics are cut off from a context in which they could approach with understanding the nature and effects of conflict in a play such as *Hamlet*.

One is tempted to the conclusion that Renaissance and neoclassical interpreters are congenitally prone to read Shakespearean tragedy as melodrama and, when the drama resists this reading, they find the work wanting. These tendencies are again apparent in critical response to *King Lear*, a tragedy so deficient in moral instruction and poetic justice that Nahum Tate thought it fit to edit Shakespeare in conformity with more generally palatable views of the good and bad fortunes due the characters in the play.[104] His making over of *King Lear* in the image of acceptable moral and literary standards seems extreme, but we should recall that a critic as tolerant as Samuel Johnson could sometimes be toward Shakespeare's breaches of convention and decorum sympathetically espoused Tate's revision. Once again, as in the case of *Hamlet*, Johnson's problems with the playwright reside largely at the ethical level. Assuming that Shakespeare's intention in *Lear* is "to impress this important moral, that villainy is never at a stop, that crimes lead to crimes, and at last terminate in ruin," Johnson proceeds to criticize the dramatist for his imperfect adherence to this end.

---

[103] *Samuel Johnson's Literary Criticism*, ed. R. D. Stock (Lincoln: University of Nebraska Press, 1974), p. 148.

[104] Tate's edition appeared in 1681. For a comparison of this version and Shakespeare's play, see Dorothy E. Nameri, *Three Versions of the Story of King Lear (Anonymous ca. 1594/1605); William Shakespeare 1607/1608; Nahum Tate 1681) Studied in Relation to One Another* (Salzburg: University of Salzburg, 1976).

But though this moral be incidentally enforced, Shakespeare has suffered the virtue of Cordelia to perish in a just cause, contrary to the natural ideas of justice, to the hope of the reader, and, what is yet more strange, to the faith of the chronicles. . . . A play in which the wicked prosper, and the virtuous miscarry, may doubtless be good, because it is a just representation of the common events of human life: but since all reasonable beings naturally love justice, I cannot easily be persuaded, that the observation of justice makes a play worse; or, that if other excellencies are equal, the audience will not always rise better pleased from the final triumph of persecuted virtue. In the present case the publick has decided. Cordelia, from the time of Tate, has always retired with victory and felicity.[105]

While Johnson focuses on the shocking fate of Cordelia at the end of the play as an unbearable insult to an audience's expectations of justice, one could say that the whole tragedy mobilizes conflicts that disrupt moral categories and ethical identities, thus rendering evaluative interpretations of character and action a hazardous business. The first act of *King Lear*, however, like the beginning of *Doctor Faustus*, appears to proceed with the models of morality drama in view. It may very well be these superficial resemblances between Shakespeare's play and a didactic work, such as Sackville and Norton's *Gorbuduc*, which also presents the hideous consequences resulting from a king's premature abdication of rule and division of state, that vexes critics, who find the action of *Lear* breaking continually beyond the generic limits it seems initially to invoke.[106]

[105] *Samuel Johnson's Literary Criticism*, p. 189, quoted by Booth, *King Lear, Macbeth, Indefinition, and Tragedy*, pp. 5–6.

[106] *Gorbuduc*, admittedly, is informed by its own ambivalences; see, for example, Altman, *The Tudor Play of Mind*, pp. 249–59. But reading this work in a didactic vein is less likely to produce the difficulties encountered by a similar reading of *King Lear*. On parallels between the two plays, see Barbara Heliodora Carneiro de Mendoça, "The Influence of *Gorbuduc* on *King Lear*," *Shakespeare Survey* 13 (1960): 41–48.

The conditions for a moralizing treatment of the material are set up when Shakespeare shows us a ruler who, by the end of the first scene, has divided his kingdom "to shake all cares and business from our age" (1.1.41), retaining only "the name, and all th'addition to a king" (1.1.138); disowned his favorite daughter, Cordelia, whose speech does not satisfy his expectations of her love; and banished the long faithful Earl of Kent, who has honored Lear "as my king, / Loved as my father, as my master followed, / As my great patron thought on in my prayers" (1.1.142–44). These assaults on propriety and bonds of loyalty by one residing at the top of the social hierarchy would produce, for a Renaissance audience, expectations of disaster that are, in a sense, realized in the action of the drama. The discord in human society and nature announced by Gloucester, in a speech that affirms the complicity of macrocosmic and microcosmic order, fulfills conventional assumptions about the probable ramifications of Lear's ill-conceived decisions.

> These late eclipses in the sun and moon portend no good to us: though the wisdom of Nature can reason it thus and thus, yet Nature finds itself scourg'd by the sequent effects. Love cools, friendship falls off, brothers divide: in cities, mutinies; in countries, discord; in palaces, treason; and the bond crack'd 'twixt son and father. This villain of mine comes under the prediction; there's son against father: the King falls from bias of nature; there's father against child. We have seen the best of our time: machinations, hollowness, treachery, and all ruinous disorders follow us disquietly to our graves.
>
> (1.2.111–23)

While the forces of cause and effect are unclear in Gloucester's discourse—does Lear's action initiate other kinds of disorder, or is it a reflection of a universe out of joint?—courtly and worldly upheavals are nonetheless closely implicated. Here, it seems, we have the beginnings of a morality play, which will demonstrate the collapse of a poorly managed kingdom and

the sorry but deserved end of a king guilty of gross misjudg-
ments. The impression is strengthened by the Gloucester sub-
plot, which introduces us to a figure like Lear in important
respects. As one critic puts it, "Any member of a Renaissance
audience would have been ready to see Gloucester's subsequent career as a demonstration that 'the dark and vicious
place' where Gloucester begot his bastard 'cost him his
eyes.' "[107] Crime and punishment, in such a reading, are com-
mensurate and enforce the hortatory value of the negative examples provided by characters in the main and subplots.

But standards of justice and injustice or of right and wrong,
on which a didactic view rests, are unsettled within the very
same dramatic movement that seems to set them in place. The
first disjunctions are subtle and unobtrusive, but they mark a
tendency toward the subversion of distinct ethical types that
becomes more troublesome as the action proceeds. For example, the error of Lear's judgment about Cordelia takes shape
largely within an adversarial setting, where the father's expectation that love can be adequately expressed in language conflicts with the daughter's sense that speech is not only insuffi-
cient to express her filial commitment but is contaminated by
the specious rhetoric of Goneril and Regan. In the situation,
the virtue and purity of Cordelia's reticent composure throw
Lear's unjust repudiation of her into relief—or so it is often
argued. But the apparent conflict between good and bad in the
scene is disturbed, if only slightly, by an attitude in Cordelia
and a manner of expression (for she does speak) that are unsettling, as critics at least since Coleridge have remarked.
Within the apparently closed circle of her purity, we are compelled to respond to suggestions that her pristine innocence is
a bit self-righteous, her emotion for her father somewhat cold,
and her honesty marred by an uncompromising with-
drawal.[108] The difficulty is not easily circumventable by ap-

[107] Booth, *King Lear, Macbeth, Indefinition, and Tragedy*, p. 47.
[108] See, for example, Booth, *King Lear, Macbeth, Indefinition, and Tragedy*, p. 54.

peal to the symbolic, nonrealistic aspects of character in this play, for example, to Cordelia's embodiment of an idea of purity that would be tainted if she let eloquence be the expression of her heart.[109] For it is precisely an idea of uncontaminated purity, of an ethical absolute established through a character's distance from language, that is being tested in the scene. Cordelia's apparent squeamishness is not the only factor at work in this process. Like her father, she talks of love as a quantifiable item, measurable according to her bond, "no more or no less." Her views, rather than being antithetical to Lear's, are variations on them and rely equally on comparison and relative value.[110]

This problem is symptomatic of an even more fundamental one: Cordelia's status as a character in drama. Her identity is bound, much more than it would be in narrative, to direct speech. In inhabiting the world of the play, she simply cannot remain true to her "ponderous love" by refusing language, although she wishes she could. We, of course, as an audience, would not know even this much about her, if she did not articulate her desire for silence in a highly paradoxical aside: "What shall Cordelia speak? Love, and be silent" (1.1.64). But she must speak and to speak at all enmeshes her ineluctably in a relational world, where "being pure" loses its absoluteness to the intrinsic variabilities of discourse and interpretation. This relativism in which Cordelia is implicated is particularly endemic to drama, since identity is constituted in speech, the understanding of which no narrative voice guides or mediates. In this very basic way, Cordelia is contaminated in the very process of trying to remove herself from the pollution of discourse.

The procedure of undercutting or complicating identity through such confrontations as those in act 1 of *King Lear* is

---

[109] See, for example, Russell Fraser's introduction to *King Lear*, Signet Classics (New York: New American Library, 1963), p. xxxi.

[110] See Booth, *King Lear, Macbeth, Indefinition, and Tragedy*, p. 54, and Lawrence Danson, "*King Lear* and the Two Abysses," in *On King Lear*, ed. Lawrence Danson (Princeton: Princeton University Press, 1981), pp. 125–27.

a familiar one in tragedy, and we have seen it at work in Sophocles' *Antigone*. Shakespeare manipulates similar techniques throughout his play and with unusually disturbing results. Take Goneril and Regan, for example. They are easily two of the most repulsive scoundrels in Shakespearean drama. Yet their early fears about having to live with their father's poor judgment and infirmity are amply substantiated in the first scene and underscored by the faithful Kent's condemnation of Lear's "hideous rashness" (1.1.153). We can understand why the demanding, testy old man grates on the nerves. In other words, the perversity of Lear in the first moments of the play gives an initial credibility to his daughters' antagonism toward him. Goneril's testimony in act 2, scene 2, that Lear's "knights grow riotous" in the palace is often regarded by critics as an example of her lying opportunism.[111] Yet an audience reasonably pauses over her complaint. Do we not expect that a king who has erred as seriously as Lear would engender unrest among his retinue? And is there not other evidence, to which I have already alluded, that bears out this contamination of subordinate orders when the ruler falters? It is simpler to deny the tenability of the evil daughter's condemnation of her father, because to do so helps us retain a steady view of her identity as an unmitigated villain. But if there are grounds for believing in the justice of Goneril's fear, then there are grounds, too, for approving the cautionary action she wishes to adopt with respect to Lear's entourage—reducing the hundred knights to fifty. She insults the king and demeans her father, of course, to strip down his numbers in this way, but her concern to maintain peace is plausible and pragmatic, given the signs of surrounding chaos, though it is crudely implemented.

I am not suggesting, in such developments, that Shakespeare draws us sympathetically into Goneril's sphere. But he disturbs the homogeneity of villainous traits in her character long enough to align us, if only temporarily, with her per-

---

[111] Booth, *King Lear, Macbeth, Indefinition, and Tragedy*, pp. 50–52.

ception of her father. We are too close to the irascibility of
Lear, at this stage, to deny her concerns as false. It is no less
true, I think, that we wish a better character than Goneril
would worry about the preservation of order. But by investing
this legitimate concern in an otherwise despicable figure,
Shakespeare complicates our moral evaluations and the understanding of distinct ethical identities on which they are
based. In short, while seeming to elicit expectations of morality drama in the first act of *King Lear*, Shakespeare destabilizes differences between good and bad, justice and injustice on
which the instructive potential of such drama rests.

The shifting of standard categories of identity is played out
in queries that reverberate across many dialogues in the
tragedy:

> KENT: How fares your Grace?
> LEAR: What's he?
> KENT: Who's there? What is't you seek?
> GLOUCESTER: What are you there? Your names?
> (3.4.127–30)

When these lines are spoken in act 3 by the characters congre-
gating on the heath, Lear has already suffered such an excru-
ciating diminishment of his noble status that his questioning
response to Kent's address sounds like an implicit denial of his
own kingly identity. But Lear's loss of grace, of course, is not
as simple as he himself suggests and not as clear-cut as a didactic reading would demand. The pervasive ambiguities of
his situation as he endures the "wrathful skies" on the heath
are conveyed partially in the fool's punning response to Kent's
earlier interrogation.

> KENT: Who's there?
> FOOL: Marry, here's grace and a codpiece;
> that's a wise man and a fool.
> (3.2.39–40)

Although at one level the fool answers the question by identifying two figures, the king and himself, the response is equiv-

ocal, since both designations "wise man" and "fool" may be applied at once to Lear and his jester. It is not only the reversibility of roles that is signaled in this pun, which makes a fool of grace and a wise man out of the bearer of a codpiece, but the doubleness of Lear, whose exposure to the elements, while repeatedly urged to take shelter, is folly and prudence, madness and an attempt to withstand it. Such reversibility and doubleness is continually pressed in act 3.

> LEAR: The art of necessities is strange,
> That can make vile things precious.
>   (3.3.70–71)
> ....
> LEAR: Thou think'st 'tis much that this contentious
>   storm
> Invades us to the skin; so 'tis to thee;
> But where the greater malady is fixed,
> The lesser is scarce felt. Thou'dst shun a bear;
> But if thy flight lay toward the roaring sea,
> Thou'dst meet the bear in th' mouth.
>   (3.4.6–11)

When the tempest in Lear's mind drives him to seek out the tyranny of the open night, he is maintaining grace and fending off a lapse into the darkness of insanity at the same time that he is confirming his wits are gone, that the wise man is a fool. Opposites converge in his experience without canceling each other out.

The difficulties of fixing Lear's identity after act 1 in accordance with the demands of morality drama are deepened by a notorious fact that cannot be accommodated to the neoclassical doctrine of poetic justice. Lear is not simply a bad man or a foolish king who rightly suffers the agonies of madness, the loss of his family, and the diminishment of his kingdom. Although he bears culpability for his daughters' usurpation of him, he is nonetheless a man more sinned against than sinning. The incommensurability of wrongdoing and suffering in this tragedy has come to stand, in modern times, as an epitome of a more general characteristic of tragic experience. But to critics of the seventeenth century, the incongruity puts in doubt the operation of justice in the universe and the possibility of comprehending the hero's catastrophe as symmetrical with an act of transgression for which he is the responsible agent. There is an excess of pathos in *King Lear* that eludes the rationalization of disaster in the doctrine of moral instruction.

The formal manifestations of this excess in the last scenes of the play have been ably elucidated by a number of recent interpreters, who have drawn our attention to the repeated deferrals of an ending in *King Lear*: each minor strand of action and its conflicts wind to a conclusion that leads to other unfinished pieces of business, until finally we are brought back to the fates of Lear and Cordelia, which are hanging in the balance. In Cordelia's death, the extenuation of suffering beyond the bounds of our expectations and hopes and beyond the structures of closure that Shakespeare repeatedly engages as the action winds down, only to press beyond them, suggests the illusory accommodations of human experience supplied by the conventions of tragic form.[112] As in the case of Marlowe's *Doctor Faustus*, *King Lear* does not settle our souls in the way Renaissance and neoclassical critics argue it should, through structural proprieties and clarity of moral vision. Nahum Tate's revision of *King Lear* might do so, but in the process it truncates those parts of the play that bring an audience in touch with the incertitudes and enigmas generated by tragic conflict and suffering.

Jacobean tragedy carries these tendencies, already well developed in Renaissance drama, to extremes. In the plays of Webster, Tourneur, and Chapman, we find dramatizations of strife so inimical to a moral understanding of the universe and the formal properties it supports that the popular traditional bases of contemporary criticism take on an increasingly re-

---

[112] See Frank Kermode, *The Sense of an Ending: Studies in the Theory of Fiction* (New York: Oxford University Press, 1967), pp. 82–83, and Booth, *King Lear, Macbeth, Indefinition, and Tragedy*, pp. 5–11.

pressive, controlling aspect.[113] Theoretical principles, affirming a hierarchical conception of the world purportedly advanced by tragedy, circumvent the vision of chaos that
pervades Jacobean plays and that the moralistic detractors of
drama continue to attack with great rigor.

In Webster's *The Duchess of Malfi* and *The White Devil*,
for example, the playwright continually frustrates aesthetic
norms of decorum by breaking the formal unity between character and linguistic or behavioral style required by sixteenth-
and seventeenth-century critics. Agents of justice and social
order, such as Ferdinand and the Cardinal or Monticelso and
Francesco, speak and act like the dangerous criminals they attempt to subdue. Their effort to restore degree to a crisis-ridden
state, crumbling under the burden of illicit relationships,
fails miserably as they become distorted images of the vices
they outwardly abhor. Attempting to set right his sister's, the
Duchess's, unlawful marriage to Antonio, Ferdinand becomes
a maniacal murderer, driven by an incestuous desire for his
sibling that he just barely sublimates and tries to purge
through a highly ritualized torture and slaughter of his "criminal" twin.[114] In the effort to turn murder into rightful sacrifice, Ferdinand recalls Othello, who, when killing Desdemona,
also tries to sacralize crime by transforming it into an act of
justice. Similarly, Francesco and Monticelso's plot to restore
order to their city by expelling Brachiano and Vittoria collapses because they become identical with the lawbreakers
they seek to exterminate. In the court scene of *The White
Devil*, Monticelso is no less than Vittoria a "devil in crystal,"
one whose "poison" is discernible under "gilded pills." And

[113] On Jacobean tragedy, see Robert Ornstein, *The Moral Vision of Jacobean Tragedy* (Madison: University of Wisconsin Press, 1960), and Irving
Ribner, *Jacobean Tragedy: The Quest for Moral Order* (London: Methuen,
1962).

[114] See James Calderwood, "*The Duchess of Malfi*: Styles of Ceremony," in
*Shakespeare's Contemporaries: Modern Studies in English Renaissance
Drama*, 2d ed., ed. Max Bluestone and Norman Rabkin (Englewood Cliffs,
N. J.: Prentice-Hall, 1970), pp. 278–91.

Francesco, when he takes on a disguise in order to avenge himself on Brachiano, perversely revels in the spectacle of torture and death that he stages.

Tourneur's *Revenger's Tragedy* and Chapman's *Bussy d'Ambois* present us with figures much like Webster's.[115] Vindice and Bussy are gradually absorbed into the sordid ways of the corrupt court, which they originally oppose. In their plotting for "justice," they become models of the distorted, scheming type of character that inhabits the world of intrigue. Their identity as agents of law and order is lost as their actions become more and more indistinguishable from those of their antagonists. Both plays in which these figures appear, and Webster's as well, are preoccupied not with validating the integrity of formal proprieties, but with inverting them to reveal the consequences of conflict.

For all three dramatists, a salient characteristic of strife is that it reduces everyone to an insidious sameness that destroys distinctions and hierarchies on which decorum rests.[116] Revenge, which is what most of the characters are after in one way or another, transforms the agents into mirror images of the guilty parties against which they are retaliating. We found the same problem of mimetic violence explored in Aeschylus's *Oresteia*. But unlike the classical agents of justice, ministers of law in Jacobean tragedy are typically consumed in their enterprise against crime into sadism and perverse revels of torture. There is an intrinsic fascination with the performative details of violence in these plays that makes them all the more disturbing, since the performance is often likened to ritual sacrifice. A more thorough study of Jacobean drama would reveal time and again that the crisis provoked by conflict is one in

---

[115] For a recent treatment of Chapman's *Bussy d'Ambois*, with a useful bibliography on the play, see Altman, *The Tudor Play of Mind*, pp. 302–20. On Tourneur's *Revenger's Tragedy*, see Ornstein, *The Moral Vision of Jacobean Tragedy*, pp. 105–7.

[116] On this aspect of conflict, see René Girard, *Violence and the Sacred*, tr. Patrick Gregory (Baltimore: Johns Hopkins University Press, 1977), pp. 39–67, though he does not address Jacobean tragedy.

which the mechanisms of legal justice lose their efficacy, becoming one and the same with the violence they seek to contain. The killing orgies so commonly found in these plays are inevitable consequences of the fact that legal sanctions actually swell rather than stem the tide of blood. In such breakdowns of demarcation between justice and perversion, formal categories dictated by standards of aesthetic appropriateness are shown to be shallow indeed. The very conditions that make moral distinctions possible simply do not hold in these plays. Characters in *The Duchess of Malfi*, *The White Devil*, *The Revenger's Tragedy*, and *Bussy d'Ambois* end up confirming, through their negative examples, not the validity of conventional norms but their precariousness and ultimate illusoriness.

These plays also end, as *Doctor Faustus*, *Hamlet*, and *King Lear* do, with disjunctive scenes, which do not so much conclude the dramatic action as force the audience to reflect on the irresolvability of the dilemmas and the inadequacy of conventional solutions. The apotheosis of the hero in Chapman's play, Antonio's assumption of control in Tourneur's tragedy, the promise of a new and better reign in *The Duchess of Malfi*, and Giovanni's sententious admonition in *The White Devil*, that "guilty men remember, their black deeds / do lean on crutches made of slender reeds"—these endings do not assure spectators that violence and strife have been curbed successfully. They are instead uncompelling, simplistic attempts to moralize an action that has utterly confounded morality.

As the example of Jacobean tragedy strikingly demonstrates, the tendency of tragic conflict to fracture the stability of formal and ethical principles challenges rather than carries out literary expectations of the period. When Tourneur presents us with a revenger who, in opposing the corrupt ducal family, turns into a monster of corruption himself and gloats over the highly stylized punishment he concocts; when Webster shows the mechanism of justice becoming hopelessly mired in savage breaches of decency and humanity; when Chapman presents us with a model of Stoic fortitude who, in antagonizing the decadent politicians of court, becomes a self-engrossed individualist, a murderer, and a scheming adulterer; when virtue takes on the gruesome appearance of vice as it consistently does in these plays, we are made to look hard at the complacency of critical views that proceed as if drama is exemplary for the moral lessons and spiritual edification it has to offer. Some modern critics maintain that the sheer negative energy in Jacobean tragedy, its horror, incites us to improvement. But the feeling we are left with in these dramatic performances is that improvement is a smug illusion in a world that yields no clear moral distinctions, that people stumble in a dark mist of cross-purposes and perverted intentions from which there is no escape.

WHILE THE DISJUNCTION between dramatic theory and practice in the sixteenth and seventeenth centuries does not reach a point of crisis that initiates serious change in critical positions, we have seen that the works of Shakespeare, in particular, can force scrutiny of inconsistencies. Accommodations on the critical side are sometimes made for the bard's breaches of convention—a fact noticeable, for example, in the writings of Samuel Johnson—but the basic principles of moral utility and formal unity remain quite firmly in place from Minturno to Dryden. There are occasions, however, when neoclassical critics directly address conflict in tragedy, in an effort to render it conformable with these principles. Such moments are rare but telling; they allow a glimpse at the strategies that seventeenth-century dramatic theorists employ to evade the threatening consequences of tragic strife. Corneille, who is both theorist and tragedian, offers a particularly insightful understanding of what can happen when the agonistic aspects of the dramatic *praxis* meet directly the pressure of rules ensuring moral instruction.

In the *Discours de la tragédie*, published in 1660, Corneille confronts a topic that his contemporaries, as we have seen, tend not to take up.[117] The subject of conflict arises in the con-

[117] Corneille's *Discours de la tragédie* appears in *Oeuvres complètes*, ed. Stegmann, pp. 830–40.

text of examining Aristotle's categorization, in chapter 9 of the *Poetics*, of incidents that excite pity and fear. All of the actions named by the Greek philosopher involve violent deeds between persons dear to each other, such as relatives and close friends. I have noted that this discussion is as close as Aristotle ever comes to addressing tragic conflict. As the previous chapter demonstrates, however, his interest is not in the struggle, but in the interplay of ignorance and knowledge between characters.[118] It is the preoccupation with *agnoia* and *anagnorisis* that motivates the classification of types in chapter 14 and that determines the best drama as one in which the agent is not aware of the true identity of the persons involved. Corneille's analysis is important not only in qualifying the Aristotelian schema of pitiable and fearful events, but in revealing the peculiar dangers posed by conflict for the neoclassical critic.

After outlining the argument of *Poetics* 14, Corneille admits that he has difficulty agreeing with Aristotle's condemnation of the type of action in which the characters recognize, undertake, but complete nothing—the case presented by Haemon's drawing his sword against his father, Creon, in Sophocles' *Antigone*. Though he concedes that a desistance from acting based on a mere shift of will, without any notable happening that obliges change, is unsatisfactory, he also believes that when the agents "do on their part all that they can, and when they are prevented from reaching a certain end by some superior power, or by some change of fortune which causes them to perish, it is beyond doubt that such makes a kind of tragedy, perhaps more sublime than the three kinds Aristotle approves."[119] He expresses his reason for preferring this type of action: when the agents recognize each other from the beginning, then a combat of passions among and within the individuals develops, which greatly enhances the emotional power of the drama. Passion against nature and duty against love, con-

---

[118] See pp. 116–17.
[119] Corneille, *Discours de la tragédie*, p. 834.

flicts composing the best tragedies, are facilitated by the species of recognition Aristotle values least.

At first glance, Corneille's discourse presents a view of the centrality of struggle in tragedy that weakens the thesis about neoclassical criticism argued in this chapter. A closer examination reveals, however, that the French writer's discussion of conflict does not controvert but affirms the theoretical norms of his contemporaries. If Corneille is unusual in giving careful scrutiny to the tension of opposites, he can venture on the topic only because he manages to take the threat out of tragic strife. He does so by insisting that the agents whose intentions precipitate conflict—the friends, for example, whose feelings of duty and love clash—for one reason or another leave off pursuing their ends. As the definition cited earlier makes clear, something happens in the play to neutralize or dissipate strife. Corneille, by implementing this strategy in his own dramatic practice, eliminates what is probably most disturbing to the neoclassical mind about the manipulation of conflict in tragedy: the failure of metaphysical or social systems to produce viable criteria for mediating a collision of values.

An example of the adjustments dictated by the need to dismantle conflict is apparent in *Oreste*, a reworking of Aeschylus's *Oresteia*. Even though the Greek trilogy arguably presents a more satisfying mediation of opposites than many other tragedies, Corneille is obviously bothered by certain features of the action. He takes offense particularly at the hero's murder of Clytemnestra, a barbarous deed that he thinks totally unnecessary.[120] Orestes should leave the punishment of his mother to God and plot against the traitor Aegisthus only. But because tradition has it that Clytemnestra in fact dies at the hands of her son, Corneille manipulates the events so that the queen is accidentally struck when she thrusts herself before Aegisthus, whom Orestes is about to kill. Thus she perishes through the agency of her son, but his action remains innocent

[120] For Corneille's discussion of this point, see *Discours de la tragédie*, pp. 836–37.

because it is unintentional. In this adaptation of the dramatic material, it is clear that Corneille eliminates the threat to social order featured in Aeschylus's trilogy by evading a conflict between filial love and righteous revenge. The difficulty of mediating between two valid moral claims is bypassed from the start.

In two of Corneille's most successful plays, *Le Cid* and *Horace*, the same strategies are found. Both pieces begin with the possibility of developing a struggle in a classical or Shakespearean mode, but the tensions are considerably weakened in the course of the action.[121] In *Le Cid*, the clash within Rodrigue, between duty to protect his father's honor and love for Chimène, against whose father he must seek revenge, is reinforced by the external opposition he eventually meets from Chimène for killing Don Gomès. But Corneille's hero in no way ends up suffering as, for example, Hamlet does. Rather, he receives honor instead of recrimination from the king and people of Seville because of his courageous protection of the state and is even allowed to hope that one day he can win back the love of his cherished Chimène—which he does in the end. Thus, we find at the heart of the drama a counterplay of emotions, but a calculated weakening of the impact of ethical conflict on the agents. Corneille's play clearly sidesteps the troublesome threat of an ethically irresolvable battle.

In *Horace*, the possibility of conflict is even more forcibly set aside. Corneille begins with all the material necessary for developing a tragic conflict in the Greek or Shakespearean vein, by setting up an opposition between duty to fatherland and ties of kinship. But in the third act, after tension has arisen with the election of the three Alban and Roman brothers, Corneille seeks to avoid the clash by having both sides agree that the chosen warriors should not be forced into battle, since they are related by blood and marriage. From then on the ac-

---

[121] See Kurt von Fritz's discussion of the plays, "Tragische Schuld und poetische Gerechtigkeit in der griechischen Tragödie," in *Antike und Moderne Tragödie: Neun Abhandlungen* (Berlin: Walter de Gruyter, 1962), pp. 42–52.

tion proceeds from personally culpable passions—the desire of the Horatii for fame above all else. The conflict dissolves under the patriotic but nonetheless censurable behavior of the Roman brothers, who show no compunction for bonds of kinship. One need only read Horace's several speeches before and after the war to see that Corneille neutralizes the conflict with which he begins.

The three plays examined here reveal Corneille's effort to mitigate the dense moral struggles of tragedy in the interest of preserving the doctrine of utility. In this respect, his literary strategies are not unlike the theoretical strategies for mediating conflict employed by Hegel. That dramatic art should present a clear delineation of vice and virtue, if not a moral teleology in which good and bad behavior gets its just deserts, is a precept expressed in the *Discours de la tragédie* and implemented in *Oreste, Le Cid,* and *Horace.* While the first two plays reveal the rewards that accrue to heroes whose intentions are innocent, the latter shows the rightful punishment falling on one whose blameworthy passion has overtaken his conduct. All three provide examples from which the audience can learn and profit. But they do so only by simplifying the complexities with which Greek and Shakespearean tragedy forcefully presents us. In Corneille, the neoclassical critical urge for moral clarity generates plays whose neutralized struggles preserve cultural order and guarantee the spectator's betterment.

NEOCLASSICAL PRECEPTS regarding form and morality in drama may reach most sophisticated prominence in the *Trois Discours* of Corneille, published in the mid-seventeenth century, but they show few signs of significant decline for at least another several decades. Not only Dryden, but Pope and Johnson, in England, and Batteux and Voltaire, in France, prove the long-lived vitality of norms composing neoclassical theories of tragedy. Against this tradition, however, we can pinpoint major intellectual shifts in eighteenth-century literary criticism that bear importantly on the issue of tragic conflict.

Two developments, in particular, contribute to the disintegration of the consolidated system of formal and moral order that excludes consideration of strife in dramatic art. First, sentimentalist accounts of tragedy, promulgated variously under Cartesian, Hobbesian, and Shaftesburian auspices, challenge the doctrine of moral instruction and poetic justice by making passionate agitation instead of reason a prime ingredient both of tragic action and of the spectator's response. Second, new theories of genius and sublimity, by devaluing the premise that poetic structure and subject matter must be regular, harmonious, and restrained, disrupt the solidarity of the formalist aesthetic and make way for more consequential developments in dramatic criticism.[122]

Before examining in detail these forces undermining Renaissance and neoclassical views, let me note briefly to what degree traditional ideas hold sway over eighteenth-century theories of drama. As others have observed, the period sustains basically the same conception of tragedy that prevailed in sixteenth-century Italy and seventeenth-century France. "Tragedy was an imitation of that portion of Nature which exhibited rule, order, and harmony. Its function was to teach and delight. It must preserve probability, poetic justice, decorum, and the Unities."[123] Though this description oversimplifies some of the more fruitful incursions of critics into new territory, it also serves as a concise reminder that the eighteenth century continues to affirm the necessity of dramatic laws for securing regularity—structural and ethical—in tragedy. When

---

[122] For a discussion of these developments, see Bate, *From Classic to Romantic*; Wimsatt and Brooks, *Literary Criticism*, pp. 283–312; Gallaway, *Reason, Rule, and Revolt in English Classicism* (1940; reprint, New York: Octagon Books, 1965), pp. 259–348; Earl R. Wasserman, "The Pleasures of Tragedy," *ELH: A Journal of English Literary History* 14 (1947): 283–307; René Wellek, *A History of Modern Criticism: 1750–1950*, 4 vols. (New Haven: Yale University Press, 1955), vol. 1.

[123] Gallaway, *Reason, Rule, and Revolt*, p. 234. Also see Clarence C. Green, *The Neo-classic Theory of Tragedy in England During the Eighteenth Century*, Harvard Studies in English no. 11 (1943; reprint, New York: Benjamin Blom, 1966), pp. 3–56.

David Hume in 1742 writes that even though poetry "can never submit to exact truth, it must be confined by rules of art, discovered to the author either by genius or observation,"[124] he is restating an opinion that John Dennis and the Earl of Shaftesbury express earlier in the century: if poetry is an art it must have an end, which can be achieved only through the proper means that we call rules.[125] Precepts of art guarantee the method and order that are still deemed the inalienable province of poetic creation.

As in the Renaissance, playing by the rules in the eighteenth century is intimately connected with the doctrine of art as idealized nature—*la belle nature* of the French neoclassicists. Not only Pope, but Doctor Johnson and Bishop Hurd speak about poetry as nature methodized, or as the particular regulated and generalized to accommodate a "universal image of truth." The expression is Hurd's, and he explains what he means by the rather elusive concept of "universal truth" when he says that the purpose of poetry "is not to delineate truth simply, but to present it in the most taking forms; not to reflect the real face of things, but to illustrate and adorn it; not to represent the fairest objects only, but to represent them in the fairest light, and to heighten all their beauties up the possibility of their natures; nay to outstrip nature."[126] Found in Hurd's edition of Horace's *Ars Poetica* (1766), this passage testifies to the vitality of the complex Horatian, Aristotelian, and Neoplatonic notion of idealized nature, which survives well beyond the formulation Sidney gives it in his *Defense of Poesie*.

Respect for regularity, ideality, and rules, then, links many contemporaries of Johnson and Hurd with their neoclassical

---

[124] David Hume, *Of the Standard of Taste*, in *Essays, Moral, Political, and Literary* (Oxford: Oxford University Press, 1963), p. 236.

[125] John Dennis, *The Grounds of Criticism in Poetry*, in *The Critical Works of John Dennis*, ed. Edward N. Hooker, 2 vols. (Baltimore: Johns Hopkins University Press, 1943), vol. 1, pp. 335–36.

[126] Richard Hurd, *Horatii epistolae*, vol. 2, pp. 140–41, quoted by Stock, *Samuel Johnson and Neoclassical Dramatic Theory*, p. 32.

predecessors—and with the neoclassical preference for closed and stable structure. This preference is reinforced by the doctrine of poetic justice, which a surprisingly large number of critics and writers continue to uphold. As one scholar observes, the eighteenth century is "inclined to accept the moral value of tragedy as a profound truth and to move on to lesser matters."[127] Figures as diverse as Johnson and Diderot maintain the necessity of representing a just distribution of deserts in drama; vice should be punished and virtue rewarded.[128] Notwithstanding the differences of these dramatic critics, their adherence to a theory of poetic justice leads to a view of tragedy as a clearly delineated, well-ordered system that brings a temporary imbalance in the moral structure of the world back to a point of stability. That tragedy reveals the governance of a moral power—Christian or deist—which could bring good out of evil is, in the words of one commentator, "intimately linked with the sublime fact that, despite occasional mysterious moves on the part of Deity, optimism [is] justified by fact."[129] Although it must be admitted that the characteristic vehicles for the moral-mindedness of the eighteenth century are the didactic poem, satire, and the social essay, tragedy becomes assimilated to the ethical expectations attached to these didactic forms. As a result, its fundamental resistance to the precept of instruction is frequently misunderstood, as it was in the sixteenth and seventeenth centuries. The adversarial nature of tragic plays, which sets them at odds with conventional notions of formal and ethical order, recedes behind a continuing emphasis on simplicity and intelligibility.

This brief sketch of the continuities between criticism of the neoclassical age and the Enlightenment suggests that the predisposition against admitting tragic conflict into theoretical

[127] Wasserman, "The Pleasures of Tragedy," p. 283.

[128] Denis Diderot, *De la poésie dramatique*, in *Oeuvres esthétiques* (Paris: Garnier Frères, 1968), pp. 259ff.; Samuel Johnson, *Preface to the Plays of William Shakespeare*, in *Samuel Johnson's Literary Criticism*, ed. R. D. Stock (Lincoln: University of Nebraska Press, 1974), p. 148.

[129] Gallaway, *Reason, Rule, and Revolt*, p. 141.

accounts of drama persists into the middle of the eighteenth century. Such a conclusion must be qualified, however, in light of some important differences that develop in the aftermath of Corneille and Dryden. Continuing emphasis on the necessity of formal rules for dramatic composition is, by the time of Johnson's *Preface to Shakespeare* (1765), no longer based so much on the a prioristic authority of the ancients as on the reasonableness or common sense that the average person would perceive in set ways for doing things. Rationality is still a component of eighteenth-century conceptions of the rules guiding the structure of tragedy, but this rationality is established and sanctioned by the clear judgments, the discriminating minds of playwrights, spectators, and critics and not simply by classical precedent.[130] If the unities of time, place, and action are espoused, it is not because they have their origins in Aristotle or Horace—as previous centuries were inclined to argue—but because they make sense and assure some minimum of artistic order. The fact is, however, that the unities are increasingly attacked in the course of the century, along with other precepts—for example, the five-act structure and the technique of *liaison des scènes*—considered more arbitrary than common-sensical.[131] Doctor Johnson maintains that breaking from convention, especially the hardened, artificial convention of the French school, is often the condition for creating greater beauties.[132]

Thus, the shift in criticism from authority to judgment leads to growing tolerance for experimentation and for divergences from customary procedure. Though formal regularity and organic coherence are still expected in drama, anomalies are

---

[130] See, for example, Stock, *Samuel Johnson and Neoclassical Dramatic Theory*, pp. 1–27; Bate, *From Classic to Romantic*, pp. 55–92; R. W. Harris, *Reason and Nature in the Eighteenth Century* (London: Blandford Press, 1968), pp. 228–50, 331–57.

[131] See Stock, *Samuel Johnson and Neoclassical Dramatic Theory*, pp. 77–80.

[132] See his defense of Shakespeare in the first pages of the *Preface* in Stock's edition, pp. 139–48.

treated with greater sensitivity and probing interest. Concessions are made to the unfettered energies of "genius." Shakespeare's tragedies, in particular, whose formal iconoclasms we have noted, profit from the new trend and receive fresh critical scrutiny. Johnson's writings on the Elizabethan playwright and Nicholas Rowe's "Some Account of the Life, etc. of Mr. William Shakespear" are an index to the shift in critical temper.[133]

Admittedly, this general loosening of firmly established precepts for structure does not immediately yield an understanding of the disjunctive, decentering effects of tragic conflict. Johnson may bear Shakespeare's banner against "the minute and slender criticism" of the staunchly neoclassical Voltaire, but he is still hard on what he considers the dramatist's unrefined and sloppy manipulation of tragic form. Having conceded the value in abandoning the three unities and the straits of decorum, he can forgive Shakespeare neither for his "loosely formed . . . carelessly pursued" plots nor for his "improbably produced or imperfectly represented endings."[134] Thus, when Johnson criticizes *Hamlet* for a catastrophe that "is not very happily produced" ("the exchange of weapons is rather an expedient of necessity, than a stroke of art") or for the neglect of poetic justice and probability, he reveals, as his seventeenth-century predecessors do, a difficulty in understanding how dislocations in dramatic structure may be deliberately engineered to reproduce the tragic insight that the world is out of joint.[135] That the suspended conflicts of Shakespeare's play are effectively registered in an unclosed, improbably concluded formal design is a point escaping the Johnsonian-minded critic, who is inclined to treat the plot of *Hamlet* as if it were bungled.

As this discussion suggests, the analytical judiciousness of Enlightenment criticism, though in many ways disintegrative

---

[133] Reproduced in *Eighteenth-Century Essays on Shakespeare*, ed. D. Nichol Smith (1903; reprint, New York: Russell and Russell, 1962), pp. 1–23.

[134] *Samuel Johnson's Literary Criticism*, ed. Stock, p. 149.

[135] *Samuel Johnson's Literary Criticism*, ed. Stock, p. 194.

of tradition, does not strike very deeply at the premises of earlier views of tragedy. A more penetrating onslaught comes
with the sentimentalist reinterpretations of drama, which
challenge not the formal conceptions of traditional criticism
(at least not directly), but the related emphasis on reason as
the shaping core of the tragic action and the audience's response. Our discussion of Renaissance and neoclassical tragic
theory revealed that the ultimate rationality of the dramatic
representation was made the condition for the spectator's rational perception of moral truth and hence his or her incite-
ment to virtuous behavior. The Stoic underpinnings of this
doctrine are most apparent in the fact that "rationally perceiving moral truth" involves the neutralization or purgation of
the passions. If the dramatic hero does not effect this stabili-
zation as an example for the beholder, then the beholder himself does by reflecting on the dangers of uncurbed emotions
and correcting his own conduct accordingly. In either case, the
intervention of *ratio* conduces to moral betterment. This is the
conception attacked by the sentimentalists. Although they still
place a high value on improving an audience, they make the
arousal—not the suppression—of passions the means of arriv-
ing at their end.

Without embarking on a detailed examination of the various sentimentalist strains in eighteenth-century theories of
tragedy, a topic discussed fully elsewhere, let me summarize
the major points of consequence for our study of conflict.[136]
In all of its versions, sentimentalism privileges the benefits of
emotional agitation. For the Cartesian, vigorous motions of
the soul produced by dramatic presentations are good in
themselves (as long as they do not disrupt the nervous system),
for they relieve lassitude; the Hobbesian claims that the stir-
rings of pity and fear please us when, as in tragedy, we recognize that we ourselves are safely removed from the distress of

---

[136] See Wasserman, "The Pleasures of Tragedy," which is substantially
about sentimentalist doctrines, and Bate, *From Classic to Romantic*, chaps. 4
and 5.

another (an idea drawn from Lucretius); and the Shaftesburian argues that the agitation elicited by tragedy, particularly pity, engages our sympathetic benevolence, an exercise that makes us feel good and betters us as human beings.[137] Though the first two positions are not inimical to reason, the second actually requiring intellectual reflection to secure the pleasure of being removed from suffering, neither allots *ratio* the place of importance it had in Renaissance and neoclassical theories. But the Shaftesburian view is more extreme, conceding reason no role at all in calling up sympathy, which depends exclusively on feeling and intuition, on the mentally unreserved identification of spectator with dramatic character.

One of the notable results of this shift from reason to passion is the emergence of a new vocabulary and conceptual framework for discussing tragedy. As interest moves from the ordered representation of the tragic play—from what and how it represents—to the feelings aroused by the drama, *excitement, disturbance, agitation, turbulence,* and *disquiet* come more and more to the forefront of discussion as acceptable terms of criticism. It is even common, especially among French critics, such as Jean-François Marmontel, to encounter *conflict* and *combat* as descriptive labels attached both to the experience provoked by tragic representation and to the dramatic action itself.[138] Instead of the neo-Stoic repose favored by Renaissance and neoclassical thinkers, the sentimentalists stress the desirability of passionate arousal and sometimes passionate struggle.

---

[137] For a fuller discussion of these three major positions, see Wasserman, "The Pleasures of Tragedy." Descartes' position is articulated chiefly in the *Traité des passions*; it is promulgated by Rapin and Dennis and best known to later English critics through DuBos and Fontenelle. The Hobbesian view is set out in the essay "Human Nature" and is espoused principally by Addison; *Characteristics*, by Anthony Ashley Cooper, the Earl of Shaftesbury, is the main source for the sympathetic strain of sentimentalism adopted by many later critics, including Edmund Burke, Adam Smith, and Lord Kames.

[138] Jean-François Marmontel, the article "Tragédie," in *Élémens de la littérature*, included in *Oeuvres complètes* (1819–1820; reprint, Geneva: Slatkine Reprints, 1968), pp. 199–228.

But do these theories bring their promulgators any closer to understanding the disjunctions of perspective and the moral impasses of classical or Renaissance dramatizations of conflict? Not really. The reason for this is that sentimentalist passion favors the pathetic situation in tragedy, the simple tale of pity that pulls our heartstrings and either makes us feel harmoniously stirred, safe in our distance from distress, or sympathetic in our identification. The Cartesian position is not friendly to jarring, disjunctive feelings, whereas the Hobbesian and Shaftesburian positions assume a simple emotional proximity to or distance from the experience presented in tragedy. None of these views embraces the troublesome culture-questioning areas of tragedy: its doubts about the viability and stability of social and moral order, its persistent way of alienating us from the simple extremes of benevolence and aloofness, its refusal to accommodate the traditional categories we would impose on characters and actions to make them safe and familiar. In short, the irregular and disturbing complexities of tragic conflict lie beyond the pale of sentimentalist views. This point is vividly affirmed in a passage from an essay by a minor theorist, George Walker, published in 1798, which summarizes the "sympathetic complex." "An untutored genius, having strong conceptions, a heart that can enter into the feelings of a fellow heart, quick in catching the most striking features of distress, judgment to select a happy tale of virtuous suffering, and simplicity to follow nature in her plain walk, will in the fabrication of tragedy reach its highest excellence."[139] The uncomplicated motives attached to the dramatic character who is virtuous but victimized by injustice and to the unsophisticated "fellow heart" that reaches out in intuitive understanding cannot go far in explaining the appeal of Greek and Renaissance tragedy.

Sentimentalism, then, undermines the rationalistic, ethical

---

[139] George Walker, "On Tragedy and the Interest in Tragical Representations," *Memoirs of the Literary and Philosophical Society of Manchester*, vol. 5 (1708): 332–33, quoted by Wasserman in "The Pleasures of Tragedy," p. 306.

basis of sixteenth- and seventeenth-century dramatic theory, whose roots are both classical and Christian, by replacing intellection with feeling. But because the new emphasis on agitation is grounded in an affinity for simplicity, critics espousing emotive doctrines still either gloss over or schematize the dilemmas of tragic plays. Concepts of emotion in the eighteenth century, however, are often linked to another complex of ideas that breaks more decisively with tradition and leads directly into the mainstream of thought surrounding the emergence of Hegel's aesthetic views, particularly his notion of conflict. This set of ideas centers on the sublime, to which we will turn in the next chapter.

CHAPTER FOUR

Kant and Schiller: Conflict and the Sublime

> The highest consciousness of our moral nature can only be sustained in a violent situation, a war.
> —Friedrich Schiller, *Über den Grund des Vergnügens an tragischen Gegenständen*

THOUGH BOILEAU brought the term *sublime* into general circulation again among critics, by publishing a translation of Longinus's *Peri Hupsous* in 1647, it is in England, not France, that the idea receives most attention during the following years.[1] This increased activity marks the coming of age of a text that was known and commented on in the Renaissance but that never achieved the prominence of Aristotle's *Poetics* or Horace's *Ars Poetica*; its orientation, though strictly speaking rhetorical, simply did not conform very well to the dominant critical spirit of the time.[2] Early English interest in the sublime is notable in John Dennis's *The Grounds of Criticism in Poetry* and in Joseph Addison's *Spectator* essays, where sublimity is the sign of a great soul, a genius, and manifests itself in deviations from the rules, in "lapses," "inadvertencies," and "irregularities" that are "infinitely preferable to the works of an inferior kind of author."[3] Implied in these early

---

[1] See T. R. Henn, *Longinus and English Criticism* (Cambridge: Cambridge University Press, 1934), and René Wellek, *A History of Modern Criticism: 1750–1950*, 4 vols. (New Haven: Yale University Press, 1955), vol. 1, 105 ff.

[2] On Longinus in the Renaissance, see Bernard Weinberg, *History of Literary Criticism in the Italian Renaissance*, 2 vols. (Chicago: University of Chicago Press, 1961), pp. 188–90, 805–6.

[3] Dennis's essay is in *The Critical Works of John Dennis*, ed. Edward N. Hooker, 2 vols. (Baltimore: Johns Hopkins University Press, 1943), vol. 1,

attempts at definition is the point that regularity and precision of form are often not sufficient to capture the magnitude and might of certain experiences that take us beyond the confines in which we usually live.[4] This basic idea, which goes well beyond the allowances for breaches of convention admitted by a critic such as Doctor Johnson, bears the seed for a full-grown revolt against classicism and against neoclassical theories of tragedy.

We can see this revolt most clearly, perhaps, in a work that also offers one of the first systematic expositions of the concept of sublimity: *A Philosophical Enquiry into the Origin of our Ideas of the Sublime and Beautiful* (1756), by Edmund Burke.[5] Unlike previous treatments of the subject, this tract is an out and out attack on the classicist aesthetic of form, particularly on the assumption that clarity, restraint, and proportion are inviolable precepts of art. Exalting sublimity over beauty, Burke prefers not the characteristics of containment, control, and design, but of vastness, irregularity, incomprehensibility, and obscurity. "Obscurity seemed to Burke to be particularly desirable," remarks one critic, "since it permitted the mind to expand into the region of indefinable forces productive of an awe that could not possibly be aroused by any force with recognizable limits."[6] Because the sublime is conceived as a disquieting and boundless experience of intense feeling that cannot be adequately presented in conventional artistic structures, it is antithetical to Renaissance views of po-

---

especially pp. 338–63. For Addison's discussions, see *Spectator*, nos. 160, 291, 592; the quotation is from *Spectator* no. 291.

[4] See William K. Wimsatt and Cleanth Brooks, *Literary Criticism: A Short History* (New York: Alfred A. Knopf, 1965), pp. 284–88; Francis Gallaway, *Reason, Rule, and Revolt in English Classicism* (1940; reprint, New York: Octagon Books, 1965), pp. 333–40; Walter Jackson Bate, *From Classic to Romantic: Premises of Taste in Eighteenth-Century England* (1945; reprint, New York: Harper and Row, 1961), pp. 153–59.

[5] Henn, in *Longinus and English Criticism*, pp. 107–14, shows that Burke is heavily indebted to Hugh Blair for many of his ideas.

[6] Gallaway, *Reason, Rule, and Revolt*, p. 336.

etic order, which stress the restraining and regulatory power of form over content.

While theories of the sublime produce some local changes of interpretation in dramatic criticism—notably in the analysis of Shakespeare—it is not until the late eighteenth and early nineteenth centuries, in German philosophy and literary theory, that these new thoughts about art merge into an essentially different, antineoclassical account of tragedy. If the sublime has no immediately penetrating impact on tragic theory in England, that is probably because, according to most theoreticians, it resides in natural forces. External objects—big, surprising, awesome, and irregular ones, like the Alps, dark cavernous landscapes, or stormy seas—are occasions of sublimity.[7] This initial orientation toward landscape and physical environment bears little relation to tragedy's focus on social, religious, or ethical institutions.

But the definition of the concept is considerably reworked by later thinkers, especially Immanuel Kant in the second book of *The Critique of Judgment* and Friedrich Schiller in a series of essays that appropriates Kant's ideas for the discussion of tragedy.[8] The importance of these essays generally has not been conceded in modern criticism or adequately studied. Their significance lies in the elaboration of a model of the sublime (*das Erhabene*) oriented toward the experience of con-

[7] See Wimsatt and Brooks, *Literary Criticism*, p. 286.

[8] I have used the English translation, by James Creed Meredith, of Kant's *Critique of Judgment* (1952; reprint, Oxford: Clarendon Press, 1973) and consulted the German text in the standard edition of the Prussian Academy of Sciences, *Kants gesammelte Schriften*, 22 vols. (Berlin: G. Reimer, 1900–1942). The important essays by Schiller on tragedy are *Über den Grund des Vergnügens an tragischen Gegenständen* (1791), *Über die tragische Kunst* (1792), *Über das Pathetische* (1793), *Vom Erhabenen* (1793), and *Über das Erhabene* (1801), in *Sämtliche Werke*, ed. Gerhard Fricke and Herbert G. Gopfert, 5 vols. (Munich: Carl Hanser, 1959). All translations of Schiller are my own. On Schiller's debt to Kant, see R. D. Miller, *Schiller and the Ideal of Freedom* (Oxford: Clarendon Press, 1970), and Renate Homann, *Erhabenes und Satirisches: Zur Grundlegung einer Theorie ästhetischer Literatur bei Kant und Schiller* (Munich: Wilhelm Fink, 1977).

flict. Thus, historically, a theory of tragedy centered on opposition and struggle seems first to emerge within the context of
philosophically oriented Romantic treatments of sublimity. It
is for this reason that such treatments deserve scrutiny in the
present chapter. If I have relegated them to a position subordinate to Hegel's in the history of dramatic theory, this is because they do not develop a theory of conflict as emphatically
and systematically as he does in his lectures on aesthetics, nor
do they appear to have an impact on criticism as immediately
influential as his. But they nonetheless shape a sense of tragedy
that has come to enjoy considerable popularity in the twentieth century, one that regards tragic nobility as a direct consequence of a great soul's confrontation with oppressive or
hostile forces inimical to his *grandeur d'âme* and moral freedom.[9] While Hegel's theory emphasizes the ethical conflict between two morally justified agents, Schiller's Kantian ideas
stress the individual hero and his isolation in the face of potentially annihilating powers such as fate.

The particular version of "tragic humanism" represented in
the Romantic criticism of Schiller, is not, however, readily discernible in recent works of interpretation. Many of its central
principles, as we will see, were so formulated that as they dis-
seminated they mingled with existentially oriented theories, to
which they bear important resemblances. Thus we find in the
twentieth century a confluence of ideas about tragedy that
have different philosophical bases but remarkably congruent

[9] For a general theory of tragedy based on this idea, see D. D. Raphael, *The
Paradox of Tragedy* (Bloomington: Indiana University Press, 1960). Its influ-
ence on views of classical tragedy is apparent in the works of Bruno Snell, *The
Discovery of the Mind: The Greek Origins of European Thought*, tr. T. G.
Rosenmeyer (Cambridge, Mass.: Harvard University Press, 1953), and *Ais-
chylos und das Handeln im Drama* (Leipzig: Dieterich'sche Verlagsbuchhan-
dlung, 1928); Cedric Whitman, *Sophocles: A Study in Heroic Humanism*
(Cambridge, Mass.: Harvard University Press, 1951); John Finley, *Pindar and
Aeschylus*, Martin Classical Lectures no. 14 (Cambridge, Mass.: Harvard
University Press, 1955); Bernard Knox, *The Heroic Temper: Studies in Sophoclean Tragedy*, Sather Classical Lectures no. 35 (Berkeley: University of California Press, 1964).

interpretational results. Some of these similarities will emerge in the course of the subsequent discussion. What I want to emphasize at this point is that, as in the case of Hegel, the view of tragic conflict developing from theories of the sublime is problematic, for it rationalizes and contains struggle within a conceptual framework that is not amenable to forces at work in tragedy, particularly Greek tragedy, to which German Romantic thinkers repeatedly turned for the development of their critical views of drama. After studying the theoretical background of the tragic sublime, we will look briefly at some of the difficulties of interpretation to which it leads.

LET US TURN NOW to part 1 of *The Critique of Judgment*, where Kant develops the concept of the sublime later incorporated into discussions of tragedy. When he talks about *das Erhabene*, Kant is concerned with a state of mind brought about by man's confrontations with nature. Echoing Burke, he argues that "Nature excites ideas of the sublime in its chaos or wildest and most irregular disorder and desolation."[10] Thus, by comparison with the experience of the beautiful, which brings a sense of the purposiveness (*Zweckmässigkeit*) of the natural world, of the definite boundaries and teleological design of phenomena, the sublime displays nothing purposive and orderly in nature. Indeed, occasions for sublimity arise only when the synthesizing power of our sensible intuition—that is, our imagination, or *Einbildungskraft*—is assaulted and threatened by a violent external force, which appears to have no form, no boundaries. However, what happens at such moments is not a humiliating defeat of man in the face of natural forces (*Naturkräfte*), but the intrusion of

[10] Kant, *Critique of Judgment*, p. 92. On Kant's sublime, see Samuel H. Monk, *The Sublime: A Study of Critical Theories in Eighteenth-Century England* (New York: Modern Language Association of America, 1935), pp. 1–9; Donald W. Crawford, *Kant's Aesthetic Theory* (Madison: University of Wisconsin Press, 1974), pp. 135–41; Thomas Weiskel, *The Romantic Sublime: Studies in the Structure and Psychology of Transcendence* (Baltimore: Johns Hopkins University Press, 1976), pp. 22–29, 38–48.

a supersensible faculty from within (*das Übersinnliche*), which asserts superiority over the threat. This power also goes under the name of reason (*Vernunft*), which, by intervening when sensible intuition fails, reminds us of our destination (*Bestimmung*) as free, autonomous beings over whom sensuous nature has no ultimate control. The generation of a higher awareness of individual freedom in the sublime moment leads Kant to speak of a purposiveness quite independent of nature, a purposiveness within the individual, whose mind uses the chaos and disorder without to reveal reason and its ideas. "For the sublime, in the strict sense of the word, cannot be contained in any sensuous form, but rather concerns ideas of reason, which although no adequate representation of them is possible, may be excited and called into the mind by that very inadequacy itself which does admit of sensuous presentation."[11] Consequently, *Erhabenes* is a quality that can be properly predicated only of the human mind and not of phenomena in the external world. "We must seek a ground external to ourselves for the beautiful of nature, but seek it for the sublime in ourselves alone."[12]

One's experience of sublimity may arise either in the face of an extreme magnitude that suggests infinity or in the face of a powerful natural force. Of these two types of confrontation, which yield respectively the "mathematical" and "dynamic" sublime, the second, the dynamic sublime, exerts most influence on later theories of tragedy, especially Schiller's.[13] In order to establish more precisely the basic components of Kant's sublime, it will be useful to look briefly at both versions. The mathematical sublime arises in our effort to grasp an enormous quantum in a single intuition, or *Zusammenfassung*. Struggling but failing in this attempt at comprehension, the faculty of sensible representation, the imagination, recognizes its inadequacy and feels crushed. At this moment of sensory

[11] Kant, *Critique of Judgment*, p. 92.
[12] Kant, *Critique of Judgment*, p. 93.
[13] See pp. 94–117 of the *Critique of Judgment* for Kant's discussion of these two forms of sublimity.

failure, however, when the vital powers are checked, reason (*Vernunft*) intervenes and presents the idea of totality or infinitude, to which the physical quantum itself is not adequate. "The mind harkens now to the voice of reason," Kant says, "which for all given magnitudes—even for those which can never be completely apprehended though in sensuous representation estimated as completely given—requires totality and consequently comprehension in one intuition."[14] In other words, the effort of imagination to comprehend the great magnitude of an object leads first to a conflict between sensory comprehension and world, then to an alienation of the individual from external surroundings. The representative faculty is overcome, for it cannot provide a concept adequate to the object. Subsequently, this struggle and alienation are internalized and reenacted at another level: the imagination tries and fails to measure up to the ideas of reason, which transcend all sensible limits and affirm their superiority in man as a being regulated by the supersensible faculty and free from domination by physical forces. The conflict between imagination and reason in Kant's sublime accounts for its affective ambivalence: for pain, on the one hand, at the failure of the imagination to figure forth an enormous magnitude and for pleasure, on the other, at the power of reason's ideas to regulate that experience for a higher end. Kant concludes in this way: "Therefore the inner perception of the inadequacy of every standard of sense to serve for the rational estimation of magnitude is a coming into accord with reason's laws, and a displeasure that makes us alive to the feeling of the supersensible side of our being, according to which it [our being] is final, and consequently a pleasure, to find every standard of sensibility falling short of the ideas of reason."[15]

While the mathematical sublime involves the perception of a great magnitude, the dynamic sublime concerns might. Whatever in nature has terrifying power will show the inade-

[14] Kant, *Critique of Judgment*, p. 102.
[15] Kant, *Critique of Judgment*, p. 106.

quacy of physical resistance. But this impotence generates, under certain circumstances in which we are not seriously threatened by force, an awareness of the supersensible within us that is above nature and outside her dominion. Again, the experience of the sublime entails a conflict, which issues in a recognition of our true *Bestimmung*. Nature occasions sublimity, Kant says, "when it challenges our power to regard as small those things of which we are wont to be solicitous, and hence to regard its might as exercising over us and our personality no such rude dominion that we should bow down before it, once the question becomes one of our highest principles and of our asserting or forsaking them."[16]

From this brief recapitulation, several points emerge that are important for understanding Schiller and certain modern conceptions of Greek tragedy indebted to him. The possibility of the sublime is opened only at a point when the mind's relation to an object breaks down. In both the dynamic and mathematical sublime, we find an excess or surplus in the field of sensible intuition that leads to an awareness of incommensurability: there is a disturbing disproportion between the outside and the inside, the world and the self. A conflict ensues in which the individual tries to overcome the disproportion by matching powers of conceptualization or strength with the threatening force from without. At the point of failure and alienation, when the person recognizes limitations in the face of a superior external force, the defeat is recuperated at another level and made a vehicle of personal salvation. The sensible faculties must be squelched, Kant suggests, in order for reason to intervene and introduce a higher purposiveness—one beyond nature. Thus Kant's theory of the sublime depends on the conflict and defeat of the sensible powers against the natural world in order to aggrandize the force of reason. The victory of *Vernunftkraft* has clear moral implications. In being freed from the compulsion or necessity of nature, the individual conforms his or her action to an inner and higher princi-

---

[16] Kant, *Critique of Judgment*, p. 111.

ple, which is absolute, since it does not "depend on any condition or aim, or indeed upon any other law, but . . . simply declares a certain action to be right in itself."[17] Abandoning material interests or pragmatic gains and following inner moral law, Kant's sublime agent exemplifies the supreme human dignity that is built on autonomy and freedom.]

It should be clear from the foregoing summary that the Kantian theory of the sublime contains several ideas easily adaptable to a theory of tragedy: the dignity of the person, nobility through conflict, conformity to inner purpose or personal law, and freedom from external constraint. But given the technical nature of Kant's discussion, these ideas may very well not have made a substantial mark on later interpretation, unless Schiller had taken them over and refined them in developing his views of drama.

In a piece entitled *Das Pathethische* (1793), Schiller appropriates the major categories of the Kantian sublime and applies them to a definition of tragedy: "The representation of suffering, as simple suffering, is never the aim of art, but it is very important as the means to the end. The ultimate aim of art is the portrayal of the supersensible, and the tragic art in particular achieves this by conveying our moral independence from natural laws in a condition of emotional disturbance."[18] Later, in the same essay, he continues: "Art must delight the mind and satisfy freedom. He who falls prey to pain is simply a tortured animal and not a man tried by suffering. For from man, above all, a moral resistance to suffering is required, a resistance through which alone the principle of freedom, the intelligence, can make itself known."[19] The dramatization of such a struggle in tragedy and the victory of moral liberty ren-

---

[17] Miller, *Schiller and the Ideal of Freedom*, p. 43. Some of the philosophical difficulties involved in Kant's discussion of freedom and the moral law are treated by Miller in chapter 3 of his book. Significant as these problems are for coming to terms with Kant's larger views of reason (particularly "practical reason") and human liberty, they are tangential to the present argument.

[18] Schiller, *Sämtliche Werke*, vol. 5, p. 512.

[19] Schiller, *Sämtliche Werke*, vol. 5, p. 516.

der the dramatic hero sublime—a point borne out further in the essay *Über das Erhabene* (1801), where Schiller gives a more elaborate description of the structure of the sublime in literary works.

We find in these passages Kant's ideas of moral autonomy, the superiority of the supersensible faculty over the senses, and dignity won through painful conflict employed in a description of the dramatic action and the tragic agent. According to Schiller, tragedy portrays human resistance to forces of nature, which include everything—instincts, emotions, and external forces of necessity and fate—that does not proceed from moral reason (*Vernunft*). During these moments of resistance, the individual asserts freedom from the compulsive power of nature (*Naturzwang*) in a battle that proves the strength of the moral self, which, it turns out, can have victory only through suffering. This point is asserted in the essay *Über den Grund des Vergnügens an tragischen Gegenständen*: "The highest consciousness of our moral nature," Schiller says, "can be sustained only in a violent situation, a war," so that personal dignity comes from the pain of violent assault. And again, "moral fitness is most fully realized when it maintains supremacy in conflict with others; the full right of moral law is revealed only when it is shown in battle with all other forces of nature and when all these forces in competition with man lose their power over a human heart."[20] The conception sketched here stresses the exalted status of the dramatic hero as a representative of human strength and integrity. Nobility through suffering is at the core of tragedy. Identified with a principle of inner freedom and decision making, man's grandeur is his own creation. He defines himself in the process of staving off threats to his autonomy and choosing without constraint his own course of action.

Tragic conflict, revealing in the hero a capacity for resistance that transcends the physical, is, in Schiller's terms, an example of the "pathetic sublime." This experience corresponds

[20] Schiller, *Sämtliche Werke*, vol. 5, p. 364.

roughly with Kant's dynamic sublime. [A basic feature of this conflict is that it simultaneously alienates the individual from his world and identifies him with his own power of moral autonomy,] which effectively forecloses defeat. Examples of this mode of sublimity on the Greek stage are, according to Schiller, Aeschylus's Prometheus, Sophocles' Philoctetes, and Euripides' Heracles and Iphigenia. Revealing a "lively susceptibility to suffering," they also show the resistance of reason to onslaughts against human dignity.[21]

While Schiller relies heavily on the Kantian sublime in formulating his theory of tragedy, he also frequently develops the idea of freedom under stress in terms that are somewhat different from those of his predecessor. Kant, as we have seen, is primarily interested in the aggrandizement of reason and its laws during sublime crises; but Schiller, though he reveals a similar valorization of reason, tends to lay greater emphasis on the will as the essence of the self and the defining characteristic of humanity (*das Geschlechtscharakter des Menschens*). In *Über das Erhabene*, for example, he begins by stating that ["all other things obey necessity; man is the being who wills,"] and he proceeds to describe the sublime in such a way that the will, with its absolutely free power to choose between the dictates of reason and the impulses of the senses, usurps the controlling role of the Kantian *Vernunft* in moments of duress.[22] To be sure, Schiller remains profoundly concerned in this essay and elsewhere (notably in *Über das Pathetische*) with the conformity of choice and action with reason. But his emphasis in discussions of the sublimity of tragedy is on a dramatic presentation that bears witness above all to personal freedom: the actual performance of reason's dictates in tragedy is less important than the ability to act without constraint and in accordance with a private, inner sense of commitment.[23] "The person who by his condition demonstrates the

---

[21] Schiller, *Sämtliche Werke*, vol. 5, pp. 514–15.

[22] Schiller, *Sämtliche Werke*, vol. 5, p. 792.

[23] Schiller, *Sämtliche Werke*, vol. 5, p. 535. Schiller actually distinguishes between the "sublime of disposition or spiritual capacity" (*das Erhabene der*

dignity of man's vocation [as a being who wills rather than submits to necessity] is a sublime object, even though we do not find this vocation realized in his person." The tragic dramatist portrays "the possibility of absolute freedom of the will" and in so doing creates an "aesthetic" rather than a "moral" object, to use Schiller's terms, by which he means an object whose predominant theme is human freedom and whose aim is not the advocacy of an ethical rule.[24] An audience's appreciation of such a spectacle is based not on the interest of reason, which would really have acted rightly, but on the interest of the imagination (*Einbildungskraft*), which could have acted rightly. From this perspective, he regards Euripides' Medea as sublime.

> Vengeance is certainly an ignoble and vulgar emotion, but this does not prevent it from becoming aesthetic, if to satisfy it we must endure painful sacrifice. Medea, when she slays her children, aims with this action at the heart of Jason, but at the same time she strikes a heavy blow at her own heart, and her vengeance becomes aesthetically sublime as soon as we see a loving mother.[25]

This example testifies clearly to the surpassing importance, in Schiller's dramatic theory, of liberty and force of will in producing the dignity typical of tragic heroes. Even though her action can hardly be said to bear out the rule of Kantian *Vernunft*, Medea is sublime because she exercises strength of will against great forces of resistance—her own maternal impulses

---

Fassung) and the "sublime of action" (*das Erhabene der Handlung*). But exercise of will figures prominently in both. "The aesthetic power with which the sublime of disposition and of action grips us is in no way based on the interest of reason [*Vernunft*], which would really have acted rightly, but on the interest of the imagination [*Einbildungskraft*], which could have acted rightly; that is, on the perception that no feeling, however strong it might be, would be able to overcome the freedom of the soul."

[24] Schiller, *Sämtliche Werke*, vol. 5, p. 528.
[25] Schiller, *Sämtliche Werke*, vol. 5, p. 536.

and public sanctions—thus adhering to her "ideal vision of her nature," as a modern critic puts it.[26]

I have given some attention to Schiller's difference from Kant in his development of a sublime theory of tragedy because of the importance that the notion of the will has in later views of the tragic hero as an autonomous and independent agent. Whereas we hear few and faint echoes of a Kantian concept of reason in modern theories of tragic humanism, we can perceive clearly the influence of[Schiller's emphasis on the heroic will as a faculty that frees one from forces impinging on oneself and shattering personal integrity.]

THE IMPACT OF Romantic concepts of the sublime on views of tragic conflict is especially notable in the case of classical drama. Some of the most popular modern works of scholarship on the Greek playwrights reveal a profound indebtedness to the German tradition, though the influence is rarely acknowledged. Cedric Whitman, for example, sees the Sophoclean tragic hero as a "disciplined individual whose guide is inner law, and whose infringement of other laws is only incidental to the enormous struggle he passes through in order to preserve himself as a type of noble behavior."[27] With its stress on "disciplined individualism," on adherence to inner moral law, and on dignity won through struggle, this formulation contains some of Kant's most characteristic ideas. Furthermore, like Kant and his successor Schiller, Whitman locates within man a stable ground for decision making, a center of orientation that directs the agent's conduct. Hostile and destructive as the environment may be, the tragic hero discovers through conflict a personal standard for action and, by implementing that standard, staves off degradation or oblivion. The views of Whitman and others are indebted to

[26] Bernard Knox's description of Medea's heroic integrity is very much in tune with Schiller's remarks; see "The *Medea* of Euripides," in *Word and Action: Essays on the Ancient Theater* (Baltimore: Johns Hopkins University Press, 1979), p. 297.

[27] Whitman, *Sophocles*, p. 80.

Bruno Snell's insights in *The Discovery of the Mind,* a work in many ways derivative of German Romantic ideas. Conceiving the tragic figure in terms of a battle between self and external forms of necessity, Snell argues a position about the centrality of free choice in fifth-century tragedy that has remained very appealing to critics. "Aeschylus is at great pains to represent the characters in his tragedies as independent agents, acting upon the bidding of their own hearts, instead of merely reacting to stimuli."[28] It is from this responsibility, Snell believes, that a new and powerful conception of human dignity is born in the Greek world, one constituted in the "wilfull determination" to direct one's affairs of life and be the ultimate cause of one's actions. In developing his thesis about the "heroic temper" in Sophoclean tragedy, Bernard Knox implements many of these same points. The tragic hero is distinguished precisely because he or she is a free and responsible agent whose extraordinary stature is established in a refusal to accept the limitations posed from without. One's action is one's alone. "Unsupported by the gods and in the face of human opposition, [the hero] makes a decision which springs from the deepest layer of his individual nature, his *physis,* and then blindly, ferociously, heroically maintains that decision even to the point of self-destruction."[29] As in the Kantian theory of the sublime, alienation of the tragic individual from the world is both reinforced and justified by the recognition of a superior law or vision within that defines human action.

Often these ideas that I have been labeling as Kantian or Romantic show a certain affinity with existentialist notions of tragedy.[30] Like Kantian theories of the sublime, existentialist interpretations stress the significance of extreme experiences

---

[28] Snell, *The Discovery of the Mind,* p. 103.

[29] Knox, *The Heroic Temper,* pp. 5–6.

[30] Whitman, for example, traces his theoretical presuppositions to the philosophical works of Kierkegaard, Sartre, and Heidegger; see "Existentialism and the Classic Hero," in *The Heroic Paradox: Essays on Homer, Sophocles, and Aristophanes,* ed. Charles Segal (Ithaca: Cornell University Press, 1982), p. 2.

or, to use Karl Jaspers' term, "boundary situations," in which the individual achieves, through suffering and conflict, a choice that constitutes or "authenticates" him.[31] The existentialist process of heroic self-formation through radical decision making and struggle against the threat of anonymity bears definite resemblances to the self-definition in which the sublime agent is involved. In both cases, the danger of annihilation is imminent, and identity takes form through the assertion of choice and action in a moment of crisis. Certainly, as I have already noted, there are very different philosophical bases for these superficial similarities between Kantian-Romantic and existentialist approaches to tragedy, differences that deserve careful study. Among other things, for example, existentialism moves away from an idea of reason as the arbiter of moral law and treats choice in an extremely personal and nonabsolutist framework, stressing the incoherent nature of human experience, once the redeeming force of cosmic order is lost and one is drawn to act without a moral context that establishes the rightness of choice. Schiller, who adapts the controlling or normative function of reason, as Kant conceives of it, to a theory of drama that centers on personal freedom and the will, may be regarded as an intermediate figure between strictly Kantian and existentialist views of tragic action. But for purposes of the present argument, such divergences are less important than the fact that theories of the sublime, stemming from Kant and Schiller, shaped a model of tragedy, which was congruent with later existentialist notions, also centered on conflict. Consequently, we find a gradual

[31] For Karl Jaspers' existentialist theory of tragedy, see *Tragedy Is Not Enough*, tr. Harald A. T. Reiche et al. (London: Victor Gollancz, 1953). Other existentially oriented theories include Murray Krieger, *The Tragic Vision: Variations on a Theme in Literary Interpretation* (Chicago: University of Chicago Press, 1960), and Robert Heilman, *Tragedy and Melodrama: Versions of Experience* (Seattle: University of Washington Press, 1968). For a useful exposition of existentialist philosophy and tragedy, see William Barrett, *Irrational Man: A Study in Existentialist Philosophy* (Garden City, N. Y.: Doubleday Anchor Books, 1958).

convergence of critical views, which produces in our century a hybrid form of interpretation.

Once the influence of Kant and Schiller has been acknowledged, the question arises whether a Kantian-based humanism is viable as a tool for interpreting Greek plays. To what extent do classical tragedies support the idea of sublime integrity constituted in a struggle for moral autonomy? Such questions have been put by critics who ponder the issue of freedom of the will and the conflict of external with internal causational forces in fifth-century drama. The debate over this problem continues, and it is unnecessary to engage its subtleties in this context.[32] Instead, I want to show that theories of Greek tragedy indebted, if only indirectly, to the Kantian sublime typically import into their arguments about heroic dignity an idea of personal autonomy or the will that is problematic in the interpretation of classical plays.

To put it simply, the works of the Attic dramatists resist the Romantic notion, adapted from Kant and found in popular modern interpretations, of an autonomous, unconstrained will that is the condition for human nobility.[33] It is not that

[32] The most recent discussions of freedom of the will in Greek literature include Albrecht Dihle, *The Theory of the Will in Classical Antiquity* (Berkeley: University of California Press, 1982); Hannah Arendt, *The Life of the Mind* (New York: Harcourt Brace Jovanovich, 1978), vol. 2, *Willing*, pp. 55–63; Jean-Pierre Vernant and Pierre Vidal-Naquet, *Mythe et tragédie en Grèce ancienne* (Paris: François Maspero, 1972), chaps. 1–2. For particular discussions of this problem in Greek tragedy, see N.G.L. Hammond, "Personal Freedom and Its Limitations in the *Oresteia*," *Journal of Hellenic Studies* 85 (1965): 42–55; Albin Lesky, "Decision and Responsibility in the Tragedy of Aeschylus," *Journal of Hellenic Studies* 86 (1966): 78–85; William Greene, *Moira: Fate, Good and Evil in Greek Thought* (Gloucester, Mass.: Peter Smith, 1968); K. J. Dover, "Some Neglected Aspects of Agamemnon's Dilemma," *Journal of Hellenic Studies* 93 (1973): 58–69; Thomas G. Rosenmeyer, *The Art of Aeschylus* (Berkeley: University of California Press, 1982), pp. 284–307.

[33] As recent discussions such as Dihle's and Arendt's suggest, the sources shaping modern critical notions of the will in Attic drama have a complicated history and are not limited by Kantian influence. While admitting this complexity, I also think that the Romantic tradition indebted to Kant was a par-

Aeschylus, Sophocles, and Euripides are especially deficient in a language for the will. Nor is it a question of their dramatizing fate as a force squelching man's ability to control his own affairs. Rather, the works by the ancient tragedians present us with human actions in ways that consistently complicate personal choice with various forms of constraint, divine and social. Choice itself, in the plays, is frequently inseparable from external necessity and is elided with powers which, in the Kantian tradition, are opposed to the will. Consequently, it is difficult to extricate from tragedy the category of an individually willed act without destroying the playwright's characteristic complexity of perspectives on the nature and origin of a human deed. To talk about the heroes of Greek plays as agents who freely will what they do against external necessity is to reduce the tension of forces that produces the uniquely tragic conception of action in fifth-century drama.[34]

Take, for example, Aeschylus's *Oresteia* and *Agamemnon*, in particular. Whatever action in the trilogy one chooses to scrutinize turns out to be informed by multiple converging motives. Agamemnon's murder of Iphigenia is provoked by the goddess Artemis in retribution for the violence that will be wreaked by the Argives against her beloved "hare," Troy: she stills the winds that are needed to make the expedition and demands the sacrifice of Agamemnon's daughter to unbind the ships of the Danaans.[35] But this divine *ananke*, or necessity, in no way mitigates the fact that the king decides, when faced with the choice of saving his child or army, to murder Iphigenia. In so doing, he does not merely submit with resignation to necessity, but rather joins his own choice to divine compulsion and acts with passion and cruelty. The chorus

---

ticularly important conduit for the importation of a theory of the will into later dramatic criticism.

[34] See A. Rivier, "Remarques sur le 'nécessaire' et la 'nécessité' chez Eschyle," *Revue des études grecques* 81 (1968): 5–39, and Vernant and Vidal-Naquet, *Mythe et tragédie*, pp. 61–74.

[35] Aeschylus, *Agamemnon*, in *Septem quae supersunt tragoedias*, ed. Denys L. Page (Oxford: Clarendon Press, 1972), ll. 126–55.

says that once he makes up his mind to take on the yoke of
necessity, he breathes with an impious, unclean, and unholy
disposition of mind: from that moment his thinking is shame-
lessly daring. The insistent intertwining of terms such as
ananke, to phronein, "understanding," and *aischrometis,*
"forming base designs," in the passage is typical of Aeschylus's
presentation of human deeds as personally and divinely motivated.[36] When we consider that the murder also falls ineluctably within the pattern of "like for like" in the *Oresteia,*
whereby the sins of the fathers are inherited by the sons, the
picture becomes even more complicated: Agamemnon's sacrifice of his child is an ironic mirroring of his own father's
murder of Thyestes' children. Hence, Artemis's compulsion,
Agamemnon's ruthless daring, and the curse on the house of
Atreus merge in a single act—the killing of Iphigenia.[37] Interpretations that either insist on the exclusiveness of necessity or
of free will or that feature one of these factors as causally explanatory of action fragment the dense web of forces in the
tragedy. Moreover, we can now begin to appreciate the difficulty of using the expression *free will* to describe the personal
choice made by Agamemnon as agent of the murder. The association of the term, at least in the Kantian tradition, with
autonomy, singular origin, and unique responsibility runs
against the grain of the Greek formulation of the act. It is for
this reason that I take exception to Albin Lesky's notion of
"double motivation" in ancient tragedy, which, although
rightly balancing the claims of divine necessity and individual
culpability, is still grounded in the language and intellectual
apparatus of a modern concept of free will.[38]

[36] Aeschylus, *Agamemnon,* ll. 218–27.

[37] See Anne Lebeck, *The Oresteia: A Study in Language and Structure*
(Washington, D.C.: Center for Hellenic Studies, 1971); Albin Lesky, "Deci-
sion and Responsibility in the Tragedy of Aeschylus," *Journal of Hellenic
Studies* 86 (1966): 80–83; K. J. Dover, "Some Neglected Aspects of Aga-
memnon's Dilemma," *Journal of Hellenic Studies* 93 (1973); Rosenmeyer,
The Art of Aeschylus, pp. 284–307.

[38] Lesky, "Decision and Responsibility in the Tragedy of Aeschylus."

As the previous analysis suggests, the conception of sublime integrity developed by Schiller and inherited by recent literary critics is undermined once individual autonomy and supremacy of the will are taken away. But Aeschylus's trilogy is not the only work that fails to answer to the recent views we have have been studying. Other plays, notably those thought to be most exemplary of tragic humanism, also contribute to a re-evaluation of Kantian-based interpretations of Greek drama. Sophocles' *Antigone* and *Ajax*, like *Agamemnon*, present heroic action as the product of diverse powers uniting in ways that are difficult to conceive within a framework that treats personal choice or individual motivation as incompatible with external constraint. Antigone, whose self-assertion and alienation have attracted theorists of individualism, is referred to frequently in the play as one not ashamed to "think apart from others" (510).[39] Guided by her own law (αὐτόνομος ζῶσα, 821), she suffers the consequence of her decision. Her *orga*, or temperament, the chorus says, is *autognotos*, "self-determined" (875). Here, it seems, we have solid evidence of a morally autonomous character, whose conduct shows all the signs of being freely willed. But as Aeschylus complicates acts of choice with forces of necessity, so too does Sophocles. Antigone's burial of Polyneices, from one point of view personally motivated, is, from another, the result of one living out the curse on Labdacus's house. About this *ate* the chorus says, "No generation releases the next, / But one of the gods brings ruin, and there is no deliverance" (596–97).

As driving motivations for Antigone's deed, choice and ancestral *ate* are integrally united, to such an extent that the cho-

[39] See, for example, Whitman, *Sophocles*, pp. 81–99, and Knox, *The Heroic Temper*, pp. 62–67. These are Knox's words on Antigone: "Two words in the long lyrical dialogue (ll. 781 ff.) precisely define the character of Antigone and the heroic temper in general: *autonomos* 'a law unto itself' and *autognotos orga* 'passion self-conceived.' The force which drives the hero on to assert his independence, like a sovereign state, is something which stems from his inner being, his *physis*, his true self: it is not to be explained by outside circumstances."

rus says elsewhere (471–72) that the peculiar characteristic directing the protagonist in self-assertive action is itself
inherited, necessitated by the unrelenting continuity of the father's "savage temper of mind" in the daughter. In a formulation typical of the Greek tragic mode, personal initiative and
external causality are not merely juxtaposed as alternative aspects of Antigone's action but are inextricably bound as an
explanation of what she does and why she does it. Sophocles'
dramatization makes it impossible to adhere to the concept of
necessity or constraint as rigorously external to an inner purpose. Tragic action marks the intersection and interpenetration of categories that we tend to regard as separate. Once
again, we see how Schiller's notion of a noble struggle against
outer threats to individual freedom is problematic as a theory
of Greek tragedy, for it sharply divides forces that the playwrights elide.

The same objection holds for interpretations of Ajax that
define the hero's dignity in terms of his radical independence
of divine or social constraints and his successful resistance
against threats to his autonomy. According to a popular modern reading, Ajax's suicide, as a freely chosen act, becomes an
instrument of self-definition that liberates him from the de-
grading humiliations he endured at the hands of Athene in the
first part of the drama.[40] Though initially subject, in a horrifying way, to the control of supernatural powers, the protagonist ultimately shapes his existence in a courageous come-
back that puts these powers to shame. But this view is partial.
While it takes into account such remarks as Tecmessa's that
no hand or agency but his own brought Ajax to death, it ignores the repeated observations at the end of the play that the
gods precipitated his act. Tecmessa herself, validating the chorus's assertion that events have happened in accordance with
the gods (θεῶν μέτα, 950), qualifies her earlier comment by
agreeing that Pallas caused (φυτεύει, 954) her husband's
death. It is also worth mentioning that Teucer, when he
grieves over his brother's corpse, speaks about the sword on

[40] See especially Whitman, *Sophocles*, pp. 59–80.

which Ajax has fallen as a weapon crafted by an Erinys, a Fury working in unison with the contrivances of the gods (1029–33). Caught in a nexus of causal factors, Ajax's suicide is no more a pure act of will than is Agamemnon's murder of Iphigenia or Antigone's burial of Polyneices.

The consistent thickening of the web of action distinguishes Greek tragedy from critical views with a humanistic bent, for they seek to locate in the autonomous will or the independent personality the source for tragic heroism. Contrary to what Kantian-based assumptions dictate, human dignity in classical drama is not constituted in a successful battle against external threats to individual freedom. What the fifth-century playwrights typically dramatize is an irreducible ambivalence, or more accurately, multivalence, in human deeds that makes it impossible to classify them according to categories of necessity and free will. At the very moments when a character seems in supreme control of his or her existence, the tragedy reveals the presence of complicating factors, such as *ate, ananke*, or *moira*. But to formulate the point in this way is to suppose a distinction between personal choice and external constraint that the tragedies, as we have seen, do not espouse. The interpenetration in Greek plays of forces that are strictly differentiated in a Kantian framework suggests all the more strongly the inadequacies of modern views indebted to the German tradition.

If the notion of will prominent in twentieth-century interpretations is problematic for a reading of classical drama, so too are the Kantian ideas of the individual and of the supreme importance of the human personality. For they have encouraged in dramatic criticism since Schiller a conception of character that is not well suited to the Greek stage. *Personality* suggests a continuity of selfhood over time, a complex continuity whose coherence is guaranteed by an ego that synthesizes experience at the same time that it differentiates itself from the events, forces, and objects in its environment.[41] Fur-

---

[41] See the essay "Personal Identity" by Terence Penelhum, in *The Encyclopedia of Philosophy*, ed. Paul Edwards, 8 vols. (New York: Collier-Macmil-

thermore, as we have seen, for Kant and Schiller the term
often has a distinctly ethical cast and is used to convey the idea
of a person "guided by laws fashioned for him according to
the principle of autonomy."[42] *Die freie Person, unsre wahre
Person*, and *Persönlichkeit* bear the notion of moral freedom
integral to Kantian thought. Such a notion cannot very well
apply to the works of the fifth-century tragedians, in which, as
we have seen, the agent is the point of intersection for diverse
forces, some of them excluded by a more modern concept of
personality.[43] The boundaries of identity in classical plays are
more fluid than those of the Kantian individual. But, from another side, they are more restricted and fixed; a tragic agent's
identity has neither historical nor biological depth. Narrowly
circumscribed by the temporal prescriptions of performance,
dramatic character in the classical tradition takes shape
around an act, usually single and liminal, staked once and for
all on the margins of existence. Such extremity and conden-
sation cut short the flow of time within which psychological,
moral, and emotional development is possible, radically
streamline character to the demands of the present, and fore-
shorten the mental space of a life lived in meditative reflection
on the past and future. *Personality*, simply on technical or formal grounds, has trouble qualifying as a viable critical term
for the interpretation of Greek drama. The assumptions that
inform it are more appropriate to the novelistic tradition, with

---

lan, 1967), vol. 5, pp. 95–107; Miller, *Schiller and the Ideal of Freedom*,
chaps. 1–2; Vernant and Vidal-Naquet, *Mythe et tragédie en Grèce ancienne*,
pp. 43–44, 47–48; Zevedei Barbu, *Problems of Historical Psychology* (London: Routledge and Kegan Paul, 1960), pp. 74–89 on individuation. Barbu's
conclusions, which need qualification, are based on Snell's work, particularly
on the idea that in Aeschylus we find full proof of the emergence within Greek
civilization of the individual as a free agent; see the chapter entitled "The
Emergence of Personality in the Greek World."

[42] See Miller, *Schiller and the Ideal of Freedom*, pp. 20–21.

[43] Some limitations of the concept of personality in the interpretation of
Greek tragedy are studied by John Gould, "Dramatic Character and 'Human
Intelligibility' in Greek Tragedy," *Proceedings of the Cambridge Philological
Society* 24 (1978): 43–67.

its extended temporal span, its introspective focus on an ego that responds to external stimuli, and its leisurely fleshing out of character.[44]

MUCH AS THE Kantian sublime enabled thinkers such as Schiller to move beyond the often narrow moralism of neo-classical dramatic theory and into direct confrontation with the culturally unsettling agonistic experiences of tragic drama, its account of struggle entailed a new series of critical exclusions. By focusing on the autonomy of moral reason or the will as the condition of heroic integrity, German Romantic critics imported into the theoretical tradition a number of assumptions about the individual and human nobility that bypassed certain kinds of dramatic evidence in classical plays. Moreover, the interpretive framework provided by the sublime, in assuming from the outset a necessary rationality in one's confrontation with violent forces, foreclosed reflection on some of the characteristic problems of identity and responsibility in tragedy. Once the tragic individual became the focal point for analysis, other elements of the dramatic action were either subordinated to a struggle for freedom and self-determination or simply excluded from a sense of what counts in a play.

From this perspective, we can see that the critical tendency to seize upon an issue in literary texts as central and to choose from the remaining mass only what seems most compliant is as characteristic of modern theories focused on tragic conflict as it is of older ones biased against it. If the Kantian and Hegelian traditions of dramatic criticism break with the past in their emphasis on agonistic structures, they do so only by regulating strife under the control of ordering principles and teleological designs. The inadequacies of these strategies of mediation, which I have tried to uncover in readings that supply

[44] See Harold Rosenberg, "Character Change and the Drama," in *The Tradition of the New* (New York: Horizon Press, 1959), pp 135–53 and Thomas G. Rosenmeyer, "Wahlakt und Entscheidungsprozess in der antiken Tragö-die," *Poetica*, vol. 10, no. 1 (1978): 1–24.

the recalcitrant material they exclude, in effect help confirm
the difficulties that strife posed for theories, such as Aristotle's, bent upon securing tragedy as a *techne* with its inherent *logos*. As the preceding chapters have shown, only when
conflict has been successfully incorporated into a larger context of order—as in Kant's sublime or Hegel's dialectic—does
it ascend to a place of prominence in theoretical reflection on
tragedy. But the condition that enables thinkers such as
Schiller and Hegel to center on strife is precisely the condition
that leads to an exclusionary appropriation of this experience
in classical and Renaissance plays, one that neutralizes or
short-circuits subversions tied to collision and thus renders
them amenable to systematic interests. This paradoxical situation, which is one also characterizing a good deal of modern
criticism indebted to the Germans, stems at least partly from
the fact that traditional Aristotelian assumptions about poetic
unity, coherence, and closure are so binding on later critical
views in the Kantian and Hegelian traditions that they end up
taming conflict, when it finally surfaces in critical discussion,
and reducing it to terms of philosophical order. The same phenomenon could be traced in an account such as Nietzsche's in
The Birth of Tragedy. While exploring under the rubric of the
"Dionysiac" various turbulent, agonistic, and unsystematic
aspects of experience in Greek tragic plays, Nietzsche nonetheless ultimately submits them to the mediating framework
of "Apollonian" form. In his emphasis on the synthesizing and
reconciling powers of dramatic structure, he carries on the tradition of Hegel, who has similar recourse to containing properties and formalistic closure in stabilizing the meaning of conflict in plays.

The resistance of tragedy, however, to such terms of order
is hardly complete or decisive, as we have seen. Neither Kant's
sublime nor Hegel's dialectic could have held so strong a grip
on critical thinking had it not generated compelling and on-
going insights. In illuminating aspects of drama that remained
unscrutinized in the classical and neoclassical traditions, these
methods of approach have broadened an appreciation of some

of the greatest literary works in the Western world and opened discussion to a pervasive experience in tragedy. But as is often the case with theories of seminal influence, the understanding that they have made possible has also enabled us to perceive the delimiting conditions giving rise to critical insight in the first place: the most fruitful and stimulating principle of the theory is secured at the price of exclusions, the scrutiny of which can in turn produce new insight.

The present study has attempted to follow this interplay between critical understanding and what it omits from its field of vigilance by focusing on one aspect of the theoretical tradition on tragedy. It is no accident that the texts in which the interplay is most productively studied are philosophical ones that strive rather more rigorously than others for systematic coherence. Within the context of these works, the tensions between interpretive expectations of dramatic order and the destabilizing, unsystematic features of tragic conflict become especially provocative sources for critical revision and self-reflection. For the urge toward rational comprehension in such theories allows us to evaluate the consequences of that motion within humans that Aristotle understood very well—the yearning for knowledge, which eliminates or at least diminishes the helplessness we feel in the face of what teases our minds and elicits our wonder. While that basic urge has produced, among other things, a vast and rich body of critical thinking about literary texts, it also has had to stand the radical challenge of tragedy and respond to points of resistance in the plays on which it exercises itself. In continually revitalizing the need to qualify and revise our critical expectations, this challenge at the same time confronts us with the inevitable inadequacies of the theoretical disposition, whose desire for explanatory fullness is always the mark of a crucial yet productive limitation.

Abel, Lionel, ed. *Moderns on Tragedy: An Anthology of Modern and Relevant Opinions on the Substance and Meaning of Tragedy* (Greenwich, Conn.: Fawcett, 1967).

Adams, Hazard. *Critical Theory Since Plato* (New York: Harcourt Brace Jovanovich, 1971).

Adkins, Arthur W. H. "Aristotle and the Best Kind of Tragedy." *Classical Quarterly*, n.s., no. 16 (1966): 78–102.

———. *Merit and Responsibility: A Study in Greek Values* (Oxford: Clarendon Press, 1960).

Aeschylus. *Septem quae supersunt tragoedias*, ed. Denys L. Page (Oxford: Clarendon Press, 1972).

Allen, Judson Boyce. *The Ethical Poetic of the Later Middle Ages: A Decorum of Convenient Distinction* (Toronto: University of Toronto Press, 1982).

Altman, Joel. *The Tudor Play of Mind: Rhetorical Inquiry and the Development of Elizabethan Drama* (Berkeley: University of California Press, 1978).

Annas, Julia. *An Introduction to Plato's Republic* (Oxford: Clarendon Press, 1981).

Arendt, Hannah. *The Life of the Mind.* Vol. 1, *Thinking.* Vol. 2, *Willing* (New York: Harcourt Brace Jovanovich, 1978).

Aristotle. *De Anima*, ed. with commentary W. D. Ross (Oxford: Clarendon Press, 1961).

———. *De Motu Animalium*, ed. and trans. with commentary Martha Craven Nussbaum (Princeton: Princeton University Press, 1978).

———. *De Partibus Animalium*, trans. D. M. Balme (Oxford: Clarendon Press, 1972).

———. *Metaphysics*, ed. with commentary W. D. Ross. 2 vols. (1924; reprint, Oxford: Clarendon Press, 1958).

———. *Nichomachean Ethics*, ed. J. Bywater (1894; reprint, Oxford: Clarendon Press, 1959).

———. *Nichomachean Ethics*, trans. Martin Ostwald (Indianapolis: Bobbs-Merrill, 1962).

Aristotle. *On the Parts of Animals*, trans. A. L. Peck (Cambridge: Cambridge University Press, 1961).

———. *Physics*, ed. with commentary W. D. Ross (1936; reprint, Oxford: Clarendon Press, 1960).

———. *Poetics*, ed. D. W. Lucas (1968; reprint, Oxford: Clarendon Press, 1980).

———. *Poetics*, ed. D. S. Margoliouth (London: Hodder and Stoughton, 1911).

———. *Politics*, ed. with commentary W. D. Ross (1957; reprint, Oxford: Clarendon Press, 1962).

———. *Prior and Posterior Analytics*. Rev. text. Ed. W. D. Ross (Oxford: Clarendon Press, 1965).

———. *Rhetoric*, ed. John Sandys, comm. Edward Cope (Cambridge: Cambridge University Press, 1877).

Arnold, E. Vernon. *Roman Stoicism: Being Lectures on the History of the Stoic Philosophy with Special Reference to Its Development within the Roman Empire* (1911; reprint, London: Routledge and Kegan Paul, 1958).

Atkins, J.W.H. *Literary Criticism in Antiquity*. 2 vols. (Cambridge: Cambridge University Press, 1943).

Avineri, Shlomo. "Consciousness and History: *List der Vernunft* in Hegel and Marx." *New Studies in Hegel's Philosophy*, ed. Warren E. Steinkraus (New York: Holt, Rinehart, and Winston, 1971), pp. 108–18.

Baker, Herschel. *The Dignity of Man: Studies in the Persistence of an Idea* (Cambridge, Mass.: Harvard University Press, 1947).

Baldwin, Charles S. *Mediaeval Rhetoric and Poetic to 1400* (Gloucester, Mass.: Peter Smith, 1959).

———. *Renaissance Literary Theory and Practice*, ed. Donald Lemen Clark (New York: Columbia University Press, 1939).

Barbu, Zevedei. *Problems of Historical Psychology* (London: Routledge and Kegan Paul, 1960).

Barish, Jonas. *The Antitheatrical Prejudice* (Berkeley: University of California Press, 1981).

Barnes, Jonathan et al., eds. *Articles on Aristotle*. 4 vols. (London: Duckworth, 1975–1979).

Barrett, William. *Irrational Man: A Study in Existentialist Philosophy* (Garden City, N. Y.: Doubleday Anchor Books, 1958).

Barthes, Roland. *S/Z* (Paris: Seuil, 1970).

———. *The Pleasure of the Text*, trans. Richard Miller (New York: Hill and Wang, 1975).

Bate, Walter Jackson. *From Classic to Romantic: Premises of Taste in Eighteenth-Century England* (1945; reprint, New York: Harper and Row, 1961).

Bluestone, Max. "*Libido Speculandi*: Doctrine and Dramaturgy in Contemporary Interpretations of Marlowe's *Doctor Faustus*." *Reinterpretations of Elizabethan Drama*, ed. Norman Rabkin (New York: Columbia University Press, 1969), pp. 33–88.

Boggess, William F. *Averrois Cordubensis Commentarium Medium in Aristotelis Poetriam*. Dissertation at University of North Carolina, Chapel Hill, 1965.

Bollack, Jean. *Empédocle*. Vol. 1 of *Introduction à l'ancienne physique*. 3 vols. (Paris: Les Éditions de Minuit, 1965).

Booth, Stephen. *King Lear, Macbeth, Indefinition, and Tragedy* (New Haven: Yale University Press, 1983).

———. "On the Value of *Hamlet*." *Reinterpretations of Elizabethan Drama*, ed. Norman Rabkin (New York: Columbia University Press, 1969), pp. 136–76.

Bowers, Fredson Thayer. *Elizabethan Revenge Tragedy, 1587–1642* (Gloucester, Mass.: Peter Smith, 1959).

Bradley, A. C. *Oxford Lectures on Poetry* (1909; reprint, London: Macmillan, 1959).

———. *Shakespearean Tragedy: Essays on Hamlet, Othello, King Lear, and Macbeth* (London: Macmillan, 1905).

Bray, René. *La formation de la doctrine classique en France* (Paris: Nizet, 1966).

Brink, C. O. *Horace on Poetry: Prolegomena to the Literary Epistles* (Cambridge: Cambridge University Press, 1963).

Bush, Douglas. *The Renaissance and English Humanism* (Toronto: University of Toronto Press, 1939).

Butcher, S. H. *Aristotle's Theory of Poetry and Fine Art, with a Critical Text and Translation of the Poetics*. 4th ed. (New York: Dover, 1951).

Buxton, R.G.A. *Persuasion in Greek Tragedy: A Study of Peitho* (Cambridge: Cambridge University Press, 1982).

Calderwood, James. "*The Duchess of Malfi*: Styles of Ceremony." *Shakespeare's Contemporaries: Modern Studies in English Renaissance Drama*. 2d ed. eds. Max Bluestone and Norman Rabkin (Englewood Cliffs, N. J.: Prentice-Hall, 1970), pp. 278–91.

Calderwood, James. *To Be and Not To Be: Negation and Meta-drama in Hamlet* (New York: Columbia University Press, 1983).

Cassirer, Ernst. *The Individual and the Cosmos in Renaissance Philosophy*, trans. Mario Domandi (New York: Barnes and Noble, 1963).

Castelvetro, Lodovico. *The Poetics of Aristotle Translated and Explained. Critical Theory Since Plato*, ed. Hazard Adams (New York: Harcourt Brace Jovanovich, 1971).

Charlton, H. B. *Shakespearian Tragedy* (Cambridge: Cambridge University Press, 1948).

Cicero. *De Oratore*, ed. A. S. Wilkins (Amsterdam: Adolf M. Hakkert, 1962).

———. *Orator. M. Tulli Ciceronis Rhetorica*, ed. A. S. Wilkins (Oxford: Clarendon Press, 1978).

Cole, A. T. "The Relativism of Protagoras." *Yale Classical Studies* 22 (1972): 19–45.

Coleridge, Samuel Taylor. *Shakespearean Criticism*, ed. Thomas Middleton Raysor. 2 vols. (Cambridge, Mass.: Harvard University Press, 1930).

Cooper, John M. *Reason and Human Good in Aristotle* (Cambridge: Cambridge University Press, 1975).

Corneille, Pierre. *Trois Discours. Corneille: Oeuvres Complètes*, ed. André Stegmann (Paris: Seuil, 1963).

Corrigan, Robert W., ed. *Tragedy: Vision and Form*. 2d ed. (New York: Harper and Row, 1981).

Crane, R. S. et al., eds. *Critics and Criticism: Ancient and Modern* (Chicago: University of Chicago Press, 1952).

Crawford, Donald W. *Kant's Aesthetic Theory* (Madison: University of Wisconsin Press, 1974).

Culler, Jonathan. *Flaubert: The Uses of Uncertainty*. Rev. ed. (Ithaca: Cornell University Press, 1985).

———. *On Deconstruction: Theory and Criticism After Structuralism* (Ithaca: Cornell University Press, 1982).

———. *Structuralist Poetics: Structuralism, Linguistics, and the Study of Literature* (Ithaca: Cornell University Press, 1975).

Danson, Lawrence, ed. *On King Lear* (Princeton: Princeton University Press, 1981).

Dennis, John. *The Critical Works of John Dennis*, ed. Edward N. Hooker. 2 vols. (Baltimore: Johns Hopkins University Press, 1943).

Derrida, Jacques. *Dissemination*, trans. Barbara Johnson (Chicago: University of Chicago Press, 1981).

———. *Of Grammatology*, trans. Gayatri Chakravorty Spivak (Baltimore: Johns Hopkins University Press, 1976).

———. *Writing and Difference*, trans. Alan Bass (Chicago: University of Chicago Press, 1978).

Diderot, Denis. *De la poésie dramatique. Oeuvres esthétiques.* 2 vols. (Paris: Garnier Frères, 1968).

Dihle, Albrecht. *The Theory of the Will in Classical Antiquity* (Berkeley: University of California Press, 1982).

Dodds, E. R. *The Greeks and the Irrational.* Sather Classical Lectures no. 25 (Berkeley: University of California Press, 1971).

———. "On Misunderstanding *Oedipus Rex*." *Greece and Rome* 13 (1966): 37–49.

Dover, K. J. "Some Neglected Aspects of Agamemnon's Dilemma." *Journal of Hellenic Studies* 93 (1973): 58–85.

Dryden, John. *An Essay of Dramatic Poesy. Literary Criticism: Plato to Dryden*, ed. Allan H. Gilbert (Detroit: Wayne State University Press, 1962).

Edwards, Paul, ed. *The Encyclopedia of Philosophy.* 8 vols. (New York: Collier-Macmillan, 1967).

Ehrenberg, Victor. *Sophocles and Pericles* (Oxford: Basil Blackwell, 1954).

Else, Gerald. *Aristotle's Poetics: The Argument* (Cambridge, Mass.: Harvard University Press, 1963).

Euripides. *Heracles*, trans. William Arrowsmith in *Euripides II. The Complete Greek Tragedies*, eds. David Grene and Richmond Lattimore (Chicago: University of Chicago Press, 1969).

———. *Heracles*, ed. Godfrey Bond (Oxford: Clarendon Press, 1981).

Fergusson, Francis. *The Idea of a Theatre: A Study of Ten Plays, The Art of Drama in Changing Perspective* (Princeton: Princeton University Press, 1949).

Finley, John. *Pindar and Aeschylus.* Martin Classical Lectures no. 14 (Cambridge, Mass.: Harvard University Press, 1955).

Finley, Moses I. "Myth, Memory and History." *History and Theory: Studies in the Philosophy of History* (The Hague: Mouton, 1965), pp. 281–302.

Foot, Philippa. "Moral Realism and Moral Dilemma." *The Journal of Philosophy*, vol. 80, no. 7 (1983): 379–98.

Foucault, Michel. *Discipline and Punish: The Birth of the Prison,* trans. Alan Sheridan (New York: Pantheon Books, 1977).

———. *Madness and Civilization: A History of Insanity in the Age of Reason,* trans. Richard Howard (New York: Vintage Books, 1973).

———. *Power/Knowledge: Select Interviews and Other Writings, 1972–1977,* ed. Colin Gordon (New York: Pantheon Books, 1980).

Fraser, Russell. *The War Against Poetry* (Princeton: Princeton University Press, 1970).

Fraser, Russell, and Norman Rabkin, eds. *Drama of the English Renaissance.* 2 vols. (New York: Macmillan, 1976).

Fritz, Kurt von. *Antike und moderne Tragödie: Neun Abhandlungen* (Berlin: Walter de Gruyter, 1962).

———. "Aristotle's Contribution to the Practice and Theory of Historiography." *University of California Publications in Philosophy,* vol. 28, no. 3 (1958): 113–37.

Furley, David J., and R. E. Allen, eds. *Studies in Presocratic Philosophy.* 2 vols. (New York: Humanities Press, 1970).

Gadamer, Hans Georg. *Hegel's Dialectic: Five Hermeneutical Studies,* trans. P. Christopher Smith (New Haven: Yale University Press, 1976).

———. *Truth and Method,* trans. Garrett Barden and John Cumming (New York: Seabury Press, 1975).

Gallaway, Francis. *Reason, Rule, and Revolt in English Classicism* (1940; reprint, New York: Octagon Books, 1965).

Garber, Marjorie. " 'Infinite Riches in a Small Room': Closure and Enclosure in Marlowe." *Two Renaissance Mythmakers: Christopher Marlowe and Ben Johnson,* ed. Alvin Kernan. Selected Papers from the English Institute, 1975–1976, n.s., no. 1 (Baltimore: Johns Hopkins University Press, 1977), pp. 3–21.

Gardner, Helen. *Religion and Literature* (London: Faber and Faber, 1971).

Gellrich, Jesse M. *The Idea of the Book in the Middle Ages: Language Theory, Mythology, and Fiction* (Ithaca: Cornell University Press, 1985).

Gernet, Louis. *The Anthropology of Ancient Greece,* trans. John Hamilton, S. J., and Blaise Nagy (Baltimore: Johns Hopkins University Press, 1981).

———. *Droit et société dans la Grèce ancienne* (Paris: Sirey, 1955).

Gilbert, Allan H., ed. *Literary Criticism: Plato to Dryden* (Detroit: Wayne State University Press, 1962).

Girard, René. *La violence et le sacré* (Paris: Grasset, 1972). *Violence and the Sacred*, trans. Patrick Gregory (Baltimore: Johns Hopkins University Press, 1977).

Glover, T. R. *Herodotus*. Sather Classical Lectures no. 3 (Berkeley: University of California Press, 1924).

Goethe, Johann Wolfgang. *Gedenkausgabe der Werke, Briefe und Gespräche*, ed. Ernst Beutler. 28 vols. (Zurich: Artemis, 1948).

Goldmann, Lucien. *Le dieu caché: Étude sur la vision tragique dans les Pensées de Pascal et dans le théâtre de Racine* (Paris: Gallimard, 1955).

Gould, John. "Dramatic Character and 'Human Intelligibility' in Greek Tragedy." *Proceedings of the Cambridge Philological Society* 24 (1978): 43–67.

Gould, Thomas. Rev. of *Aristotle's Poetics: The Argument*, by Gerald Else. *Gnomon* 34 (1962): 641–83.

Grace, Joan C. *Tragic Theory in the Critical Works of Thomas Rymer, John Dennis, and John Dryden* (Rutherford, N. J.: Fairleigh Dickinson University Press, 1975).

Gray, J. Glenn. *Hegel and Greek Thought* (1941; reprint, New York: Harper and Row, 1968).

Green, Clarence C. *The Neo-classic Theory of Tragedy in England during the Eighteenth Century*. Harvard Studies in English no. 11 (1941; reprint, New York: Benjamin Blom, 1966).

Greenblatt, Stephen. "Marlowe and Renaissance Self-Fashioning." *Two Renaissance Mythmakers: Christopher Marlowe and Ben Johnson*, ed. Alvin Kernan. Selected Papers from the English Institute, 1975–1976, n.s., no. 1 (Baltimore: Johns Hopkins University Press, 1977), pp. 41–69.

———. *Renaissance Self-Fashioning: From More to Shakespeare* (Chicago: University of Chicago Press, 1980).

Greene, William. *Moira: Fate, Good and Evil in Greek Thought* (Gloucester, Mass.: Peter Smith, 1968).

Grene, David, and Richmond Lattimore, eds. *The Complete Greek Tragedies* (Chicago: University of Chicago Press, 1969).

Grimaldi, William. *Aristotle, Rhetoric I: A Commentary* (New York: Fordham University Press, 1980).

———. *Studies in the Philosophy of Aristotle's Rhetoric*. Hermes Einzelschriften no. 25 (Wiesbaden: Franz Steiner, 1972).

Grube, G.M.A. "Educational, Rhetorical, and Literary Theory in Cicero." *Phoenix*, vol. 15, no. 4 (1962): 234–57.

Habermas, Jürgen. *Knowledge and Human Interests*, trans. Jeremy J. Shapiro (Boston: Beacon Press, 1971).

Hammond, N.G.C. "Personal Freedom and Its Limitations in the *Oresteia*." *Journal of Hellenic Studies* 85 (1965): 42–55.

Hampshire, Stuart. "On Tragedy." *Moderns on Tragedy: An Anthology of Modern and Relevant Opinions on the Substance and Meaning of Tragedy*, ed. Lionel Abel (Greenwich, Conn.: Fawcett, 1967), pp. 267–71.

Hardie, W.F.R. *Aristotle's Ethical Theory*. 2d ed. (Oxford: Clarendon Press, 1980).

Hardison, O. B. *The Enduring Monument: A Study of the Idea of Praise in Renaissance Literary Theory and Practice* (Chapel Hill: University of North Carolina Press, 1962).

———. "The Place of Averröes' Commentary on the *Poetics* in the History of Medieval Criticism." *Medieval and Renaissance Studies: Proceedings of the Southeastern Institute of Medieval and Renaissance Studies, Summer, 1968*, ed. John L. Lievsay (Durham: Duke University Press, 1970).

Harris, R. W. *Reason and Nature in the Eighteenth Century* (London: Blandford Press, 1968).

Hathaway, Baxter. *The Age of Criticism: The Late Renaissance in Italy* (Ithaca: Cornell University Press, 1962).

———. *Marvels and Commonplaces: Renaissance Literary Criticism* (Ithaca: Cornell University Press, 1961).

Havelock, Eric A. *The Greek Concept of Justice: From Its Shadow in Homer to Its Substance in Plato* (Cambridge, Mass.: Harvard University Press, 1978).

———. *Preface to Plato*. (1963; reprint, Cambridge, Mass.: Harvard University Press, 1982).

Haydn, Hiram. *The Counter-Renaissance* (Gloucester, Mass.: Peter Smith, 1966).

Hazlitt, William. *Characters of Shakespeare's Plays* (London: J. M. Dent and Sons, 1906).

Hegel, G.W.F. *G.W.F. Hegel: Werke in zwanzig Bänden*, ed. Eva Moldenhauer and Karl Markus Michel. 20 vols. (Frankfurt: Suhrkamp, 1970).

———. *Hegel on Tragedy*, eds. Anne and Henry Paolucci (1962; reprint, New York: Harper and Row, 1975).

————. *Hegels Sämtliche Werke*, ed. Hermann Glockner. 20 vols. (Stuttgart: Friedrich Fromann, 1927–1930).

————. *Reason in History*, trans. H. B. Nisbet (Cambridge: Cambridge University Press, 1975).

————. *Die Vernunft in der Geschichte*, ed. Johannes Hoffmeister (Hamburg: F. Meiner, 1955).

Heidegger, Martin. *Being and Time*, trans. John Macquarrie and Edward Robinson (New York: Harper, 1962).

Heilman, Robert. *Tragedy and Melodrama: Versions of Experience* (Seattle: University of Washington Press, 1968).

Henn, T. R. *The Harvest of Tragedy* (1956; reprint, London: Methuen, 1961).

————. *Longinus and English Criticism* (Cambridge: Cambridge University Press, 1934).

Herodotus. *Histories*. 3d ed. ed. C. Hude. 2 vols. (Oxford: Clarendon Press, 1975).

Herrick, Marvin T. *The Fusion of Horatian and Aristotelian Literary Criticism, 1531–1555* (Urbana: University of Illinois Press, 1946).

————. *The Poetics of Aristotle in England* (New Haven: Yale University Press, 1930).

Hesiod. *Works and Days*, ed. M. L. West (Oxford: Clarendon Press, 1978).

Hester, D. S. "Sophocles the Unphilosophical: A Study in the *Antigone*." *Mnemosyne*, 4th ser., vol. 24, no. 1 (1971): 11–59.

Hintikka, Jaako. *Time and Necessity: Studies in Aristotle's Theory of Modality* (Oxford: Clarendon Press, 1973).

Holscher, Uvo. "Weltzeiten und Lebenszyklus." *Hermes* 93 (1965): 7–33.

Homann, Renate. *Erhabenes und Satirisches: Zur Grundlegung einer Theories aesthetischer Literatur bei Kant und Schiller* (Munich: Wilhelm Fink, 1977).

Homer. *Homeri Opera*, eds. David B. Munro and Thomas Allen. 2 vols. (1920; reprint, Oxford: Clarendon Press, 1962).

Hoopes, Robert. *Right Reason in the English Renaissance* (Cambridge, Mass.: Harvard University Press, 1962).

Horace. *Ars Poetica. Opera*, eds. Edward Wickham and H. W. Garrod (Oxford: Clarendon Press, 1975).

How, W. W., and J. Wells. *A Commentary on Herodotus*. 2 vols. (Oxford: Clarendon Press, 1912).

278   Bibliography

Hume, David. *Of the Standard of Taste: Essays, Moral, Political and Literary* (Oxford: Oxford University Press, 1963).

Hyppolite, Jean. *Genesis and Structure of Hegel's Phenomenology of Spirit*, trans. Samuel Cherniak and John Heckman (Evanston, Ill.: Northwestern University Press, 1974).

Irwin, Terence. "Euripides and Socrates." *Classical Philology*, vol. 78, no. 4 (1983): 183–97.

Jaeger, Werner. *Paideia: The Ideals of Greek Culture*, trans. Gilbert Highet (New York: Oxford University Press, 1939).

Jameson, Frederic. *Marxism and Form: Twentieth-Century Dialectical Theories of Literature* (Princeton: Princeton University Press, 1971).

Jaspers, Karl. *Tragedy Is Not Enough*, trans. Harald A. T. Reiche et al. (London: Victor Gollancz, 1953).

Johnson, Samuel. *Samuel Johnson's Literary Criticism*, ed. R. D. Stock (Lincoln: University of Nebraska Press, 1974).

Jones, John. *On Aristotle and Greek Tragedy* (New York: Oxford University Press, 1962).

Kahn, Charles. *Anaximander and the Origins of Greek Cosmology* (New York: Columbia University Press, 1960).

———. "Anaximander's Fragment: The Universe Governed by Law." *The Presocratics: A Collection of Critical Essays*, ed. Alexander R. D. Mourelatos (Garden City, N. Y.: Anchor Books, 1974), pp. 99–117.

———. *The Art and Thought of Heraclitus* (Cambridge: Cambridge University Press, 1979).

Kakridis, Johannes. *Homeric Researches* (Lund: C.W.K. Gleerup, 1949).

Kant, Immanuel. *Critique of Judgement*, trans. James Creed Meredith (1952; reprint, Oxford: Clarendon Press, 1973).

———. *Kants gesammelte Schriften*. 22 vols. (Berlin: G. Reimer, 1900–1942).

Kaufmann, Walter. *Hegel: Reinterpretation, Texts, and Commentary* (Garden City, N. Y.: Doubleday, 1965).

Kelly, H. A. "Aristotle-Averröes-Alemannus on Tragedy: The Influence of the *Poetics* on the Latin Middle Ages." *Viator: Medieval and Renaissance Studies* 10 (1979): 161–209.

Kerferd, G. B. *The Sophistic Movement* (Cambridge: Cambridge University Press, 1981).

Kermode, Frank. *The Genesis of Secrecy: On the Interpretation of Narrative* (Cambridge, Mass.: Harvard University Press, 1979).

————. *The Sense of an Ending: Studies in the Theory of Fiction* (New York: Oxford University Press, 1967).

Kernan, Alvin, ed. *Two Renaissance Mythmakers: Christopher Marlowe and Ben Johnson.* Selected Papers from the English Institute, 1975–1976, n.s., no. 1 (Baltimore: Johns Hopkins University Press, 1977).

Kierkegaard, Soren. *Fear and Trembling*, trans. Robert Payne (New York: Oxford University Press, 1939).

Kimmelman, George. "The Concept of Tragedy in Modern Criticism." *Journal of Aesthetics and Art Criticism* 4 (1945–1946): 141–60.

Kirk, G. S., and J. E. Raven, eds. *The Presocratic Philosophers: A Critical History with a Selection of Texts* (1957; reprint, Cambridge: Cambridge University Press, 1975).

Knapp, Steven, and Walter Benn Michaels. "Against Theory." *Critical Inquiry*, vol. 8, no. 4 (1982): 723–42.

Knox, Bernard. *The Heroic Temper: Studies in Sophoclean Tragedy.* Sather Classical Lectures no. 35 (Berkeley: University of California Press, 1964).

————. *Word and Action: Essays on the Ancient Theater* (Baltimore: Johns Hopkins University Press, 1979).

Kreiger, Murray. *The Tragic Vision: Variations on a Theme in Literary Interpretation* (Chicago: University of Chicago Press, 1960).

Kristeller, Paul Oskar. "The Place of Classical Humanism in Renaissance Thought." *Journal of the History of Idea*, vol. 4, no. 1 (1943): 59–62.

Lebeck, Anne. *The Oresteia: A Study in Language and Structure* (Washington, D.C.: Center for Hellenic Studies, 1971).

Lesky, Albin. "Decision and Responsibility in the Tragedy of Aeschylus." *Journal of Hellenic Studies* 86 (1966): 78–85.

Levick, Barbara, ed. *The Ancient Historian and His Materials: Essays in Honor of C. E. Stevens on His Seventieth Birthday* (Farnborough, England: Gregg International, 1975).

Levin, Harry. *The Question of Hamlet* (New York: Oxford University Press, 1959).

Levy, G. Rachel. *The Gate of Horn: A Study of the Religious Conceptions of the Stone Age, and Their Influence upon European Thought* (London: Faber and Faber, 1948).

Lobel, E. *Greek Manuscripts of Aristotle's Poetics* (London: Oxford University Press, 1933).

Long, A. A. "Empedocles' Cosmic Cycle in the Sixties." *The Presocratics: A Collection of Critical Essays*, ed. Alexander R. D. Mourelatos (Garden City, N. Y.: Anchor Books, 1974), pp. 397–425.

Lovejoy, Arthur. *The Great Chain of Being: A Study of the History of an Idea* (New York: Harper and Row, 1936).

MacIntyre, Alastair. *After Virtue: A Study in Moral Theory*. 2d ed. (Notre Dame: Notre Dame University Press, 1984).

Mack, Maynard. "The World of *Hamlet*." *Tragic Themes in Western Literature*, ed. Cleanth Brooks (New Haven: Yale University Press, 1955), pp. 502–33.

Maggi, Vincenzo. *Vincentii Madii Brixiani et Bartholomaei Lombardi Veronensis in Aristotelis De Poetica Communes Explanationes* (1550; reprint, Munich: W. Fink, 1969).

Man, Paul de. *Allegories of Reading: Figural Language in Rousseau, Nietzsche, Rilke, and Proust* (New Haven: Yale University Press, 1979).

————. *Blindness and Insight: Essays in the Rhetoric of Contemporary Criticism* (New York: Oxford University Press, 1971).

————. *The Resistance to Theory*. Theory and History of Literature no. 33 (Minneapolis: University of Minnesota Press, 1986).

Mandel, Oscar. *A Definition of Tragedy* (New York: New York University Press, 1961).

Marcus Aurelius Antoninus. *The Communings with Himself, Together with his Speeches and Sayings*. Greek text with trans. C. R. Haines (1916; reprint, Cambridge, Mass.: Harvard University Press, 1961).

Marcuse, Herbert. *Reason and Revolution: Hegel and the Rise of Social Theory*. 2d ed. (New York: Humanities Press, 1954).

Marmontel, Jean-François. *Élémens de la littérature. Oeuvres complètes*. 1819–1820 (Geneva: Slatkine Reprints, 1968).

McElroy, Bernard. *Shakespeare's Mature Tragedies* (Princeton: Princeton University Press, 1973).

McMahon, A. P. "Seven Questions on Aristotelian Definitions of Tragedy and Comedy." *Harvard Studies in Classical Philology* 11 (1929): 99–108.

Mendoça, Barbara Heliodora Carneiro de. "The Influence of *Gorbuduc* on *King Lear*." *Shakespeare Survey* 13 (1960).

Michel, Laurence, and Richard B. Sewall, eds. *Tragedy: Modern Essays in Criticism (1963; reprint, Westport, Conn.: Greenwood Press, 1978).

Miller, R. D. *Schiller and the Ideal of Freedom* (Oxford: Clarendon Press, 1970).

Minturno, Antonio. *L'Arte Poetica. Literary Criticism: Plato to Dryden*, ed. Allan H. Gilbert (Detroit: Wayne State University Press, 1962).

Monk, Samuel H. *The Sublime: A Study of Critical Theories in Eighteenth-Century England* (New York: Modern Language Association of America, 1935).

Moulton, Carroll. "Antiphon the Sophist, *On Truth*." *Transactions of the American Philological Association* 103 (1972): 329–66.

Mourelatos, Alexander R. D., ed. *The Presocratics: A Collection of Critical Essays* (Garden City, N. Y.: Anchor Books, 1974).

Mure, William. *A Critical History of the Language and Literature of Ancient Greece*. 5 vols. (London: Longman, 1854).

Myers, Henry. "The Tragic Attitude Toward Value." *Tragedy: Modern Essays in Criticism*, eds. Laurence Michel and Richard B. Sewall (1963; reprint, Westport, Conn.: Greenwood Press, 1978), pp. 161–74.

Nameri, Dorothy E. *Three Versions of the Story of King Lear (Anonymous ca. 1594/1605; William Shakespeare 1607/1608; Nahum Tate 1681) Studied in Relation to One Another* (Salzburg: University of Salzburg Press, 1976).

Nietzsche, Friedrich. *The Birth of Tragedy*, trans. Francis Golffing (Garden City, N. Y.: Doubleday, 1956).

Nill, Michael. *Morality and Self-Interest in Protagoras, Antiphon, and Democritus* (Leiden: E. J. Brill, 1985).

O'Brien, George Dennis. *Hegel on Reason and History: A Contemporary Interpretation* (Chicago: University of Chicago Press, 1975).

Ornstein, Robert. *The Moral Vision of Jacobean Tragedy* (Madison: University of Wisconsin Press, 1967).

Page, Denys L., ed. *Lyrica Graeca Selecta* (1968; reprint, Oxford: Clarendon Press, 1973).

Palmer, Richard E. *Hermeneutics: Interpretation Theory in Schleiermacher, Dilthey, Heidegger and Gadamer* (Evanston, Ill.: Northwestern University Press, 1969).

Plant, Raymond. *Hegel: An Introduction* (Bloomington: Indiana University Press, 1973).

Plato. *Hippias Major*, trans. Paul Woodruff (Indianapolis: Hackett, 1982).

———. *Platonis Opera*, ed. John Burnet (Oxford: Clarendon Press, 1974).

———. *Republic*. ed. John Burnet (1903; reprint, Oxford: Clarendon Press, 1965).

Pöggeler, Otto, "Hegel und die griechische Tragödie," *Hegel-Studien*. Supplement of "Heidelberger Hegel-Tage" (1962): 285–305.

Quintilian. *Institutio Oratoria*, ed. M. Winterbottom. 2 vols. (Oxford: Clarendon Press, 1970).

Rabkin, Norman. *Shakespeare and the Common Understanding* (New York: Free Press, 1967).

———, ed. *Reinterpretations of Elizabethan Drama* (New York: Columbia University Press, 1969).

Raphael, D. D. *The Paradox of Tragedy* (Bloomington: Indiana University Press, 1960).

Reinhardt, Karl. *Sophocles*, trans. Hazel Harvey and David Harvey (New York: Barnes and Noble, 1978).

Reiss, Timothy. *Tragedy and Truth* (New Haven: Yale University Press, 1980).

Ribner, Irving. *Jacobean Tragedy: The Quest for Moral Order* (London: Methuen, 1962).

Rivier, A. "Remarques sur le 'nécessaire' et la 'nécessité' chez Eschyle." *Revue des études grecques* 81 (1968): 5–39.

Robinson, Forrest G. *The Shape of Things Known: Sidney's Apology in Its Philosophical Tradition* (Cambridge, Mass.: Harvard University Press, 1972).

Robortello, Francesco. *Francesci Robortelli Utinensis in librum Aristotelis De Arte Poetica Explicationes* (1548; reprint, Munich: W. Fink, 1968).

Rodgers, V. S. "Some Thoughts on *Dike*." *Classical Quarterly* 21 (1971): 284–301.

Rorty, Amelie O., ed. *Essays on Aristotle's Ethics* (Berkeley: University of California Press, 1980).

Rosenberg, Harold. *The Tradition of the New* (New York: Horizon Press, 1959).

Rosenmeyer, Thomas G. *The Art of Aeschylus* (Berkeley: University of California Press, 1982).

———. *The Masks of Tragedy: Essays on Six Greek Dramas* (Austin: University of Texas Press, 1963).

————. "Wahlakt und Entscheidungsprozess in der antiken Tragödie." *Poetica*, vol. 10, no. 1 (1978): 1–24.

Ross, W. D. *Aristotle*. 5th ed., rev. (New York: Barnes and Noble, 1964).

Rymer, Thomas. *A Short View of Tragedy. The English Stage: Attack and Defense, 1577–1730*, ed. Arthur Freeman (New York: Garland, 1974).

Sanders, Wilbur. "Marlowe's *Doctor Faustus*." MCR 7 (1964): 78–91.

Scaliger, Julius Caesar. *Select Translations from Scaliger's Poetics*, ed. and trans. F. M. Padelford. Yale Studies in English no. 26 (New York: Holt, 1905).

Schiller, Joseph Christoph Frederich von. *Sämtliche Werke*, eds. Gerhard Fricke and Herbert G. Gopfert. 5 vols. (Munich: Carl Hanser, 1959).

Schlegel, A. W. *A Course of Lectures on Dramatic Art and Literature*, trans. John Black. 2 vols. (London, 1815).

Schopenhauer, Arthur. *The World as Will and Idea*, trans. R. B. Haldane and J. Kemp. 3 vols. English and Foreign Philosophical Library, vols. 22–24 (London: Trubner, 1883–1886).

Segal, Charles. *Dionysiac Poetics and Euripides' Bacchae* (Princeton: Princeton University Press, 1982).

————. *Tragedy and Civilization: An Interpretation of Sophocles* (Cambridge, Mass.: Harvard University Press, 1981).

Seneca. *Ad Lucilium Epistolae Morales*, ed. L. D. Reynolds (Oxford: Clarendon Press, 1965).

Shakespeare, William. *Hamlet*, ed. Edward Hubler (New York: New American Library, 1963).

————. *King Lear*, ed. Russell A. Fraser (New York: New American Library, 1963).

Sidney, Philip. *Defense of Poesie. Literary Criticism: Plato to Dryden*, ed. Allan H. Gilbert (Detroit: Wayne State University Press, 1962).

Smith, Barbara Herrnstein. *Poetic Closure: A Study of How Poems End* (Chicago: University of Chicago Press, 1968).

Smith, D. Nichol, ed. *Eighteenth-Century Essays on Shakespeare* (1903; reprint, New York: Russell and Russell, 1962).

Smith, G. Gregory, ed. *Elizabethan Critical Essays*. 2 vols. (Oxford: Oxford University Press, 1904).

284   Bibliography

Smithson, Isaiah. "The Moral View of Aristotle's *Poetics*." *Journal of the History of Ideas*, vol. 44, no. 1 (1983): 3–17.

Snell, Bruno. *Aischylos und das Handeln im Drama* (Leipzig: Dieterich'sche Verlagsbuchhandlung, 1928).

———. *The Discovery of the Mind: The Greek Origins of European Thought*, trans. Thomas G. Rosenmeyer (Cambridge, Mass.: Harvard University Press, 1953).

———. "Das frühste Zeugnis über Sokrates." *Philologus* 97 (1948): 125–35.

Solmsen, Freidrich. "Love and Strife in Empedocles' Cosmology." *Phronesis* 10 (1965): 109–48.

Sophocles. *Antigone*, ed. Sir Richard Jebb (Cambridge: Cambridge University Press, 1928).

———. *Antigone*, Commentary J. C. Kamerbeek (Leiden: E. J. Brill, 1978).

———. *Fabulae*, ed. A. C. Pearson (Oxford: Clarendon Press, 1971).

Sorabji, Richard. *Necessity, Cause and Blame: Perspectives on Aristotle's Theory* (Ithaca: Cornell University Press, 1980).

Spingarn, Joel Elias. *A History of Literary Criticism in the Renaissance*. 2d ed., rev. and aug. (New York: Columbia University Press, 1954).

Spitzer, Leo. *Classical and Christian Ideas of World Harmony; Prolegomena to an Interpretation of the Word "Stimmung,"* ed. Anna G. Hatcher (Baltimore: Johns Hopkins University Press, 1963).

Ste. Croix, G.E.M. de. "Aristotle on History and Poetry (*Poetics* 9, 1451a36–b11)." *The Ancient Historian and His Materials: Essays in Honour of C. E. Stevens on His Seventieth Birthday*, ed. Barbara Levick (Farnborough, England: Gregg International, 1975), pp. 45–58.

Steinkraus, Warren E., ed. *New Studies in Hegel's Philosophy* (New York: Holt, Rinehart, and Winston, 1971).

Stepelevich, Lawrence S., and David Lamb, eds. *Hegel's Philosophy of Action* (Atlantic Highlands, N. J.: Humanities Press, 1983).

Stinton, T.C.W. "*Hamartia* in Aristotle and Greek Tragedy." *Classical Quarterly* 25 (1975): 221–54.

Stock, R. D. *Samuel Johnson and Neoclassical Dramatic Theory* (Lincoln: University of Nebraska Press, 1973).

Taylor, Charles. *Hegel* (Cambridge: Cambridge University Press, 1975).

———. "Hegel and the Philosophy of Action." *Hegel's Philosophy of Action*, eds. Lawrence S. Stepelevich and David Lamb (Atlantic Highlands, N. J.: Humanities Press, 1983).

Theognis. *The Elegies of Theognis and Other Elegies Included in the Theognidean Sylloge*. Rev. text. Comm. T. Hudson-Williams (New York: Arno Press, 1979).

Urmson, J. O. "Aristotle's Doctrine of the Mean." *American Philosophical Quarterly* (July 1973): 223–30.

Vernant, Jean-Pierre, and Pierre Vidal-Naquet. *Mythe et tragedie en Grèce ancienne* (Paris: François Maspero, 1972).

Vlastos, Gregory. *Equality and Justice in Early Greek Cosmology*. Vol. 1 of *Studies in Presocratic Philosophy*, eds. David J. Furley and R. E. Allen. 2 vols. (New York: Humanities Press, 1970), pp. 56–91.

Waldock, A.J.A. *Hamlet: A Study in Critical Method* (Cambridge: Cambridge University Press, 1931).

Wasserman, Earl R. "The Pleasures of Tragedy." *ELH: A Journal of English Literary History*, vol. 14, no. 4 (1947): 283–307.

Weinberg, Bernard. *A History of Literary Criticism in the Italian Renaissance*. 2 vols. (Chicago: University of Chicago Press, 1961).

———. "The Poetic Theories of Minturno." *Studies in Honor of Frederick W. Shipley*. Washington University Studies in Language and Literature no. 14 (Lancaster, Penn: Lancaster Press, 1942), pp. 101–29.

———. "Robortello on the *Poetics*." *Critics and Criticism: Ancient and Modern*, eds. R. S. Crane et al. (Chicago: University of Chicago Press, 1952), pp. 319–48.

Weiner, Andrew D. *Sir Philip Sidney and the Poetics of Protestantism: A Study of Contexts* (Minneapolis: University of Minnesota Press, 1978).

Weiskel, Thomas. *The Romantic Sublime: Studies in the Structure and Psychology of Transcendence* (Baltimore: Johns Hopkins University Press, 1976).

Wellek, René. *A History of Modern Criticism: 1750–1950*. 4 vols. (New Haven: Yale University Press, 1955).

White, Nicholas P. *A Companion to Plato's Republic* (Indianapolis: Hackett, 1979).

Whitman, Cedric. *The Heroic Paradox: Essays on Homer, Sophocles, and Aristophanes*, ed. Charles Segal (Ithaca: Cornell University Press, 1982).

Whitman, Cedric. *Sophocles: A Study of Heroic Humanism* (Cambridge, Mass.: Harvard University Press, 1951).

Willey, Basil. *Tendencies in Renaissance Literary Theory* (Cambridge: Bowes and Bowes, 1922).

Wimsatt, William K., and Cleanth Brooks. *Literary Criticism: A Short History* (New York: Alfred A. Knopf, 1965).

Winnington-Ingram, R. P. *Sophocles: An Interpretation* (Cambridge: Cambridge University Press, 1980).

Library of Congress Cataloging-in-Publication Data

Gellrich, Michelle.
Tragedy and theory.

Bibliography: p.
Includes index.
1. Tragedy. 2. Conflict (Psychology) in literature. I. Title.
PN1892.G38 1988   809.2′512   87–25868
ISBN 0–691–06738–4 (alk. paper)

Michelle Gellrich is an Associate Professor of English
and Foreign Languages at Louisiana State University.